Social Problems

Social Problems

JOEL BEST

W. W. NORTON & COMPANY

NEW YORK LONDON

Editor: Karl Bakeman
Editorial assistant: Rebecca Arata
Manuscript editor: Stephanie Hiebert
Project editor: Rebecca A. Homiski
Production manager: Ben Reynolds
Book design: Margaret M. Wagner
Composition: Matrix Publishing Services
Manufacturing by the Maple-Vail Book Group, Binghamton

Library of Congress Cataloging-in-Publication Data

Best, Joel.
    Social problems / by Joel Best.—1st ed.
        p. cm.
    Includes bibliographical references and index.
    ISBN-13: 978-0-393-92877-8 (paperback)
    ISBN-10: 0-393-92877-2 (paperback)
    1. Social problems. I. Title.
HN28.B45 2008
361.1—dc22

                            2006103182

W. W. Norton & Company, Inc., 500 Fifth Avenue, New York, N.Y. 10110
www.wwnorton.com
W. W. Norton & Company, Ltd., Castle House, 75/76 Wells Street,
London W1T 3QT

1 2 3 4 5 6 7 8 9 0

Contents

v

Figures

Boxes

A Note to the Reader

Many, many books titled *Social Problems* have been published in the last hundred years. Their tables of contents look a lot alike: they begin with a brief discussion of the nature of social problems, then consider a list of different problems. Each chapter presents more or less up-to-date information about a particular social problem: there is a chapter about crime, another about racism, and so on. If your parents, grandparents, or even great grandparents read a social problems textbook, that book almost certainly fit this pattern.

This is not your parents' social problems textbook.

The chapters in this book do not deal with different problems. Instead, each chapter deals with a different stage in the *social problems process*—the process by which particular problems become a focus of concern. Why do we worry about, say, the risks of breast implants in one year, road rage in another, and identity theft in still another? This book seeks to explain how and why attention to different issues rises and falls.

If you're a student who's been assigned to read this book, it probably already seems long. All I can say is that it could have been a lot longer. Lots of people have written about the rise and fall of social problems; hundreds of studies have been published on the topic, particularly since the 1970s. But I have decided to cite relatively few sources. Often where I've cited one source, I could have cited dozens. In general, I have chosen to cite sources that appeared relatively recently. In addition, because this book is intended as an introduction to thinking about social problems, I have tried to hold jargon to a minimum. If you go on to read more of what sociologists have written on the topic—and I hope that this book will get you interested enough to do just that—you will find that other authors have explored the ins and outs of studying social problems in far more detail, and that they have developed many specialized terms and concepts to help us think about the social problems process. However, my goal is not to summarize everything that has been written about what I call the constructionist approach to social problems. Rather, I want to give you a basic framework for understanding this approach. This book is intended to help you become a more critical thinker; it provides some tools that can help you better analyze what you read and hear about social problems.

Acknowledgments

I particularly want to thank Karl Bakeman, Norton's editor for sociology. Over the years, I have been approached by several publishers who said they wanted me to write a book about social problems. I had a standard response: "You don't want to publish the book I want to write, and I don't want to write the book you want to publish." That was enough to discourage everyone—except Karl. I appreciate his willingness to take a chance on the book I wanted to write.

I also want to thank Kathe Lowney, who read the entire manuscript and gave me a lot of good advice. I also benefited from the comments of the other reviewers: Alison Alkon, University of California, Davis; Nancy Berns, Drake University; Vincent Carter, Emory University; Tracy Citeroni, Mary Washington University; Joseph E. Davis, University of Virginia; Stephanie Decker, University of Kansas; Jen Dunn, Southern Illinois University at Carbondale; Heather Feldhaus, Bloomsburg University; Jessica Greenebaum, Central Connecticut State University; Scott Harris, St. Louis University; Ann Herda-Rapp, University of Wisconsin–Marathon; Jim Holstein, Marquette University; Pam Hunt, Kent State University; Michelle Jacobs, Mira Costa College; Ellis Jones, University of

California, Davis; Jeanne Mekolichick, Radford College; Bryce Merrill, University of Colorado at Boulder; David Meyer, University of California, Irvine; Dorothy Pawluch, McMaster University; Gina Petonito, Miami University–Ohio; Meredith Redlin, South Dakota State University; Theodore Sasson, Middlebury College; Stu Shafer, Johnson County Community College; Ira Silver, Framingham State University; and Loreen Wolfer, University of Scranton.

Finally, I want to thank the other folks at Norton who helped me pull the book together. In particular, Stephanie Hiebert did the copyediting.

Social Problems

1

The Social Problems Process

The title of this book identifies its subject: social problems. But what are *social problems*? If asked, most people have no difficulty listing some examples: crime, suicide, racism, sexism, terrorism, global warming. Most people have a commonsense notion of what the term means, but actually defining the concept turns out to be much trickier.

Suppose we agree that suicide and global warming are both social problems. What, exactly, do the two have in common? They seem very different: we usually think of suicide as an extremely personal act, committed by individuals who feel isolated and in despair, whereas global warming involves physical climate change across a whole planet. What sort of definition can cover both individual acts and global transformations?

TWO WAYS TO DEFINE SOCIAL PROBLEMS

Social Problems as Harmful Conditions: The Objectivist Outlook

The usual answer is to define social problems as conditions that somehow harm society. For example, another recent book that shares the title of this book, *Social Problems*, offers this definition: "A social problem is a condition that undermines the well-being of some or all members of a society and that is usually a matter of public controversy" (Macionis, 2005, p. 7). In other words, some conditions have the characteristic of "undermining well-being" that makes them social problems. Although the precise wording of their definitions varies, most books on the topic characterize social problems as harmful conditions.

This approach to defining social problems is sometimes called **objectivist** because it tries to couch the definition in terms of objectively measurable characteristics of conditions. Once we define social problems as harmful conditions, we can look around until we spot a harmful condition and then identify it as a social problem. Most books titled *Social Problems* have chapters devoted to crime, racism, and other conditions that presumably have been objectively determined to be harmful.

Objectivist definitions seem fine—until we start to think about them. Then some problems with the objectivist approach become obvious. The first difficulty is that conditions that might be deemed harmful aren't always identified as social problems. Take sexism. Virtually all the books titled *Social Problems* and published in the United States in recent decades discuss sexism; it is widely understood to be a social problem. And yet, although social arrangements that discriminate against females have had a very long history, often they have been taken for granted, viewed as normal and natural—not at all a problem. Even today, many people around the world believe that their religions or traditions justify—even require—such discriminatory social arrangements. In fact, even American books about social problems published before 1970 rarely mentioned sexual discrimination. Only in recent decades has the term *sexism* emerged to refer to a form of discrimination seen as analogous to racism (which already was widely understood to be a social problem).

If we ask people to explain why racism is a social problem, they are likely to emphasize justice or fairness. It is, they will explain, unjust to discriminate against people simply because they belong to a particular race. Some may add that racism also harms society in that victims of racial discrimination are blocked from making all of the contributions they might make to the larger society, so that not only are those victims harmed, but the larger society is damaged because it misses out on what the victims could contribute; moreover, society is harmed further because racial tensions create conflict that makes the society less productive and harmonious. In other words, it is easy to argue that racism is a harmful condition and should be recognized as a social problem.

Obviously it is possible to make analogous arguments about sexism—that it is unfair, blocks women from fulfilling their potential, and fosters conflict, and therefore harms the larger society. Thus, by objective standards, we might assume that racism and sexism should both be seen as social problems, although we know that—at other times or in other places—people have treated both racist and sexist practices as normal, even as the way things ought to be.

Note, however, that we might make essentially the same arguments about discrimination based on height. Studies show that taller people have various advantages; for example, they are more likely to be hired and more likely to be promoted. Thus, short people can be seen as victims of height discrimination (Judge & Cable, 2004). Such discriminatory treatment also might be considered unfair, and ultimately harmful to society in much the same ways that racism and sexism are harmful. By objective standards, then, shouldn't "heightism" also be considered a social problem?

The first difficulty with objectivism becomes apparent: although we might argue that racism, sexism, and heightism all have analogous effects on society, as social problems these three forms of discrimination have not received anything like the same degree of attention. Racial discrimination has long been understood to be a serious social problem; sexism has only recently been added to the list of significant social problems; and heightism rarely receives mention as a social problem. As far as I know, no book about social problems includes a chapter about height discrimination. The different treatment of these three forms of discrimination makes it difficult to argue that there is an evenly applied objective standard for identifying what is or is not a social problem.

A second challenge to objectivism is that the same condition may be identified as a social problem for very different reasons; that is, people may disagree about why a certain condition is harmful. For example, some commentators argue that contemporary society discriminates against people who are overweight; heavier people find it more difficult to get jobs, are the objects of scorn, and so on. In this view, weight discrimination, like racial, gender, or—yes— height discrimination, should be considered a social problem because it is unjust and blocks some individuals from opportunities. More recently, however, attention has focused on obesity itself as a social problem. Here the argument is that heavier people are less healthy, and that obesity costs society many millions of dollars in additional health care costs. Critics taking this view consider obesity a social problem not because it leads to discrimination, but because it is a drain on societal resources (see Box 1.1).

Note that, although both arguments suggest that there is a social problem related to weight, they make very different claims: the former suggests that discrimination against overweight people is unfair (presumably, this position might lead to suggestions that society ought to become more tolerant of weight differences and that such discrimination should be discouraged); the latter views obesity itself as a source of harm (and would presumably lead to calls to reduce obesity). This example reveals a second problem with the objectivist view of social problems: very different—even contradictory— objective standards may be used in identifying a condition as a social problem.

Box 1.1 A WEIGHTY DISAGREEMENT

Many Americans are heavy. Is this a social problem? If so, what exactly is the nature of this problem? Is it a discrimination/civil rights problem? Or is it a medical/public health problem?

Since 1969, the National Association to Advance Fat Acceptance (NAAFA), "a non-profit human rights organization dedicated to improving the quality of life for fat people," has argued that heavy people face discrimination: "Fat people are discriminated against in employment, education, access to public accommodations, and access to adequate medical care. In addition, fat people are stigmatized, and are the victims of tasteless jokes and assaults on their dignity." NAAFA insists that what it calls *size discrimination* is a social problem in the same way that racial discrimination and sexual discrimination are social problems.

In contrast, many medical authorities and government agencies argue that obesity should be understood as a disease. They present statistical evidence that obesity is associated with such dangerous medical conditions as hypertension, stroke, diabetes, respiratory problems, and some forms of cancer. Not only do obese people live shorter lives, but they burden society by incurring higher health care costs. These authorities speak of obesity as an *epidemic*. In this view, obesity should be considered a medical or public health problem analogous to the problem posed by tobacco smoking, and steps should be taken to reduce obesity.

These different views on obesity illustrate that even people who agree that a particular condition is a social problem may disagree about the *sort* of social problem it is.

Sources: www.naafa.org; Morrill & Chinn, 2004.

A third problem with objectivism has already been suggested: our lists of social problems include wildly diverse phenomena. They usually range from problems affecting particular individuals, such as suicide or mental illness, to global trends, such as overpopulation, globalization, or global warming. Any objective definition that tries to cover such a broad range of topics must be fairly vague, and speak in only the most general terms about harm, undermining well-being, or anything else. Although objectivists argue that social problems are harmful conditions, they don't specify what constitutes harm. Instead, harmfulness becomes a big conceptual umbrella, covering a huge array of phenomena, ranging from, say, the pain experienced by those who knew someone who committed suicide, through all of the economic and ecological costs that might be incurred as global temperatures rise. In practice, then, objective definitions of social problems turn out to be so vague as to be almost meaningless.

For all of these reasons, it is quite difficult to devise an objective definition of social problems that can distinguish between the things that people consider social problems and the things that they don't. So let's ask the question again: what, exactly, do suicide and global warming have in common? Once we think about it, we realize that there is really only one quality that all of the diverse phenomena considered social problems share: they are all considered social problems. The point is not so much that some conditions cause harm, but that people think of some conditions as being harmful.

Social Problems as Topics of Concern: The Subjectivist Outlook

Imagine two societies with arrangements that discriminate against women; in one, people consider these arrangements normal and natural; in the other, some people consider these arrangements wrong. From the point of view of the first society's members, sexism is not a social problem; some members of the second society, though, do regard sexism to be a social problem. Of course, people's views may change. In recent decades, Americans have come to view social arrangements that treat men and women differently as problematic, so even though sexism was formerly not considered a social problem, it has become one.

We might think of this as a **subjectivist** approach, in that it defines social problems in terms of people's subjective sense that something is or isn't a problem. If people don't think that heightism is a social problem, then it isn't one; but if height discrimination began receiving a lot of concerned attention, heightism could become a social problem. If people consider both suicide and global warming to be social problems, then both are.

Once we start thinking about social problems in terms of subjective judgments, we realize that people often disagree about what should be considered social problems. We might expect people of above-average height to dismiss arguments that height discrimination should be considered a social problem, and those of below-average height to be more receptive to those claims. Similarly, the views of individuals outside a society may differ from those of its members. When Americans criticize sexism in other countries, they are identifying a social problem, even if most of the occupants of those countries disagree. Remember, there is no objective standard that lets us declare, "*X* is a social problem, but *Y* is not." Rather, whether a condition is a social problem depends on different people's points of view—and they won't always agree.

In this view, social problems will come and go as people's subjective judgments change. Announcements of discoveries of a new disease or a new environmental threat can vault previously overlooked conditions onto people's lists of social problems. Other social problems fade away. For example, during the 1950s many commentators worried that young Americans were apathetic, but apathy stopped being considered a social problem during the 1960s, when campus demonstrations led critics to charge that students had become too concerned, too involved in political activity.

From the subjectivist outlook, it is not an objective quality of a social condition, but rather the subjective reactions to that condition, that make something a social problem. Therefore, social problems should not be viewed as a type of social condition, but as a *process* of responding to social conditions. Thus, we can define social problems as efforts to arouse concern about conditions within society. Or, to quote one influential definition, social problems are "the activities of individuals or groups making assertions of grievance and claims with respect to some putative conditions" (Spector & Kitsuse, 1977, p. 75). In other words, the study of social problems should focus not on conditions, but on claims about conditions.

At first glance, this approach may seem wrongheaded. If we're interested in, say, poverty, then shouldn't we be studying poverty as a condition? We might try to measure the number of poor people, determine the causes of poverty, and so on. In other words, shouldn't we adopt a more objectivist approach and focus on the condition of poverty, rather than on claims about poverty? Of course, it is possible to study poverty and other social conditions, and there is nothing wrong with doing so. But that has nothing to do with studying poverty *as a social problem.*

Studying poverty as a social problem requires asking how and why people came to consider poverty problematic. After all, poverty has been around for a long time; throughout history, many people in many societies have taken poverty for granted, seeing it as necessary, normal, even just. Some societies with very large populations of poor people have not viewed poverty as a social problem. In contrast, in the United States and many other modern societies, the widespread view is that poverty should be considered a social problem, and that we ought to do something about it. Studying poverty *as a social problem* requires studying how that view emerged and spread.

In other words, efforts to find a workable definition of social problems based on the objective characteristics of social conditions have proved futile. Thinking systematically about social problems requires adopting a subjectivist approach that focuses on the process by which people identify social problems. That process involves what sociologists call *social construction*.

SOCIAL CONSTRUCTION

By **social construction**, we mean the way people assign meaning to the world. People use language; language is essential to our understanding of the world that surrounds us (just try thinking without using words). One of the principal accomplishments of infancy and early childhood is learning to recognize, understand, and use words. Through language, we learn to categorize the world, to understand that some things are edible (*food*) while others are dangerous and must not be eaten (*poison*), and so on. This is obviously a social process: we do not invent our language; rather, we learn to use the language of our parents and the other people around us. The meanings of their words—their categories for classifying the world—are the ones that we learn. Children grow up speaking English, or French, or whatever language the people in the group around them speak, and they learn to assign that group's meanings to the world.

Language is flexible: as people learn new things about the world, they devise words with new meanings. In this way, people continually create—or construct—fresh understandings about the world around them. Because this is a social process, sociologists refer to it as *social construction* (Berger & Luckmann, 1966).

Sociologists do not view social construction as a completely arbitrary process; it is constrained by the physical world within which people find themselves. We can imagine all sorts of ridiculous meanings that people might, in theory, construct. For instance, an imaginary society might, in theory, teach its young that rocks are edible, or that people can fly by flapping their arms, but this is hardly likely. Although this could happen, it probably wouldn't, because those lessons would prove worthless, even dangerous. In general, the meanings people construct need to make sense of the world they inhabit.

The point is not that people could assign ridiculous meanings to the world, but rather that they must assign some meanings to at least some of their surroundings. Probably every human society throughout history has categorized people as either male or female. The distinction is relatively clear-cut: we can look at virtually any newborn infant and confidently declare that it falls into one category or the other. If this doesn't seem to be a social process, remember that a tiny fraction of infants (about one in every thousand) are born with anomalous sexual organs that do challenge the simple male/female classification, and societies have to decide how to deal with those cases (Preves, 2003). There are various solutions: Many Native American societies defined hermaphrodites as having a special status as *berdaches*—a sort of third sex outside the standard male/female divide. By contrast, in contemporary America surgeons often "correct" the anomalies, to give the infant either a male or a female appearance, and foster an unambiguous gender identity.

This example reminds us that even something as apparently straightforward as sorting people into males and females is a social process of constructing meanings. Note, too, that the precise meanings assigned to these categories—the qualities attributed to males or females—vary from one society to another. Both the two-category male/female classification and the specific qualities associated with each category are instances of social construction. All meanings, including how we designate planets in the solar system and all other elements in the physical world, are socially constructed (see Box 1.2).

Sociologists sometimes illustrate social construction by pointing to problems that seem ridiculous. These examples offer a sort of analytic leverage: they lay bare the process of social construction. Witch hunts are a favorite historical example; UFO abductions and satanic ritual abuse offer more contemporary cases. Critics might

Box 1.2 Pluto: A Planetary Problem?

For decades, schoolchildren learned that there were nine planets, but that changed in 2006, when astronomers demoted Pluto from the list, reclassifying it as a *dwarf planet*. Pluto is unlike the other planets in several ways: (1) It is much smaller. (2) It has a different composition; the four inner planets (Mercury, Venus, Earth, and Mars) are basically rocks, and the four giant planets (Jupiter, Saturn, Uranus, and Neptune) are composed of gas, but Pluto is basically a big lump of ice. (3) It has a less circular, more elliptical orbit than the other planets, so sometimes it is closer to the Sun than Neptune is. And (4), unlike the other eight planets, whose orbits fall more or less along a single plane, Pluto has an orbit that is at an angle to that plane.

No one denies that Pluto exists; the question is whether it makes more sense to classify it as a planet or as belonging to a different category. When Ceres—the largest asteroid—was discovered in 1801, it was initially considered a planet, but astronomers dropped that classification once they realized that there were many asteroids. Now Ceres joins Pluto in the new category of dwarf planet. These examples remind us that *planet* is a social construction, a category that people use to assign meaning to the world. Our words are social products: we create them and teach them to one another. Because we understand our world through language, sociologists view all knowledge as socially constructed.

Sources: Freedman, 1998; Overbye, 2006.

argue that there is no convincing evidence that witches, UFOs, or child-abusing satanists exist (ignore, for the moment, those people who remain convinced that these are real phenomena). Therefore, the sociologists declare, witchcraft, UFOs, and satanic blood cults are clearly social constructions.

This conclusion is true, but its implication is quite false. UFO abductions are a social construction, in the sense that this term was created and disseminated by people. But the implication—that only unprovable claims are socially constructed—is wrong. Poverty is just as much a social construction as UFO abductions are. The term *poverty* is another category that people have created to make sense of the world. Just as some people have drawn attention to UFO abductions, others have campaigned to raise concern about poverty (during the 1960s, for example, President Lyndon Johnson declared "war on poverty"). Saying that poverty is a social construction does not mean that poverty doesn't exist, that it somehow doesn't occur in the real world; obviously some people have much less money than others. But the words we choose to describe those people (*impoverished*, for instance, rather than *wretched* or *depraved*—terms that were once used to describe the poor), how we explain their condition, and what we recommend doing about it are meanings that people create and use. In that sense, poverty—like everything else we know about—is a social construction.

Once we recognize that social problems are social constructions, and that what the conditions constructed as social problems have in common is precisely that construction, then it becomes apparent that social problems should be understood in terms of a **social problems process**. That is, the study of social problems should focus on how and why particular conditions come to be constructed as social problems. How and why did poverty—or UFO abductions—emerge as topics of interest and concern at particular moments, and in particular places? Why do people decide that something needs to be done about some conditions, and how do they decide exactly what should be done? This approach to studying social problems is called **constructionist**, and it is the perspective adopted in this book.

THE BASIC FRAMEWORK

The constructionist approach requires understanding a few basic terms. These will reappear throughout the chapters that follow. The first is **claim**. Constructing a social problem involves a process of **claimsmaking**: that is, someone must bring the topic to the attention of others, by making a claim that there is a condition that should be recognized as troubling, that needs to be addressed. For constructionist sociologists, social problems are defined in terms of this claimsmaking process, because it is claimsmaking—and only claimsmaking—that all social problems have in common.

Note that claims may be supported by very different sorts of evidence: someone making claims about poverty might present poverty statistics, photographs of poor people, or all manner of other evidence; claims about UFO abductions tend to rely on first-person accounts by people who say they recall having been abducted. Whether other people find a claim convincing is a separate issue. At one extreme, we can imagine a claim that no one finds convincing: picture a man standing on a street corner warning passersby that invisible, undetectable aliens from planet Zorax have infested the very air that they're breathing. This may be a claim, but if everyone who hears it dismisses or ignores it, it will have no impact. The social problems process requires not only that someone make a claim, but that others react to it.

The people who make claims are, of course, **claimsmakers**. They are the ones who seek to convince others that something is wrong, and that something should be done about it. Obviously not all claimsmakers are equal: we tend to treat some claims more seriously, simply because they seem more plausible, or because they are promoted by people we respect—experts, officials, and so on. Successful claims spread, so that they become the subject of media coverage and debates over public policy.

These few concepts—claim, claimsmaking, and claimsmaker—provide a foundation upon which we can build a more elaborate analysis of the social problems process. Throughout this book, we will distinguish between claims and the conditions about which claims are being made. We will refer to **troubling conditions**—that is, the conditions that become subjects of claims. The word *troubling* focuses our attention on people's subjective reactions: a condition is troubling if it bothers someone. Note that it isn't necessary for everyone to accept the claim; some people may consider UFO abductions troubling, even though others regard such claims as fantastic. We can consider both poverty and UFO abductions troubling conditions, regardless of whether we agree that they both exist.

Adopting a subjectivist stance can seem confusing at first. In particular, two sorts of confusion arise. We have already discussed the first: people sometimes wrongly imagine that *social construction* refers only to imaginary, nonexistent phenomena. Again, this is wrong—all human knowledge is socially constructed through our language, which means that all social problems are socially constructed.

The second source of confusion is that we must acknowledge that sociologists are themselves engaged in social construction. Like all other people, sociologists must use language to make the world meaningful; they devise their own categories—such as *claims* and *claimsmakers*—that they use to classify the world. This book, for instance, can be understood as a set of sociological claims about the social problems process.

Some people worry that, if sociology is one more social construction, we can't really have confidence in sociological knowledge. The response, of course, is that we can have exactly the same sort of confidence in sociology that we have in our other sorts of knowledge. When we encounter claims in everyday life—when someone gives us a compliment, politicians ask for our votes, or advertisers try to sell us their products—we neither accept everything we hear at face value nor assume that it is all meaningless. Rather, we learn to evaluate claims, to look for evidence, and so on. Similarly, sociologists can offer support for their arguments, and this book will try to suggest the nature of that support. (For more detailed discussions of various theoretical and methodological aspects of the constructionist approach, see Holstein & Miller, 1993, 2003a; and Loseke, 2003).

THE PLAN OF THE BOOK: THE NATURAL
HISTORY OF SOCIAL PROBLEMS

To understand the approach that this book takes in its look at social problems, it may help to begin with a familiar example from U.S. history: the 1960s civil rights movement against segregation. After World War II, the southern states retained customs and laws maintaining racial segregation: African Americans were blocked from voting; intermarriage was illegal; whites and blacks attended different schools; and other institutions were segregated, so that the races ate in different restaurants, sat in different sections on buses, and used racially separate restrooms and drinking fountains. Organized protests against this system of segregation became more common; in particular, the 1955–56 bus boycott in Montgomery, Alabama, brought national attention to the leadership of the Reverend Martin Luther King Jr.

By the early 1960s, there were numerous civil rights organizations—including King's Southern Christian Leadership Conference (SCLC), the Congress of Racial Equality (CORE), and the Student Nonviolent Coordinating Committee (SNCC, pronounced "snick")—leading marches, boycotts, freedom rides, voter registration campaigns, and other sorts of protests. Television news programs showed dramatic scenes of police beating and arresting protesters, and public opinion—particularly outside the South—increasingly sympathized with the civil rights campaign. In 1963, the great March on Washington called for congressional action, and Congress eventually passed the Civil Rights Act of 1964 and the Voting Rights Act of 1965. By the end of the 1960s, segregation in the South had generally lost its legal standing, although of course other forms of racial inequality remained.

We can use the story of the civil rights movement's campaign against segregation to illustrate a more general phenomenon: the natural history of a social problem. The term **natural history** refers to a sequence of stages that tends to appear in lots of different cases.

Figure 1.1 diagrams the natural history of the social problems process. This natural history identifies six stages: claimsmaking, media coverage, public reaction, policymaking, social problems work, and policy outcomes. The figure sketches a general framework. Describing a natural history helps us organize our thinking about a typical social problems process, although not every instance of social problems construction will fit this model. In fact, other sociologists have offered different natural histories of the social problems process (see Blumer, 1971; and Spector & Kitsuse, 1977). Figure 1.1 is a simplified diagram intended to give an overview of what is actually a much more complicated process. In later chapters, we will expand this diagram to consider some of those complexities, but this version gives us a starting point.

Stage One: Claimsmaking

The first stage in Figure 1.1 concerns claimsmaking. During this stage, claimsmakers make claims; that is, they argue that a particular troubling condition ought to be recognized as a social problem, and that someone ought to do something about that problem. In the case of the civil rights movement, the claimsmakers were the social movement activists and demonstrators who protested against the system of racial segregation. We can distinguish between claimsmakers and their claims. *Claims* are arguments, efforts to persuade others that something is wrong, that there is a problem that needs to be solved. For example, the civil rights movement claimed that racial segregation was wrong, that it was unjust, and violated the basic American belief in equality. The social problems process always begins with claims, so we will begin this book by exploring various aspects of claims in Chapter 2.

Typically we think of claimsmakers as **activists**, members of social movement organizations such as the civil rights movement's SCLC, CORE, or SNCC. Lots of people want to make claims, but

Figure 1.1 Basic Natural History Model of the Social Problems Process

Claimsmaking →	Media Coverage →	Public Reaction →	Policymaking →	Social Problems Work →	Policy Outcomes
People make claims that there is a social problem, with certain characteristics, causes, and solutions.	Media report on claimsmakers so that news of the claims reaches a broader audience.	Public opinion focuses on the social problem identified by the claimsmakers.	Lawmakers and others with the power to set policies create new ways to address the problem.	Agencies implement the new policies, including calls for further changes.	There are various responses to the new arrangements.
Example: Civil rights activists, such as Martin Luther King Jr., call for an end to racial segregation in the South, hold marches and demonstrations.	**Example:** Reporters from newspapers and television describe the conflict over the civil rights campaign.	**Example:** People become more concerned about racial segregation and more supportive of the campaign against it.	**Example:** Congress passes the Civil Rights Act of 1964 and the Voting Rights Act of 1965.	**Example:** Under the new federal laws, states and localities are forced to end formal policies of racial segregation.	**Example:** People call for additional changes to reduce racism, as well as campaigns to promote the rights of women and other groups.

it is often hard to get others to pay attention. Activists must devise ways of drawing attention to their cause; civil rights demonstrators conducted sit-ins, boycotts, freedom rides, and marches as ways of attracting notice. Activists also need to recruit people to join their movement, manage the movement's operations, and maintain interest in their cause. Chapter 3 examines the role of activists as claimsmakers, as well as some of the challenges that social movements confront.

Not all claimsmakers are social movement activists. Claims also come from various sorts of **experts**, such as physicians, scientists, lawyers, and officials. These people claim to speak with special authority because they have special knowledge; for example, scientists may have done research that shows the nature or extent of a particular troubling social condition, or lawyers may argue that the law related to the condition needs to be reinterpreted. During the civil rights movement, for example, social scientists and psychiatrists claimed that segregation had harmful consequences, while lawyers devised strategies to challenge segregation in the courts. Many societies grant authority to those seen as having special, expert knowledge; Chapter 4 considers how experts can use their authority as claimsmakers.

Stage Two: Media Coverage

The second stage shown in Figure 1.1 is media coverage. Claimsmakers often seek such coverage to bring their claims to the attention of a wider audience. Stories and photographs in newspapers and magazines, as well as reports broadcast on radio and television news programs, can make both the public and policymakers more aware of claims. Civil rights demonstrators depended on this reporting; traditionally it had been easy for Americans outside the South to ignore segregation, but dramatic clashes between protesters and police created major news stories that focused national attention on civil rights. The media face practical considerations that affect how they address social problems, and media coverage inevitably reshapes claims. This is the topic of Chapter 5.

Stage Three: Public Reaction

The general public, then, learns about claims either directly from claimsmakers or indirectly through media reports. The public's response to these claims forms the third stage in Figure 1.1. Usually efforts to understand the public's reactions involve public opinion polls that seek to measure people's attitudes. In some cases, claimsmaking can have dramatic effects on public opinion; during the civil rights movement, for instance, polls indicated an increase in the proportion of Americans who considered civil rights a major problem, and who disapproved of the South's segregation policies. Such shifts are considered important in a democracy because voters may elect officials who reflect their changed views. Chapter 6 looks at polling, as well as other, less traditional ways of understanding the public's reactions.

Stage Four: Policymaking

The fourth stage in Figure 1.1's natural history is **policymaking**. Social policies are the means that society adopts to address troubling conditions, and such policies can be made in various ways. Most obviously, laws can be changed, as when Congress passed and President Johnson signed the Civil Rights Act of 1964 and the Voting Rights Act of 1965—the principal federal responses to the civil rights movement (over time, state legislatures and local city councils also had to modify their laws regarding segregation). But legislation is not the only form of policymaking; all sorts of bodies set social policies: government agencies establish standards for, say, clean water; schools create dress codes for their students; and so on. Policymakers respond to claimsmakers, media coverage, and public opinion, but their own considerations also shape the policies they create. Policymaking is the focus of Chapter 7.

Stage Five: Social Problems Work

Declaring that there will be a new social policy is not the end of the matter; policies have to be implemented, carried out by police officers, social workers, teachers—whoever is responsible for enforcing the particular policy. This is **social problems work**—the fifth stage in Figure 1.1. Often claimsmakers, the media, the public, and policymakers discuss social issues in fairly abstract, theoretical terms: here's what's wrong, and this is what ought to be done. In contrast, social problems workers confront these issues as practical matters. They must deal with particular cases and address a messy real world that often seems quite complicated. For example, civil rights laws had to be translated into specific enforcement practices. It is one thing to say, for instance, that an all-white police force should be integrated, but even if everyone agrees on that principle, they may disagree about practical details regarding how officers should be selected. Chapter 8 tackles the complexities of social problems work.

Stage Six: Policy Outcomes

The sixth and final stage in Figure 1.1 is **policy outcomes**, reactions to the social problems process. Several sorts of outcomes are possible. Some relate directly to the ways in which social policies are implemented. Critics may argue that the new policies are ineffective—that they don't do enough to address the troubling condition, or that the policies actually cause new problems, even making things worse. For instance, the federal civil rights laws passed in the 1960s have been criticized for not going far enough; even though the formal system of legal segregation was dismantled, all sorts of racial inequality remained (thus, blacks continue to have lower incomes, shorter life expectancies, and so on). Other critics may argue that a policy goes too far, as with charges that the affirmative action policies that emerged from the civil rights movement themselves create unequal arrangements. There may be efforts to measure the policy's impact, to evaluate its effectiveness, but how should effectiveness be judged? Often such complaints and questions lead to new claims, and the social problems process begins anew. Such reactions to social policies are the topic of Chapter 9.

In contrast, Chapter 10 explores a broader set of outcomes that often extend over time and space. Consider the impact of the civil rights movement. The dramatic, heavily publicized campaign against segregation inspired other claimsmakers, both within the United States and around the world. Civil rights activists learned valuable practical lessons about how to organize a social movement, attract media coverage for their cause, and so on. Veterans of civil rights protests began to apply their new skills in other social movements, becoming involved in protests over the war in Vietnam or campaigns to advance women's rights, or gay and lesbian rights. Claimsmakers in other nations also tried to duplicate the success of the American civil rights movement by organizing protests over troubling conditions in their own countries. In addition to examining how claims spread, Chapter 10 considers cycles in claimsmaking—a pattern in which claims rise to attract a good deal of attention, then recede, before rising again years later.

Finally, Chapter 11 uses the discussion of Chapters 2 through 10 to revisit Figure 1.1 and develop a more elaborate natural history of the social problems process. Chapter 11 also discusses the uses and future of the constructionist approach.

ADDITIONAL THEMES

Chapters 2 through 11 are organized according to the natural history model illustrated in Figure 1.1. In general, we will discuss top-

Figure 1.2 RESOURCES AND RHETORIC AFFECT EACH STAGE OF THE
SOCIAL PROBLEMS PROCESS

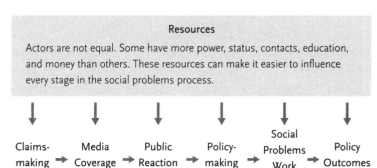

Resources

Actors are not equal. Some have more power, status, contacts, education, and money than others. These resources can make it easier to influence every stage in the social problems process.

Claims-making → Media Coverage → Public Reaction → Policy-making → Social Problems Work → Policy Outcomes

Rhetoric

Any troubling condition can be understood in various ways. At each stage in the social problems process, a troubling condition can be reconstructed to fit the concerns of the actors involved in that stage.

ics in the order in which they occur in the social problems process; this is the book's central organizing principle. In addition, two other themes will run through every chapter: resources and rhetoric. As Figure 1.2 suggests, these themes influence each stage in the social problems process.

Resources

The first theme concerns the **resources** that people bring to the social problems process. A society's members are not equal; some have more money than others, or more power, more status, more education, more social contacts, and so on. These are resources that people can draw upon in the social problems process. We will discover that each stage in Figure 1.1 involves competition: claims-makers compete to attract attention to their claims, claims compete for media coverage and attention from the public and policymakers, and so on. At each stage in the social problems process, some claims succeed in moving to the next stage, while others fail to attract much notice. History is filled with claims that never attracted many adherents, and were ignored, dismissed, or discredited.

Resources affect this competition. In general, people with more money, power, and other resources find it easier to have their claims heard. The resources available to major corporate leaders give them considerable influence over social policy; they have money to spend on political contributions that allow them and their lobbyists access to policymakers. In contrast, the story of the civil rights movement is inspiring precisely because most African Americans living under segregation had such limited resources; they had relatively little in the way of money or political influence, yet they mounted a campaign that successfully changed social policy. At every stage in the social problems process, inequality—whether based on race, class, gender, or something else—means that people bring different resources to the process. It is much easier for those with ample resources to make claims and get them heard, than it is for those with fewer resources.

Rhetoric

The second theme that runs through each chapter is rhetoric. **Rhetoric** is the study of persuasion. Social problems construction is inevitably rhetorical. Whenever people make claims, they are trying to convince others that something is a problem, that it is a problem of a particular sort, and that specific action needs to be taken to deal with this problem. These arguments evolve with each stage in the social problems process; that is, every problem is constructed and reconstructed. Even people who are allied in a claimsmaking campaign may adopt different rhetoric; the claims of activists and experts often emphasize different elements. The media, when they cover claimsmaking campaigns, reshape claims to fit their needs, just as the public's awareness of social problems tends to emphasize some aspects and downplay others. Similarly, when policymakers try to devise means of addressing troubling conditions, they, too, offer their own constructions of what is at issue. And when social problems workers try to implement policies, the practical requirements of their tasks lead them to focus on particular aspects—yet another reconstruction. Finally, at the stage of policy outcomes, there are likely to be all sorts of reinterpretations of previous claims and the policies they inspired. Thus, rhetoric is a central theme in the chapters that follow because social problems claims are not static; rather they shift and morph at each stage in the larger social problems process as the rhetoric changes.

The themes of resources and rhetoric remind us that the social problems process occurs within a broader structural and cultural context. Existing social structural arrangements—resources—give some actors advantages in claimsmaking; having more money or more power makes it easier to promote particular constructions. At the same time, the larger culture makes particular claims—rhetoric—more or less compelling. At each stage in the social problems process, then, actors compete to devise claims that others will find persuasive.

Feedback

Finally, there is a third theme that both Figure 1.1 and Figure 1.2 overlook. These diagrams oversimplify the social problems process. In both, the arrows between stages of the social problems process point in only one direction; that is, claimsmaking is shown as affecting media coverage, media coverage in turn shapes public reaction, and so on. In fact, the social process is more complicated, involving a great deal of **feedback**. That is, claimsmaking does affect media coverage, but claimsmakers are also affected by that coverage (for example, if the press ignored a civil rights demonstration in the 1950s and '60s, activists knew that they needed to adjust what they were doing, in order to attract better coverage for future demonstrations). Similar feedback processes can occur at every stage in the social problems process because the actors at the various stages—the claimsmakers, people who work in the media, and so on—don't just act, but also pay attention to how others react to what they have done, and then respond to those reactions by adjusting what they're doing.

At several points in the book we will consider more elaborate diagrams that illustrate some of these feedback processes; in addition, Chapter 11 will discuss feedback processes in more detail. Remember, Figure 1.1 is designed to help us start thinking about the social problems process; it is by no means the last word.

SUMMARY

This book explores the constructionist approach to social problems. Rather than assuming that social problems are conditions that share an objectively defined characteristic, it defines social problems as a process of raising subjective concerns. This process follows a typical course, a natural history that provides a framework for the rest of the book.

The chapters that follow will focus on specific stages in the social problems process. Taken together, these chapters develop a general framework for thinking about the construction of social problems. The chapters contain many brief mentions of examples that illustrate whatever principle is being discussed. In addition, each chapter features several boxes (somewhat more detailed discussions of how a specific theme in the text is related to a particular social problem), and each chapter ends with a longer case study that explores how the ideas developed in that chapter can be applied to a particular case. Of course, all of these examples are merely illustrative. The goal of this book is to give you a better way of thinking about whatever social problems strike you as interesting.

MAKING CONNECTIONS

- *A social constructionist approach to social problems focuses on the process by which people identify social problems.*

- *As you read the upcoming chapters on claims and claimsmaking, keep in mind how claimsmakers use rhetoric to convince others that a troubling condition is a social problem.*

- *In Chapter 10 you will learn how claims about troubling conditions change depending on the time period and geographic location.*

2

Claims

/

A nyone who follows the news cannot help but hear claims about new social problems. Newspaper stories announce that doctors have identified a new disease, or that scientists have discovered a new environmental threat. Magazine covers warn that a dangerous new drug is spreading, or that law enforcement is battling a new crime. Television commentators discuss new problems brought on by technological developments or changing lifestyles.

Often the new problem has a catchy name, such as *road rage, identity theft, the digital divide,* or *racial profiling*. Suddenly, the brand-new term seems to be on everyone's lips. In many cases, interest in the new problem will prove to be short-lived; people will worry about it for a time, but then their attention will wander. But other terms—think of *sexism*, which first entered the language around 1970—seem to take up permanent residence in our society's vocabulary and consciousness, and the problems they identify remain topics of concern.

Constructing a new social problem involves making claims—that is, calling attention to a troubling condition. Claims are the first element in the social problems process, and they are this chapter's focus. After examining the basic structure of claims, we will consider how audiences respond to them, how they evolve, and where they fit in the larger culture.

THE RHETORIC OF CLAIMS

Every social problems claim makes a persuasive argument; it is an effort to persuade others, to convince them that a particular troubling condition ought to be recognized as a social problem, that that problem has certain characteristics, that the problem demands attention, and that it should be addressed in a specific way. When we analyze claims as arguments or statements, it matters less whether the claims are true or false than whether the people who make the claims and the audiences for those claims find the reasoning convincing.

One of the lessons of this chapter is that claims tend to take standard forms, because people who share a culture are likely to find the same sorts of arguments persuasive. Claims need to be tailored to their audiences, but of course the people who make claims usually belong to the same society as their audience, so when they devise claims that they themselves find sensible, those claims are likely to persuade their audiences. For example, members of a highly religious society may find claims based on theological reasoning compelling, whereas members of another society may be more likely to be swayed by scientific evidence. As a result, within a given society, even claims about very different problems are structured in similar ways. This means that a claim you find utterly convincing will probably contain persuasive elements that resemble those in a claim you consider completely unreasonable. Keep in mind that our topic is how claims work, and understanding this does not require knowing whether the claims are, in fact, true.

The study of persuasion is called *rhetoric*, and we can analyze the rhetoric of claims. Persuasive arguments share a rhetorical structure with three fundamental components: grounds, warrants, and

Figure 2.1 THE STRUCTURE OF SOCIAL PROBLEMS CLAIMS

Grounds ────────────────────▶ Conclusions

Information and
evidence about the
troubling condition—
typifying examples,
statistics, etc. (Also
called the *diagnostic
frame*.)

Warrants

Justifications, appeals
to values—reasons why
something must be
done about the
troubling condition.
(Also called the
motivational frame.)

Recommended
changes, new policies,
etc. to address the
problem. (Also called
the *prognostic frame*.)

Sources: Best, 1990; Snow and Benford, 1988; Toulmin, 1958.

conclusions (Best, 1990; Toulmin, 1958). In social problems claims, *grounds* are statements about the nature of the problem, *warrants* justify taking action, and *conclusions* explain what that action should be. Figure 2.1 illustrates the connections among grounds, warrants, and conclusions. We will consider each in turn.

Grounds

Every social problems claim begins by identifying a troubling condition. Two sorts of statements are involved: those describing the condition, and those explaining why it should be considered troublesome. The former are the grounds; the latter are the warrants (discussed in the next section).

The Basic Rhetorical Recipe. A claim's **grounds** usually are assertions of fact; that is, they argue that the condition exists, and offer supporting evidence. Claims in the contemporary United States often establish their grounds by following a rhetorical recipe containing three ingredients:

1. *Typifying example.* Claims often begin with a **typifying example**, a description of a particular instance of the condition. Typifying examples are, in fact, rarely typical. Usually they are chosen to illustrate the seriousness of the problem, so they tend to be especially extreme, dramatic, disturbing, memorable cases. For instance, claims about child abuse might start with an atrocity story, a description of a very young child who was beaten to death (Johnson, 1995). This would not be a typical case; most child abuse is not fatal. However, using a child's death to typify abuse is compelling rhetoric; the example characterizes the problem in melodramatic terms, in that it depicts a vulnerable, innocent youngster being menaced by a more powerful, villainous adult. This example suggests that child abuse is a very serious problem, because it can involve real, terrible harm. Because the example is so disturbing, people are likely to pay attention, to start worrying about innocent children being threatened by this evil.

2. *Name.* Next the claim **names** the problem. The fatal beating in our example would be identified as an instance of the larger problem of child abuse. Sometimes a new name is attached to an old behavior. Bad driving has long been a familiar problem, but calling it *road rage* is a relatively recent development (Best & Furedi, 2001). Note that naming a problem is not the same as defining it. Many claimsmakers avoid defining a problem by instead focusing on typifying examples. In spite of all of the attention that *child abuse* and *road rage* have received in the media, it can be very difficult to find precise definitions of either term in that coverage. Rather, the people who make up the audience for these claims probably assume that they understand the nature of these problems because they are familiar with one or more typifying examples.

3. *Statistic.* A third ingredient in the basic recipe that establishes the grounds for many claims is some sort of **statistic**, a number that sug-

gests the scope of the problem. In our child abuse example, we might be told that authorities receive nearly three million reports of suspected child abuse annually. In contemporary American culture, statistics imply accuracy and precision—that someone must have counted something. In practice, this is not necessarily true. When claimsmakers are first trying to draw attention to a social problem, they often argue that this problem has been neglected or overlooked. But if people have been ignoring a particular social condition, they probably haven't been carefully measuring its extent, which means no one has been keeping accurate statistics. As a result, early claims often feature figures that are ballpark estimates or educated guesses (Best, 2001a). And just as claimsmakers favor dramatic typifying examples, they usually prefer big numbers, statistics that suggest that the problem is widespread, because a big number implies there is a big problem. Particularly at the beginning of the social problems process, claims often feature big numbers that are really little more than rough estimates.

The three ingredients in the basic rhetorical recipe—a disturbing typifying example, a name, and a big number—combine to create a troubling impression. For example, a description of a small child being beaten to death, coupled with both an explanation that this death is just one instance of the larger problem of child abuse and a statement that three million cases of suspected abuse are reported each year, conveys a sense that millions of children are in danger—possibly of losing their lives. This basic recipe offers a quick, compelling case for recognizing a new social problem. It is an effective rhetorical formula, one that can be spotted in many social problems claims (see Box 2.1).

Additional Grounds. Claims often feature grounds beyond the basic recipe's three ingredients. Many different rhetorical devices can appear as grounds in social problems claims; what follows is just a sampling.

BOX 2.1 THE BASIC RECIPE: GROUNDS FOR MAKING IDENTITY THEFT A SOCIAL PROBLEM

One of *USA Today*'s first stories about identity theft began with a *typifying example*: an Ohio man whose Social Security number had been used to apply for credit, which was then used to charge $111,000 worth of merchandise (Fields, 2000). The man's wife was forced to "put her career on hold" to try and straighten out the resulting mess, which required spending hundreds of hours communicating with creditors. The story then *named* the problem this case exemplified, calling it "identity theft."

The article went on to offer a *statistic* that suggested the problem's scope: "'There is anywhere from $2 billion to $3 billion in fraud losses on credit cards annually,' said James Johnson, Treasury Department undersecretary. 'Much of that is attributable to identity theft'" (Fields, 2000). Another newspaper article from 2000 reported that an estimated "400,000 people across the nation fall victim to identity theft each year" (Gallagher, 2000).

Disturbing examples and big numbers help arouse concern. But even if the worst estimates were accurate and 400,000 people lost $3 billion to identity theft in 2000, those figures average out to false claims of $7,500 per victim—far less than the $111,000 in the typifying example. In addition, these *were* estimates (note the round numbers and the billion-dollar range cited by the official). Typically, in the early stages of constructing a social problem, no accurate statistics are available; for instance, a newspaper story from 2001 quoted another estimate from one credit rating service that there had been 750,000 cases of identity theft the previous year, yet noted that "the Federal Trade Commission's office on ID theft can verify only 25,000 complaints" (Williams, 2001).

- *Worsening situation.* Very often, claims insist that the problem is getting worse. Words like *epidemic* and *crime wave* convey a sense of urgency: the problem is spreading, and—unless something is done—it may soon spiral out of control.

● *Familiar type of problem.* Claims often categorize a problem as being of a recognizable type, such as a crime or a disease. These types are characterized by familiar patterns: we think of crime as being perpetrated by a criminal who intentionally preys on an innocent victim, and diseases as striking vulnerable individuals who should not be considered responsible for getting sick. When a claim classifies the new problem as belonging to a particular type, the claim's audience immediately has a sense of how to think about the problem.

● *Kind of people affected.* Most claims identify categories of people involved in the troubling condition, and explain how their involvement should be understood (Loseke, 2003). Among the most common person categories are *victims* (those harmed by the problem, who may be characterized as bearing no responsibility for their plight, and therefore meriting society's support and sympathy) and *villains* (those responsible for the problem, usually depicted as deserving blame and punishment). Typifying examples often illustrate the principal categories of people involved in the troubling condition (such as an innocent, abused child, and an abusive parent).

● *Range of people affected.* Another popular ground for claims is the suggestion that the problem affects a broad range of people—rich and poor, white and black, and so on. Sometimes it is argued that the problem strikes "randomly" (Best, 1999). Of course, if a problem strikes at random, then it might affect anyone, including anyone listening to the claim. Such randomness suggests that each person who hears the claim has a personal interest in doing something to deal with the problem—before it affects him or her.

● *Challenge to older interpretations.* Claims also may challenge existing or alternative interpretations of the social problem. For instance, students who don't do well in school traditionally were held responsible for their poor performance, which was attributed to their inattention, lack of discipline or effort, and so on. But recent decades have featured claims about learning disabilities arguing that many students should not be blamed, because their poor performance is due to biologically based learning disabilities that deserve accommodation (Conrad & Potter, 2000; Erchak & Rosenfeld, 1989). Such claims challenge older, more familiar constructions. These challenges may be quite explicit; claims may list—and debunk—what they describe as "myths," widely held beliefs about the problem that the claim dismisses as wrong. For example, claims that seek to reconstruct the problem of rape criticize "rape myths" for distorting people's thinking about that crime (Lonsway & Fitzgerald, 1994).

Again, these are just a few of the many kinds of grounds statements found in claims. Taken together, a claim's grounds give a sense of the problem—its nature, scope, and future prospects. Effective grounds convince listeners that the condition is real, thereby setting the stage for the claim's warrants.

Warrants

A claim's **warrants** justify doing something about the troubling condition; they explain why something *ought* to be done. Warrants invoke values. That is, warrants argue that the condition identified in the grounds is inconsistent with what we value, and therefore we need to do something about it. Thus, claims suggest that the troubling condition violates our sense of justice, fairness, equality, or other values.

Values tend to be expressed as vague principles that most—if not all—people can endorse. Most Americans can be expected to hold freedom, justice, equality, protecting the vulnerable, and humanitarianism as cherished values. But what does this mean in practice? It is not always clear how abstract values apply in real-world situations. It is not unusual for opponents in debates over social issues to endorse the same values, even as they support opposing policies. Thus, both those who favor and those who oppose restricting access to abortion tend to invoke *rights*: pro-life abortion opponents speak of the "unborn child's right to life," while pro-choice abortion advocates speak of a "woman's right to choose." Similarly, those who favor affirmative action argue that affirmative action programs foster equality by giving advantages to those who have been disadvantaged, yet affirmative action opponents insist that the programs subvert equality because they don't treat everyone evenhandedly. Although virtually all Americans can be expected to affirm their beliefs in rights or equality, obviously they can disagree over how those abstract values should be translated into practical policies.

Warrants rise and fall in popularity. Sometimes new warrants—new ways of justifying claims—emerge, and change how social problems are characterized. For example, in recent years the rising costs of medical care have inspired a new warrant: arguments that some troubling conditions need to be addressed because they create costly health care burdens for the larger society. For instance, laws requiring motorcycle riders to wear protective helmets have been justified by the high costs of providing long-term medical care to head injury patients, just as campaigns to restrict smoking and reduce obesity have emphasized how those conditions add many millions of dollars to the nation's medical costs (see Box 2.2).

Warrants based on medical costs seem to have emerged to counter arguments that defended motorcycle riding and other risky activities using another, older warrant: personal freedom. That is, motorcycle riders, smokers, and overweight individuals have long argued that they ought to have the freedom to make their own choices, even if those choices involve risks. American culture generally considers freedom an important warrant, particularly if the person taking the risks is not harming others. Using medical costs as a warrant tries to counter this older defense based on individual liberty by arguing that helmetless motorcycle riders and other

Box 2.2 Have You Got a Warrant? Health Care Costs as a Justification

Health care costs continue to rise faster than inflation, inspiring public discussions about how to bring these costs under control, and fostering the emergence of a new warrant for social problems claims. Increasingly we encounter arguments that some conditions should be considered social problems, in part, because they increase health care costs.

Early on, this warrant was used to justify state laws requiring motorcycle riders to wear protective helmets. Claims argued that helmets could reduce head injuries among motorcyclists, and thereby reduce the costs of providing expensive, long-term care to patients. According to one newspaper story, "Helmet proponents say Texas taxpayers pay millions of dollars each year to care for head injuries alone that could have been avoided, or minimized, with a helmet" (LaFranchi, 1987).

Other claims offer parallel warrants. During the 1990s, the attorneys general of several states successfully sued tobacco manufacturers to recover the health care costs that states paid to treat smokers. More recently, a *Newsweek* cover story titled "The Meth Epidemic" offered a similar warrant: "When [methamphetamine] labs explode, they not only kill and maim the cooks; they wreak financial havoc on the facilities that treat them, since the vast majority of meth victims lack health insurance" (Campo-Flores, 2005, p. 44). These claims argue that (1) these social problems harm not just motorcycle riders, smokers, and meth users, but the larger society that has to foot the bill; and (2) society has a right to try to control the economic costs of such harms.

risk takers are not just endangering themselves, but are also harming everyone else, in that their risky behavior raises health care costs across the board, and society has a right to try to discourage people from taking such costly risks.

Because claims can invoke many different values, and because those values are abstract and subject to conflicting interpretations, claims often feature multiple warrants, so different people may agree that something needs to be done about a troubling condition even though they disagree on the reasons for taking action.

Conclusions

Every claim, then, offers a justification for taking action: the grounds identify a troubling condition, and the warrants explain why something should be done about it. Thus, all claims lead to **conclusions**, statements that specify what should be done, what action should be taken to address this social problem. The nature of the conclusions is shaped by the grounds and warrants. If a claim's grounds have depicted a condition that causes terrible suffering, and the warrants speak to humanitarian concerns about the need to alleviate suffering, then the conclusions are likely to focus on ways to help the afflicted. On the other hand, if the grounds emphasize the terrible nature of a particular crime, and if the warrants focus on society's need to protect its members from such evils, then the conclusions will probably advocate cracking down on this crime.

Often conclusions include both short-range and long-range goals. Within the short term, claimsmakers may be trying to arouse concern—to make others aware of the problem, to get people to join their campaign, or to encourage the media to cover the issue. Longer-range goals typically seek policy changes, by arguing that people need to pass a new law, fund a program, or otherwise deal with the troubling condition in a new, more effective way. Usually the short-range goals are seen as steps toward making these long-range changes possible.

Conclusions range from vague endorsements of change to extensive, detailed agendas for action. Early in the social problems process, when claimsmakers' primary aim is to raise awareness of the troubling condition, grounds and warrants tend to receive more emphasis. At later stages in the process, when concern about the problem has become widespread, policy choices become a more central focus, and conclusions are likely to receive greater, more detailed attention.

Summary

Grounds, warrants, and conclusions, then, are standard elements in most arguments (Toulmin, 1958). In the case of social problems claims, this rhetorical structure explains what is wrong, why it is wrong, and what should be done about it. But who hears these claims? Which audiences are these claims meant to persuade, and how do they respond?

CLAIMS, THEIR AUDIENCES, AND THE SOCIAL PROBLEMS MARKETPLACE

Every claim involves communication between at least two parties: those who make the claim (*claimants* or *claimsmakers*), and an **audience** whom the claim is meant to persuade. The audience for claims can include all of the other participants in the social problems process: people who might be enlisted in the cause, other claimsmakers, members of the media who might publicize the claims, the general public, policymakers, and so on. Audiences differ in what they find persuasive, so effective claims need to be tailored to fit their audiences' concerns. How claimsmakers understand those concerns should affect their rhetorical choices. Because there is little point in presenting claims that an audience will not find convincing, claimsmakers must devise arguments that they believe will persuade their audience.

Some claims face little resistance, quickly gaining widespread acceptance among those who hear them. For example, claims about child abuse, child pornography, and other similar threats to children tend to be well received (Best, 1990). American culture views children as vulnerable innocents who deserve societal protection. Therefore, claims that children are being menaced by adults can arouse widespread concern. The arguments seem so compelling that it is difficult to imagine anyone opposing such claims; how could child abuse possibly be defended? Political scientists sometimes refer to claims that inspire this sort of general agreement as **valence issues** (Nelson, 1984).

At the other extreme are claims related to entrenched controversies that probably never will lead to consensus. The debate over abortion remains intense because it features people who have taken intractable, opposing positions: some pro-life advocates argue that abortion is murder and should never be tolerated, while some pro-choice proponents insist that women must be able to control their own bodies and therefore must be free to choose to have abortions. It is very unlikely that a new pro-life claim will persuade those who hold hard-core pro-choice beliefs to change their minds, and equally unlikely that pro-choice arguments can be devised that will change the opinion of those firmly committed to a hard-core pro-life position. When addressing such contested issues, or **position issues**, claimsmakers know that they cannot persuade everyone; they can expect their claims to encounter opposition from at least some people who hear them (Nelson, 1984).

The audience for claims is not an undifferentiated mass. Rather, it can be subdivided—or **segmented**—by race, age, social class, gender, region, and so on. Different segments of the audience tend to have different interests and ideologies. People may respond to a claim by recognizing that they stand to gain or lose if the claims succeed: claims probably seem more compelling to segments of the audience who perceive themselves as directly threatened by the troubling condition, while other segments may resist claims that might adversely affect them by, for example, restricting their freedom or raising their taxes.

Such perceptions of interest are often linked to ideologies or systems of beliefs; different segments of the population are likely to view the world differently, to place different emphasis on particular values, explanations, justifications, and so on. As a general rule, those who benefit from existing social arrangements are more likely to view those arrangements as just, fair, and reasonable, and they are less likely to be sympathetic to claims arguing that those arrangements need to be overturned. Thus, both their interests and their ideologies make them a tough audience, while those disadvantaged by the troubling condition are more likely to be receptive to such claims. Different segments of society, then, view the world differently, and persuasive claims need to match the various worldviews of the segments of the audience toward which they are directed.

Claimsmakers devise various methods to deal with audience segmentation. One tactic is to preach to the choir—that is, to direct claims toward those segments of the audience most likely to respond favorably. For example, abortion activists often direct their claims toward those who they believe already share their beliefs—as when they speak to sympathizers at pro-choice or pro-life rallies. Directing claims to those most likely to be supportive can be a particularly important tactic at the beginning of the social problems process, when claims are first being made: addressing a presumably sympathetic audience first can make more people aware of an issue, rally supporters to the cause, give claimsmakers a chance to hone their claims to make them as persuasive as possible, and create some momentum for carrying the claim to a broader, more diverse audience (such tactics for mobilizing supporters into a social movement are discussed further in Chapter 3).

An alternative approach is to craft claims so as to maximize their appeal to the broadest possible audience. Claims can incorporate multiple grounds, warrants, and conclusions that appeal to different people, thereby seeming to offer something for, if not everyone, at least lots of people. For instance, many advocates of vegetarianism see ethical issues as central to their cause, and they oppose meat eating as morally wrong. However, they also know that these ethical claims encounter widespread resistance; most Americans enjoy eating meat and don't consider it wrong, so moral arguments alone are unlikely to persuade a large audience (Maurer, 2002). However, other grounds and warrants are available: vegetarians can argue that eating meat is unhealthy, in that it fosters heart disease and other ailments; or they can claim that raising animals for food damages the environment. Such arguments add additional grounds and warrants to vegetarians' claims that might appeal to people who are worried about their health or the environment, even if they don't have moral qualms about eating meat. Expanding claims in this way offers vegetarians a chance to persuade people who could be expected to resist narrower ethical arguments that eating meat is wrong.

Well-crafted claims sometimes create surprising alliances among people who usually don't agree, inspiring consensus and converting potential conflict into a valence issue. For instance, political liberals and conservatives often disagree about educational policies. During the 1990s, however, many liberals and conservatives joined forces to promote policies requiring public school students to wear uniforms (Brunsma, 2004). Liberals argued that uniforms would make social class differences among students less visible, reduce pressure on parents to purchase expensive clothes for children, and enhance students' self-esteem; conservatives claimed that uniforms would encourage discipline and orderly behavior among students. Both sides insisted that school uniforms could reduce violence and improve learning. In this case, people who usually disagree found themselves promoting the same solution, even though they disagreed about the precise nature of the problem.

Similarly, advocates representing a wide range of ideologies support efforts to exclude troubling material from elementary and secondary school textbooks: liberals call for excluding material that might reinforce gender or racial stereotypes, fundamentalist Christians want to block content mentioning witches or other supernatural elements, and so on (Ravitch, 2003) (see Box 2.3). Mandating school uniforms and regulating textbook content are just two examples of claims constructed in ways that build broad-based consensus among people who often disagree on other educational issues.

It is important to recognize that the audiences for claims are not passive. People who hear claims react, and claimsmakers must take those reactions into account, by adjusting, revising, and fine-tuning their claims to make them more effective, more persuasive. In other words, claims should not be viewed as one-way messages, transmitted from claimsmakers/senders to their audiences/receivers. Rather, claimsmakers need to be sensitive to their audiences' reactions, to figure out which parts of their claims are working and which are not persuasive and need to be revised. In other words, claimsmakers and their audiences engage in a **dialog** in which the audience's feedback leads claimsmakers to modify their claims (L. T. Nichols, 2003).

If a particular ground or warrant fails to elicit a good reaction, claimsmakers may strike it from their claims and substitute something that they hope will evoke a more favorable response from their audience. For instance, Fujiwara (2005) describes how activists campaigning to halt impending cuts in programs that had provided support to immigrants began with general claims ("immigrant rights are human rights") that proved ineffective. However, they soon found that the media and politicians responded more favorably to claims about the vulnerability of elderly, disabled immigrants, so they refocused their campaign on these more sympathetic cases.

Claimsmaking is usually not a one-shot effort; it takes time to develop effective claims. Most claimsmakers have to try again and

Box 2.3 No Child Left Offended: The Broad Appeal of
Textbook Censorship

The perception that children are vulnerable invites all sorts of claims
about the need to protect kids. For instance, there are efforts to
shield children from exposure to troubling messages, such as the
rating systems used by movies and television to designate the appropriate ages for audiences. Educational critic Diane Ravitch (2003)
writes about parallel efforts to eliminate disturbing content from
textbooks for elementary and secondary school students. These
claims have led to the establishment of extensive guidelines that list
what should be avoided—such as language that might encourage
stereotypical thinking, as well as content that might be construed
as endorsing particular spiritual or political views. A wide range of
claimsmakers—from feminists to fundamentalists—argue for eliminating from children's schoolbooks such troubling words as *actress*,
chief, *Devil*, *fat*, *God*, *homosexual*, *jungle*, *masterpiece*, *poor*, or *wait-
ress*. In a sense, groups who might be expected to disagree come
to a consensus: I won't object to eliminating the content you wish
to forbid, if you support striking the content I want to exclude.

Ravitch—who is, of course, making claims of her own—argues,
"The censorship that has spread throughout American education
has pernicious and pervasive effects" (p. 159). She argues that students are poorly (oops!) served by the books they read being watered
down in hopes that no child—or parent—will be disturbed by the
books' content. In her view, consensus over textbook content may
have more damaging consequences than the conflict that educators
have sought to avoid by trying to please everyone.

again to achieve widespread attention for their claims; they must
try out claims, assess the audience's response, revise the claims, and
so on, until they develop a persuasive argument. After all, claims
compete within a **social problems marketplace** (Best, 1990; Hil-

gartner & Bosk, 1988). At any given moment, countless claims-makers are struggling to get their particular claims heard—far more than can hope to capture the audience's limited attention. Moreover, it is usually impossible to control either the other claims competing to attract the audience's notice or what the audience will choose to notice. Imagine a claimsmaker who had scheduled a major event—say, a combination press conference and demonstration—for September 12, 2001. Because the 9/11 terrorist attacks monopolized the nation's attention for days, no one would have paid any attention to anything the claimsmaker had to say on the twelfth. Although extreme, this example illustrates that claims do not operate in a vacuum.

The competition to capture the audience's attention helps explain some of the features of social problems rhetoric that we noted earlier. Why do claimsmakers so often begin claims with disturbing typifying examples? Why do claims usually settle for naming the problem—often with a catchy label like *road rage*—and avoid giving detailed (and therefore boring) definitions of the problem? Why do claimsmakers favor statistics that suggest the problem is surprisingly large? Each of these rhetorical devices is arresting, eye-catching; each can draw people's attention to this claim (and away from those other claims competing for the audience's attention). The goal is to grab and hold the audience. This competition in the social problems marketplace means that claimsmakers are encouraged to devise dramatic, disturbing, easily grasped claims that will command attention over competing claims. Simpler, stronger arguments work better.

In sum, claimsmakers present what they hope will be persuasive arguments, but they must then attend to the audience's responses, and those responses and their own sense of how they need to revise their rhetoric in turn may be affected by all the other claims and events that are competing for the audience's attention in the social problems marketplace.

EVOLUTION AND OPPOSITION

Social problems claims are not static; rather, they keep evolving. This process continues even after the audience becomes concerned about the problem. Once a claim has attracted recognition and acceptance, we can consider it *well established*; that is, there is widespread agreement that this troubling condition ought to be considered a social problem. Yet this is not the end of the matter; even well-established claims need to change. However compelling claims may seem when they first gain acceptance, they tend to become familiar, stale, boring (Downs, 1972). Audiences find it easier to forget about or ignore claims that can be dismissed as old news, particularly because other, newer claims are always competing for their attention. Audiences also may become frustrated by problems that aren't easily solved—where efforts to address the problem don't seem to make much progress. Each time a claim is repeated, it seems more familiar, less interesting—and less persuasive.

Therefore, claimsmakers often find it necessary to revise and repackage their claims, just to make them seem fresh and interesting. They may add additional grounds, more warrants, or fresh conclusions to give their claims a new look. For instance, instead of simply criticizing the general problem of sexism, the women's movement has been successful at calling attention to a long series of women's issues, each revealing a different aspect of sexist practices, through claims about sexual harassment, date rape, the glass ceiling (which blocks female executives from rising to the top of corporations), and so on. Constantly identifying additional forms of sexism keeps the women's movement's claims fresh.

Once a claim has gained acceptance, it is often possible to build additional claims on that foundation. One possibility is **domain expansion** (Best, 1990). As we have seen, initial claims often emphasize disturbing typifying examples. In the 1960s, for example, claimsmakers described the *battered child syndrome*, the problem of brutal beatings of infants or very young children. Terrible examples tend to make claims more interesting and effective; they help raise concern about an issue. In turn, once this concern has been established, it becomes possible to argue that other conditions are just as bad as—really just another form of, or the moral equivalent of—the initial problem.

In the case of child beating, battered child syndrome was soon renamed *child abuse*, and then the boundaries of what was considered abusive began to expand: Abuse also could affect older children and even adolescents. People began to recognize new types of abuse; beatings were now termed *physical abuse*, as distinguished from emotional abuse, sexual abuse, and so on. And advocates began applying the now widely accepted *child abuse* label to a range of other phenomena, so smoking around children, failing to strap kids into protective car seats, and circumcision, among other things, were claimed to be forms of child abuse. In other words, over time, the domain of child abuse expanded to include more and more phenomena. This sort of domain expansion can occur whenever initial claims become well established (see Box 2.4).

In a related process, claimsmakers choose to **piggyback** a new troubling condition on a well-established problem (Loseke, 2003). Again, child abuse is a good example. The popularity of the label *child abuse* inspired other claimsmakers to characterize their troubling conditions as varieties of *abuse*—so people began speaking of wife abuse, sibling abuse, elder abuse, and so on. Similarly, the successes of the civil rights movement led, in turn, to other campaigns promoting the *rights* of various groups—such as women's rights, gay rights, children's rights, prisoners' rights, and animal rights. And mid-1990s claims about road rage (typified as drivers becoming frustrated and violently attacking others) led journalists to begin identifying all sorts of other *rages*: air rage (among airline passengers), desk rage (office workers), even shopping cart rage (Best & Furedi, 2001). In each of these cases, a well-established social problem created opportunities to construct claims about

Box 2.4 Expanding the Domain of Hate Crimes

In the early 1980s, advocates began drawing attention to what they called *bias crimes*—assaults and other crimes directed at members of racial and religious minorities. Around the same time, gay and lesbian activists in some cities started calling for action against *gay bashing*—criminal attacks that victimized homosexuals. By the middle of the decade, these two campaigns had merged in opposition to what were now renamed *hate crimes*—crimes motivated by the offender's hatred of the victim's ethnicity, religion, or sexual preference. The federal government and most states passed new laws against hate crimes.

Soon other claimsmakers began arguing that the domain of hate crimes was too narrow and ought to be expanded. Some feminists, for example, argued that all rapes were, by definition, motivated by gender hatred, and that crimes against women ought to fall under the hate crime statutes. Advocates for the disabled claimed that crimes against people with disabilities should be considered hate crimes, and it was argued that crimes against the elderly also ought to be categorized as hate crimes. These arguments led to different results depending on the jurisdiction; some state laws continue to define hate crimes narrowly, but other states wound up with more expansive laws. All of these claims, however, illustrate the logic of domain expansion—how the successful construction of a social problem invites efforts to extend that problem's boundaries.

Source: Jenness & Grattet, 2001.

other troubling conditions as being somehow analogous to the familiar original—in effect arguing that there was a sort of family resemblance among types of abuse, rights, or rages—that if the familiar case deserved to be considered a social problem, then so, too, did these other troubling conditions.

Claims do not have to use the same terms— *abuse*, *rights*, *rage*, and so on—to piggyback on successful constructions. In some cases the rhetorical formula used to construct one social problem can be applied to other problems of the same general sort. There is, for example, a fairly standard recipe for identifying new drug problems: claims are made that a drug is a particularly harmful drug, that its use is rapidly spreading, and so on (Reinarman, 1994). This familiar, well-established formula means that contemporary arguments about the dangers of Ecstasy or crystal meth do not look a great deal different from nineteenth-century warnings about opium smoking. Similarly, claims about new forms of victimization often use a well-established rhetorical formula arguing that victimization is widespread and serious yet remains hidden, so that extraordinary measures are needed to identify it, and so on (Best, 1999). In other words, the structure of successful claims—combinations of grounds, warrants, and conclusions that have proved effective in bringing attention to one drug problem or one form of victimization—can be copied and brought to bear on other, analogous issues.

Claims often inspire **counterclaims**, arguments in direct opposition to the original claims. Again, think of the pro-life and pro-choice movements' struggle over abortion; or the claims that global warming is a serious problem exacerbated by humans' activities, and the counterclaims that global warming may be neither as serious as has been feared nor caused primarily by people's actions. In such cases, advocates with opposing views develop full-fledged arguments—each with its own set of grounds, warrants, and conclusions, and each trying to make the most persuasive case (see Box 2.5).

Such debates often revolve around confrontations over grounds or warrants. Each side may challenge the evidence—the grounds—presented by their opponents, charging that those opponents have misunderstood or misrepresented the nature of the troubling condition. "Stat wars" may arise in which each side denounces its opponents' statistics and argues that its own numbers are more accurate (Best, 2001a). Similarly, opponents may insist that some warrants ought to be more compelling than others; in the abortion debate,

Box 2.5 Fighting about Pigeons

Beginning in 1934, Hegins, Pennsylvania, celebrated Labor Day with a community-sponsored pigeon-shooting contest. Each year, about nine thousand birds were placed in boxes and released; on average, contestants managed to shoot about 70 percent of the pigeons (Bronner, 2005).

The Hegins pigeon shoot attracted the notice of animal rights activists, who conducted annual protests between 1987 and 1997. The protesters denounced the pigeon shoot as not just a form of animal cruelty, but a "massacre" or "murder." They linked the celebration to larger social problems, such as genocide, serial murder (claims argued that, while still children, serial murderers often begin mistreating animals), and violence against women (most of the shooters were male, and most of the protesters were female).

The pigeon shoot's defenders offered counterclaims. They argued that this was a traditional celebration, a part of the community's way of life. They challenged the worth of pigeons ("rats with wings"), and they dismissed the protesters as outsiders with peculiar values ("bunny huggers"). They also argued that the protests interfered with the exercising of their rights, and they saw protests against the pigeon shoot as part of a larger campaign to restrict gun ownership.

The Pennsylvania Supreme Court eventually canceled the Hegins pigeon shoot, but claims and counterclaims continue about other animal rights issues (including somewhat different forms of pigeon shooting).

for example, there are sharp disagreements about whether the rights of the fetus or those of the pregnant woman ought to be considered more important.

Many claims emerge within and are promoted as linked to particular **ideologies**—that is, more or less coherent sets of beliefs, such as libertarianism, feminism, liberalism, conservatism, or the various religious doctrines. Ideologies usually emphasize particular warrants; for example, libertarianism views liberty as a central value, and feminism opposes social arrangements that block opportunities for women. Often, too, those familiar with an ideology favor particular grounds; feminists, of course, look for evidence of sexism, and so on. In addition, ideologies often recognize competing belief systems, so liberals and conservatives anticipate disagreeing over many issues. These ideological disputes make it very easy to mount counterclaims; the news that someone associated with a rival ideology is making a claim invites counterclaims.

Claims often have to be modified in response to counterclaims. Opposition means that one's arguments will be subjected to sharper scrutiny and criticism, and those elements that prove easiest to challenge may need to be changed or reinforced. A statistic that has been debunked by one's opponents may be dropped and a more defensible number added to fill the gap, and so on. At the same time, the fact that there is opposition can be incorporated into one's claims. It may be possible to characterize one's opponents as part of the problem, turning the fact of opposition into a new ground for the claims. At least for those who share our ideology, news that the opposition is making counterclaims can reassure us that we're correct.

In sum, claims are constantly in play. They evolve, and they can inspire both other claims and opposition, so new claims are almost always shaped by those that preceded them.

CULTURAL RESOURCES

Theoretically, claimsmakers are free to assemble claims in any form they choose. In practice, however, claims have to make sense—both to the claimsmakers who choose to make them, and to the audiences whom the claimsmakers hope to persuade. This means that claims must draw upon the larger culture; they must be consistent with people's understandings of how the world works. In some societies, attributing misfortune to the acts of witches has been seen as a perfectly sensible explanation. In contemporary American society, however, claims about witchcraft are likely to be rejected out of hand by most people—although not by all. Most would-be claimsmakers recognize that this is the prevailing view, so they tend to avoid blaming witches or, more generally, constructing problems along lines that they and their audiences will find unconvincing.

Every culture, then, can be seen as a large repository of evolving, more or less familiar ideas about how the world works—and how it should work. These **cultural resources** are available to be exploited whenever claims are created. Our culture, for example, tends to idealize children as vulnerable innocents, and claims that warn about threats to children often elicit sympathetic reactions. This is such a widely shared view that we have trouble imagining people thinking any other way. However, New England's Puritans had a much darker view of children: they worried that children were born in a state of sinful willfulness, and they believed that children needed to have their wills broken to become properly God-fearing (Fischer, 1989, pp. 97–101).

Such different assumptions lead to quite different visions of, say, discipline. For some modern Americans, spanking is seen as harmful, even as a form of child abuse—one more way that adults inflict injuries on innocent children (P. W. Davis, 1994). Although the Puritans considered spanking a last resort, they used a variety of physical restraints and shaming devices, such as forcing a child to wear a wooden bit; such practices, which seem quite shocking to us, were standard ways of disciplining children, designed to teach them to be submissive and to understand God's wrath. It's easy to imagine that some claims about endangered children that might seem very powerful to us would have fallen on deaf ears among the Puritans.

Claims, then, draw on a society's cultural resources—the fund of words, ideas, and images that most people understand to be reasonable. It is easier to arouse contemporary Americans' concern about threats to children or violence against women—two groups that are widely understood to be relatively vulnerable to victimization and therefore in need of protection—than to promote claims about endangered adult males. Nevertheless, although culture does limit the range of possible claims to some degree, it still offers a broad array of choices. For example, various segments of the U.S. population attribute different social problems to quite diverse causes—causes such as acts of God (for instance, to explain natural disasters), germs, conspiracies, belief systems (for example, particular religious or political ideologies), people's upbringing, and so on. Of course, part of being familiar with a culture is having the ability to predict which audiences will find which explanations appropriate for which problems.

Note that the fund of cultural resources is large, diverse, and not necessarily logically consistent. The point is not that all social problems have to be constructed in the same way, but that any culture offers various ideas and images that might be incorporated into successful claims. Just as American culture supports values that can sometimes conflict with one another, so, too, it encompasses other competing, conflicting notions.

This cultural diversity means that most social problems might be constructed in very different ways. For example, debates over poverty often feature dramatically different interpretations: Some commentators argue that the poor bear much of the responsibility for their plight, that they make bad choices (such as dropping out of school) that make poverty a likely outcome. Other critics insist that poverty is largely a product of a social structure that blocks too many opportunities, creating obstacles (such as a shortage of high-paying jobs) that make it hard for people to overcome poverty. Both the idea that individuals must bear responsibility for their own decisions, and the idea that a fair society should offer opportunities for advancement are familiar; both belong to the stock of cultural resources from which claims can be assembled. Such competing accounts of poverty's causes—although derived from the same culture—can reveal bitter differences within the culture.

Claimsmakers may charge that rival claims are morally irresponsible because they apply inappropriate explanations, that they ignore God's laws, blame victims who should not be blamed, or err in some other way. Not everyone subscribes to every element in the larger culture—certainly not all of the time.

Moreover, the cultural context for claims is continually shifting. Ideas, values, imagery, explanations—all the elements of culture—can go in and out of fashion. In part, this fluctuation reflects people's ongoing quest for novelty: both claimsmakers and their audiences can become bored when claims seem stale—too familiar—so claims must be continually repackaged to make them seem fresh and interesting. In addition, genuinely new elements are added to the stock of cultural resources; a scientific discovery, the spread of a new disease, a new invention, or a dramatic event can have far-reaching consequences. Such novelties can reverberate through society generally, and through the social problems marketplace in particular, in complex ways.

Consider the identification of AIDS as a new disease in the early 1980s. No sociologist could have predicted all of the consequences that derived from that development: shifts in funding priorities for medical research and reforms in the methods used to test new treatments; the promotion of AIDS prevention policies (including condom distribution and needle exchange programs), all manner of art portraying aspects of the epidemic, and on and on. Or consider how the spread of cell phones has spawned new social problems claims—about the risks when drivers are distracted while talking on their phones, about the propriety of carrying on phone conversations where they can be overheard by others, about allegations of health hazards from cell phones, and so on.

Cultural shifts are reflected in social problems claims. Many social problems—for instance, gangs, cults, racism, and poverty—have been the subject of claims going back many decades, even centuries, but the particular constructions of these problems in different periods reflect current cultural developments during those

Box 2.6 Linking Trauma and Sexual Abuse

During the 1970s, public attention came to be focused on adults who had been sexually abused as children—a category of people who had not been the subject of much notice in earlier decades. In particular, claims argued that childhood sexual abuse was often traumatic, continuing to shape the victims' adult lives. Why did these particular claims emerge when they did?

A set of shifts in the larger culture combined to shape these claims (J. E. Davis, 2005). During the early 1970s, advocates for Vietnam veterans convinced the American Psychiatric Association to classify post-traumatic stress disorder (PTSD) as a mental illness. Although originally understood as a reaction to terrible combat experiences, other sorts of experiences began being classified as "traumatic stresses." Meanwhile, the feminist movement boomed during the 1970s, drawing attention to rape, incest, and other forms of sexual exploitation by males, and particularly to the lasting effects of victimization—which, it was argued, included PTSD. By 1980, Christian fundamentalists had begun claiming that there was a vast, underground conspiracy of satanists that sexually abused children in rituals. Often these various claims insisted that sexual abuse victims might have repressed all memories of their abuse; this meant that adults with troubled lives—people who felt unhappy or were overweight, for example—might be responding to childhood abuse, and therapists began trying to recover memories of this suspected abuse.

These apparently unrelated developments—in this case involving veterans' advocates, feminists, fundamentalists, and mental health professionals—all contributed to a readiness to worry about the long-term consequences of trauma generally and of childhood sexual abuse in particular. No one could have foreseen that a campaign to help troubled veterans would influence how people thought about sexual abuse, but it did. In short, cultural shifts can have unexpected effects on thinking about social problems.

periods (see Box 2.6). This means that cultural conditions during particular historical periods affect how social problems are constructed during those times. For example, the theme of expanding individual rights during the 1960s (as reflected in the civil rights movement and the sexual revolution), or the shift toward more conservative values that began in the late 1970s (as reflected in growing concerns about sex and drugs), can be seen as having influenced claims about many different social problems (Jenkins, 2006). (Chapter 10 will have more to say about the historical context of claims.)

Cultural resources, then, both constrain and enrich claims. Claims almost always use familiar language, imagery, forms of explanations, and other cultural elements. After all, the claimsmakers are themselves members of the culture, and they are almost forced to construct claims that they themselves view as sensible, claims that they also believe will receive a receptive hearing from their audiences. Thus, cultures constrain the sorts of claims that are likely to emerge. However, cultures are complex enough, multifaceted enough, that claimsmakers still have considerable leeway in choosing and shaping the arguments they present. Although we can note similarities among claims, such as cases in which new claims seem modeled on others, and we can imagine claims (about, say, witchcraft) that seem too far-fetched to succeed in our society, it is still true that claimsmakers have a lot of flexibility in devising their arguments.

UNDERSTANDING CLAIMS

This chapter has explored various aspects of social problems claims. It began by considering claims as rhetorical arguments—the ways in which grounds, warrants, and conclusions structure claims. To be effective, though, claims have to persuade audiences, so claimsmakers must understand who their audiences are and shape their

Figure 2.2 DYNAMICS SHAPING CLAIMS

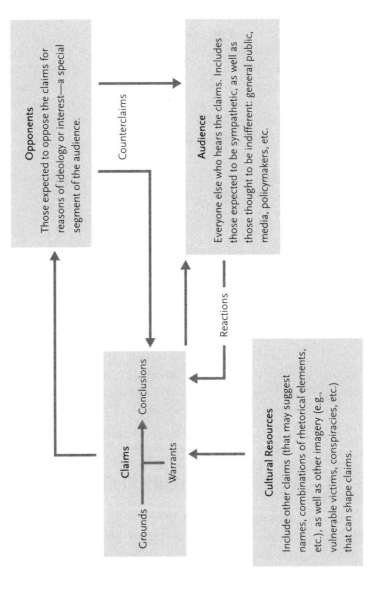

Opponents

Those expected to oppose the claims for reasons of ideology or interest—a special segment of the audience.

Audience

Everyone else who hears the claims. Includes those expected to be sympathetic, as well as those thought to be indifferent: general public, media, policymakers, etc.

Counterclaims

Claims

Grounds

Warrants

Conclusions

Reactions

Cultural Resources

Include other claims (that may suggest names, combinations of rhetorical elements, etc.), as well as other imagery (e.g., vulnerable victims, conspiracies, etc.) that can shape claims.

arguments to fit those audiences' concerns. As a result, claims-makers and audiences find themselves in a dialog as they respond to one another's ideas. Claims also are influenced by other claims. They evolve over time; claims need to be periodically revised to make them seem fresh. They are also shaped by the successes and failures of earlier claims: successful claims invite domain expansion or other efforts to piggyback on their success, just as claimsmak-ers try to avoid the mistakes of failed claims. And for highly con-tentious issues, claims face counterclaims, and opponents must respond to one another's constructions within the larger social problems marketplace. Finally, the broader culture provides a con-text for claims: language, imagery, and other cultural resources offer raw material from which claims can be built. Figure 2.2 illustrates all these various processes.

Of course, claims are social products; they do not exist inde-pendently of people. People assemble—construct—claims in hopes of persuading others. Although this chapter has focused on the claims themselves, the remainder of this book will concentrate on the various sorts people who create, distribute, alter, challenge, or otherwise react to claims—the actors in the various stages of the social problems process.

MAKING CONNECTIONS

- *Claims are rhetorical arguments structured by grounds, warrants, and conclusions.*

- *The concepts of claims and claimsmakers introduced in this chapter set the stage for the next two chapters' discussion of activists as claimsmakers and experts as claimsmakers.*

- *In Chapter 5 you will learn how claimsmakers use the media to present their claims. You will also learn how the media alter the claims they present. As you read that chapter, keep in mind what you have learned in this chapter about cultural resources.*

CASE STUDY
CLAIMS ABOUT GAY MARRIAGE

In the fall of 2003, gay marriage abruptly became a far more visible social issue. The Massachusetts state supreme court ruled that that state's constitution did not prohibit same-sex marriages and declared that, unless the legislature acted, the state would be required to grant licenses to homosexual couples. (Massachusetts began issuing marriage licenses to same-sex couples who resided in the state six months later.) Shortly after the Massachusetts court's ruling, the mayor of San Francisco announced that, in his interpretation, California also could not legally refuse marriage licenses to homosexual couples, and he ordered San Francisco to begin issuing licenses to gay and lesbian applicants. Thousands of couples applied for and received licenses; the lines of applicants waiting outside city hall allowed television cameras to make gay marriage visible. In the coming weeks, officials in other cities copied San Francisco's example, although none of the new policies lasted once the courts weighed in; the California state supreme court, for example, ruled that San Francisco's mayor had overstepped his authority and ordered the city to stop issuing marriage licenses to gay and lesbian couples.

Courts in some other states seemed likely to follow the Massachusetts example; meanwhile, other states passed laws explicitly stating that marriage would be restricted to couples composed of one man and one woman. News reports indicated that several European countries had legalized same-sex marriages, and Canada followed suit in 2005 (Smith, 2005). Claims advocating gay marriage inspired counterclaims opposing the change.

Americans tend to think of marriage in sentimental terms, as an expression of commitment between people who love one another. In fact, early claimsmaking by advocates of same-sex marriage often focused on the emotional aspects of marriage: why, they asked, shouldn't people in love be able to marry? By 2004, however, the claims by proponents of gay marriage increasingly emphasized practical issues (Rauch, 2006). Advocates argued that marriage is far more than a sentimental commitment between two people, that it grants the married couples significant legal rights and protections. For instance, married partners can hold property in common; in many states, a surviving spouse has legal inheritance rights upon the partner's death. Many hospitals grant spouses special privileges to be with and make decisions on behalf of a sick or dying partner. Increasingly, the typifying examples presented by proponents of gay marriage pointed to cases in which individuals whose expressed wishes—to designate their partners as the ones who should inherit their property or make medical decisions in their behalf—had not been respected, cases in which courts or hospitals had refused to honor those wishes, even when they were stated in wills and other formal documents, because the partner was not a legal spouse.

Advocates of gay marriage drew upon a variety of warrants. They pointed to freedom and individualism, by arguing that individuals ought to have the right to choose whom they love, to choose to pass their property along to those loved ones without penalty, and to choose who should oversee their care when they can no longer care for themselves. Proponents also focused on questions of equality, insisting that being blocked from marriage constituted unequal treatment under the law and thus discriminated against gays and lesbians.

Counterclaims depicted the issue in very different terms. In earlier years, opposition to same-sex marriage had often emphasized that homosexuality was simply wrong and should not be condoned by the state. Although many opponents of gay marriage may have continued to see the issue as one of morality, they began to craft somewhat different claims. In particular, they argued that marriage had traditionally been defined as a union between one man and one woman, and that gay marriage would violate the fundamental nature of marriage. They further argued that the purpose of marriage was procreation, and that children benefit from being raised by married couples. They warned that, if gay marriage gained approval, society would start down a slippery slope, where other forms of marriage, such as polygamy, might also become legal. Once tradition was cast aside, who knew where it might lead? The issue, they argued, was not the rights of gays and lesbians, but preservation of the traditional family—a fundamental social institution.

The audience for these claims was itself divided. Certainly a segment of the population strongly disapproved of homosexuality and viewed calls for legalizing gay marriage as very troubling. In particular, a large share of religious conservatives opposed gay marriage, and during the 2004 and 2006 election years, conservative politicians sought to court those voters by, for instance, endorsing a constitutional amendment to forbid same-sex marriage.

More generally, the arguments of both proponents and opponents of gay marriage proved persuasive. Many people found the proponents' arguments for equal rights persuasive, and some polls showed that most people supported proposals to establish "civil union" laws (Brewer & Wilcox, 2005). (*Civil unions* were arrangements designed to offer the same legal protections that married partners received, although without calling their relationship a marriage.) When the issue was same-sex *marriage*, however, only a minority approved.

Meanwhile the debate continued. There were more court cases and more legislative debates. And many gay and lesbian couples were arranging marriage ceremonies (sometimes held within established churches, although these were not legally binding unless a marriage license had been issued).

Would gay marriage become a legal, routine social arrangement? The new claims—particularly those focusing on the legal protections given to married spouses—suggested that the issue's outcome was at least uncertain.

QUESTIONS

1. What grounds, warrants, and conclusions do advocates for gay marriage and their opponents use?

2. How did claims in favor of gay marriage evolve from those of the earliest advocates to the more recent campaigns after the ruling by the Massachusetts state supreme court?

3. How did opponents to gay marriage change their counterclaims to respond to new arguments by advocates of gay rights?

3

Activists as Claimsmakers

C laims cannot exist by themselves; people—claimsmakers—must advance them. It's tempting to equate claimsmakers with activists—people like Martin Luther King Jr.—who become passionately involved with an issue, dedicate their lives to a cause, and march and demonstrate until their claims receive attention. Indeed, this is part—but only part—of the story.

When we think of activists, we envision people who stand outside the halls of power. Because they do not hold powerful political offices or have strong ties with those who do, it is fairly difficult for these **outsider claimsmakers** to get others—the media, the general public, and particularly the officials who can make policies that might actually do something about the troubling social condition—to pay attention to their claims (Best, 1990). This is why activists so often resort to attention-grabbing tactics: demonstrations, sit-ins, and so on. Activists hope that these activities will lead to media coverage, and that attracting publicity for their cause will bring their claims to the attention of the public, so that, in turn, both the media and the public will press policymakers to take action. That is, activists envision the claimsmaking process as shown in Figure 3.1a, where the thicker arrow between the claimsmakers and the

Figure 3.1 CLAIMSMAKING BY OUTSIDER AND
INSIDER CLAIMSMAKERS

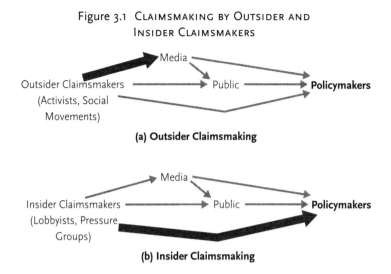

(a) Outsider Claimsmaking

(b) Insider Claimsmaking

media identifies the media as the most important audience for outsiders' claims.

However, there is an alternative, more direct route to successful claimsmaking. Some people already have contacts with policymakers. Such people include lobbyists, major political contributors, government officials, and well-established interest groups such as the National Rifle Association (NRA), which is concerned with protecting the rights of gun owners, or the National Association for the Advancement of Colored People (NAACP), which is concerned with advancing the rights of African Americans. Those who are already well connected to policymakers form what is sometimes called the **polity** (Useem & Zald, 1982); the polity consists of those groups whose interests are routinely considered by policymakers, so they are often able to influence policymaking. People with such connections can act as **insider claimsmakers**; often they pursue their claims outside the glare of the media spotlight, without arousing much public attention. The activities of insider claimsmakers are depicted in Figure 3.1b, where the thicker arrow runs directly from claimsmakers to policymakers.

The activities of insider claimsmakers will be considered in Chapter 4; this chapter will focus on outsider claimsmakers—in particular, activists such as Dr. King. Activists often belong to broad **social movements**, general causes such as the civil rights movement or environmentalism. Each social movement may contain several distinct **social movement organizations** (SMOs), such as the civil rights movement's SNCC (Student Nonviolent Coordinating Committee) and CORE (Congress of Racial Equality), or the environmentalist movement's Greenpeace and Sierra Club. As we shall see, although the larger society may view a movement's SMOs as allies that share a common cause, activists frequently think of other SMOs within the same social movement as rivals.

Social movements frequently face opposition. Movements seek to promote change, and the status quo inevitably has its defenders. The most vigorous defenses usually come from those who have vested interests in the status quo; these opponents benefit from existing social arrangements in ways that would be threatened if the changes promoted by the movement were to occur. For example, some white southerners, who saw themselves as benefiting from legal segregation, opposed the civil rights movement. Moreover, it takes effort to change social arrangements, and even when people may not strongly oppose activists' claims, they may see no good reason to exert the effort that change requires; sociologists refer to such reluctance to alter existing social arrangements as **inertia** (Becker, 1995).

Chapter 2 described position issues—that is, topics that evoke controversy, inciting active disagreements about whether a particular condition should be considered troubling, or what that condition's causes might be, or what should be done to address the condition. In such position issues, claims inspire counterclaims, and **countermovements** may arise to promote these counterclaims.

Some sociologists associate the term *social movement* with liberal or progressive causes and prefer to restrict the term *counter-movement* to more conservative causes. However, it makes better analytic sense to speak of social movements as calling for change, and of countermovements as resisting change. When abortion was generally illegal, there was a movement of abortion rights advocates, which was opposed by a countermovement that favored restricting abortion. Once abortion became widely legal, however, it became more reasonable to speak of a pro-life movement calling for change, and a pro-choice countermovement trying to defend the existing right to abortion. This example illustrates that countermovements are conservative in the sense that they seek to preserve the status quo; when political liberals support existing social arrangements (such as laws protecting the right to abortions), they may organize countermovements to oppose claimsmaking by political conservatives (such as the pro-life movement).

Because most social movements—and countermovements—promote claims about social problems, and because images of activists tend to come to mind when we think of claimsmakers, this chapter will focus on key aspects of social movements and the role of activists as claimsmakers. (Chapter 4 will consider other sorts of claimsmakers.) We will begin this chapter's discussion of activist claimsmakers by examining three recent approaches adopted by sociologists to study social movements: framing, resource mobilization, and opportunity structures.

FRAMING

Most social movements present claims; they identify a troubling condition and call for social changes to address the problem (Benford & Hunt, 2003). These claims can, of course, be studied in terms of their rhetoric—that is, by using the concepts developed

Chapter 2. Social movement scholars, however, often adopt a slightly different vocabulary: they speak of **framing** to describe how activists construct their claims.

Like the frame around a picture, activists' frames place a social movement within a larger context; frames locate the key issues and set them off so that they are easily understood. Like the wooden frame of a house, activists' frames provide a structure, a framework around which elaborate claims can be assembled.

The same issue might be framed in many different ways. Some frames emphasize morality, appealing to people's sense of right and wrong. Other frames evoke particular ideologies or political philosophies, such as Marxism or libertarianism. Still other frames emphasize political struggles between groups with competing interests. What may seem to be a single social movement—the civil rights movement, the environmental movement, and so on—can be composed of activists who frame the issue in very different ways (see Box 3.1).

Frames encourage viewing the world from a particular perspective; they give meaning to what might otherwise seem confusing, so that once someone adopts a given frame, everything seems to be clearer, to make sense. For example, the feminist movement calls attention to the various ways in which social arrangements disadvantage women; a feminist frame gives activists a particular vantage point from which they can view women's place in the world.

There are obvious parallels between constructionist scholars' examinations of claimsmaking rhetoric (as discussed in Chapter 2), and social movement analysts' discussions of frames. Frames have three components: **diagnostic frames** identify the nature of the problem (that is, *diagnostic frame* is another term for what constructionists call *grounds*); **motivational frames** explain why action needs to be taken (akin to the constructionists' *warrants*); and **prognostic frames** specify what needs to be done (similar to the constructionists' *conclusions*) (Snow & Benford, 1988). For our purposes, these are essentially similar classification schemes, one

Box 3.1 Frames for Peace

The American peace movement of the 1980s was an alliance that drew together activists who framed issues of peace and war in very different ways. John Lofland (1993, pp. 25–36) identifies six very different frames, or theories, for how the movement could foster peace:

1. *Transcender theory* was an idealistic frame that viewed "international conflict as a giant error or misunderstanding" that could be easily resolved if nations only reexamined their differences.

2. *Educator theory* argued that peace could be achieved if activists provided more factual information and taught people to think more clearly about peace issues.

3. *Intellectual theory* sought to generate new theories or research that might influence the debate over peace issues and thereby bring about change.

4. *Politician theory* sought to shape the democratic process by running candidates committed to peace policies, lobbying the government, and otherwise joining the political process.

5. *Protester theory* led to a variety of demonstrations, marches, and other activities designed to draw attention to the cause of peace and, in some cases, to disrupt the system that supported war.

6. *Prophet theory* called for spiritual regeneration, in which people experienced an inner transformation that left them committed to the cause of peace.

These different theories are evidence that the peace movement encompassed quite different approaches to thinking about—framing—the issue of peace, and what ought to be done to bring about change. Of course, particular activists might, on different occasions, adopt different frames. But references to *the* peace movement overlook what were sometimes important differences in how activists understood the issues. Many social movements encompass similarly diverse arrays of frames.

favored by those who think of themselves as sociologists of social problems, the other by scholars of social movements.

One reason that social movement analysts favor the language of framing is their interest in how social movements recruit new members. A key issue for most activists is enlisting supporters to their causes. Social movements need to attract new members, to convince people to share the activists' concerns and support the movement through donations and investments of time and energy. Because social movements typically promote unfamiliar ways of looking at society and its problems, they must frame issues in ways that will appeal to prospective members. In other words, activists need to align their frames with those of the people they hope to enlist in their movements.

Frame alignment refers to the ways in which social movements must address the existing frames or ways of looking at the world held by prospective members (Snow, Rochford, Worden, & Benford, 1986). Movement participants—activists—have a particular frame, with its diagnostic, motivational, and prognostic elements, but the people they might like to recruit to the movement already have their own ways of understanding the world. The goal is to bring these frames into alignment, so that others will come to adopt the activists' frame (and presumably join the movement). For example, the feminist movement seeks to introduce people to a feminist frame so that they can recognize how sexism affects their lives, and so that they will support feminist efforts to challenge sexual discrimination. Frame alignment usually takes one of four forms:

1. *Bridging.* In **frame bridging**, activists seek support from people thought to hold frames similar to their own. For example, liberal activists interested in a new issue are likely to seek supporters among those already known to be sympathetic with other liberal causes, just as conservative activists generally try to bring their new concerns to

the attention of known conservatives. That is, activists seek to enlist people who have already supported other, similar causes because it should be easy to build a bridge between fundamentally similar frames.

2. *Amplification.* In **frame amplification**, activists call upon values or beliefs that they presume many people hold in order to rally others to their cause. Although the prospective supporters may not have been active in other movements, they are presumed to hold basic assumptions that should make them sympathetic to the activists' cause. For instance, recent campaigns to register sex offenders and then restrict their rights have drawn upon popular stereotypes about the predatory nature of sex offenses, and people's sense that society ought to be protected from such predators. Frame amplification often seeks to arouse emotional reactions, such as compassion or outrage, so that people feel compelled to join the movement.

3. *Extension.* In **frame extension**, activists extend their frame to encompass concerns that prospective supporters are thought to have. In this case, the activists' core values or beliefs may not overlap those of their prospective supporters until they extend their frame. To return to an example raised in Chapter 2, vegetarian activists tend to be concerned with primarily ethical issues: they believe that it is morally wrong to eat meat (Maurer, 2002). However, relatively few Americans share that concern, and vegetarians have had more success gaining support by extending their frame to emphasize the health and ecological benefits of vegetarian eating—appeals that can attract supporters who worry about health or environmental issues more than the morality of eating meat.

4. *Transformation.* In **frame transformation**, activists call upon prospective supporters to reject the familiar worldview that they take for granted and adopt a new and different frame. This transformation may be limited to how one thinks about a specific troubling condition (for example, the campaign to redefine drunk driving sought to persuade

people to stop thinking of it as a somewhat amusing, minor offense, and start viewing it as a serious crime that all too often leads to terrible consequences). In other cases, activists may try to convert supporters to a completely different view of the world (think of efforts to recruit adherents to unfamiliar religions).

These four forms of frame alignment pose increasingly difficult challenges to activists. Frame bridging is the most straightforward task: claims are made to prospective recruits who are thought to be ideologically predisposed to being sympathetic to the claims. Frame amplification depends on emphasizing values and beliefs that the activists already share with the audience for their claims, in order to mobilize them to action; and frame extension requires activists to modify their own frame to make it more attractive to potential recruits. Frame transformation presents the greatest challenge: recruits are asked to abandon their familiar view of the world in favor of the activists' frame.

Different SMOs within the same social movement may have distinct frames that appeal to different prospective members. Often, for instance, a movement may contain both moderate and radical SMOs, the former advocating limited reforms to the existing social system, while the latter call for more significant changes. Activists from a movement's moderate and radical wings usually frame the troubling condition and its solution differently, and they may clash in **frame disputes**, disagreements over how to think about the problem (Benford, 1993). In many cases, activists from different camps within the same social movement present their frames to different audiences: as a general rule, moderates seek to appeal to older people in the middle class (who have relatively secure places within the existing social system, and who therefore are likely to resist radical calls for dramatic social change); and radicals are more likely to seek supporters among those who are younger or poorer (who have far less invested in maintaining the status quo, and who therefore should be more open to pursuing fundamental changes).

Successful framing draws upon cultural resources; it incorporates familiar values, beliefs, imagery, and other cultural elements that prospective members find persuasive and convincing. Feminists, for instance, invoke familiar notions of fairness and equality, and argue that women have a right to equal treatment. But framing cannot be a one-way process. When activists interact with prospective members, they usually discover that some appeals are more persuasive than others in convincing people to join the movement. After all, prospective social movement members have many messages competing for their attention—television shows, news reports, advertisements, and on and on. Activists cannot simply present a frame and wait for the world to take notice; that would leave too much to chance because it would be too easy for the activists' frame to be overlooked. Rather, activists must seek out potential supporters, try to frame their message in ways that others will find interesting and convincing, and then pay close attention to what does and doesn't work. If activists find that their claims have generated counterclaims, they may need to reframe the issue to take this opposition into account. Similarly, when one version of a frame fails to elicit much response, it will need to be modified until it begins to be effective (see Box 3.2).

This need to devise frames that will attract supporters, counter opposition, and eventually influence social policy can raise issues of integrity for activists (Benford, 1993). Activists at the core of an SMO often have more ideologically coherent frames than many other movement supporters have, and they may view frame extension—altering their frame in order to make it more appealing—as a violation of their principles, as "selling out." Frame disputes within a movement often revolve around questions of compromise: should activists present what they believe to be a more correct, more principled view of the issue even if it risks rejection by many prospec-

Box 3.2 Reframing the Tobacco Problem

Modern activists' efforts to restrict tobacco smoking received a major boost in 1964, when the U.S. surgeon general issued a heavily publicized report declaring that smoking significantly increases risks of developing lung cancer and other serious illnesses. This announcement led to campaigns to educate smokers (placing warning labels on cigarette packs) and to discourage the spread of smoking (banning cigarette companies from advertising on television). The antismoking movement framed the issue in terms of the increased risks to smokers.

By 1980, however, the movement seemed to be losing momentum; although a number of restrictive laws had been passed, smokers and the tobacco industry could make counterclaims based on the value of freedom. They argued that smokers ought to have the right to take whatever risks smoking involved.

Antismoking activists responded to these counterclaims by reframing the issue to emphasize the dangers of secondhand smoke. They argued not only that smoking poses a health danger to smokers, but also that nonsmokers face increased risks from inhaling the smoke from other's cigarettes. Activists warned that smokers jeopardize the health of others, including innocent children. Shouldn't nonsmokers be free to avoid exposure to the risks of secondhand smoke? This new frame proved very effective; it led to the passage of additional laws restricting the settings where people could smoke (smoking was forbidden in airplanes, in many restaurants and workplaces, and so on). Adopting a new frame gave the antismoking movement new life (Troyer, 1989).

tive supporters who will find it too difficult to understand, or even unpalatable; or should they frame the issue in weaker but more appealing terms so that prospective members will find it easier to digest? Frames inevitably reflect a combination of how activists view the world, and what they believe will be an effective message.

RESOURCE MOBILIZATION

Adopting a frame that justifies belief in a cause is not enough to make a claim successful; activists cannot trade on outrage alone. Social movements also need to deal with a variety of mundane problems. Organizing a successful demonstration means picking a good time and place, to maximize participation. People who might be willing to participate must be contacted and encouraged to come (demonstrations designed to attract a big crowd might require Internet postings, posters, telephone calling systems, and other ways of getting the word out); it might even be necessary to make arrangements to transport people to the event. Large demonstrations also require a lot of planning: tasks might include training people in dos and don'ts, scheduling speakers and other events, assigning monitors to supervise demonstrators, preparing first-aid stations, and possibly even arranging to post bail for people who get arrested. In addition, press releases need to be issued to inform the media that the demonstration will be taking place, and it may be a good idea to designate spokespeople to explain the demonstrators' purpose to the reporters covering the event.

In other words, one way to think about activists is in terms of the resources required by a social movement's activities. Movements need money, members, skills, and so on. These may seem like mundane considerations, especially if we think of social movements in romantic terms, consisting of plucky little guys struggling against powerful interests. But without sufficient resources, movements will have difficulty getting started, let alone enduring. Successful movements must assemble the resources they need. Sociologists refer to this gathering of resources as **resource mobilization** (McCarthy & Zald, 1977).

The resources that activists need are almost always scarce: it is hard to raise enough money, because the people who give money have lots of other ways to spend it; it is hard to get people to devote time to the movement, because there are other things they could do; and so on. The struggle to assemble resources means that SMOs—even SMOs that are theoretically allies in the same social movement—find themselves in competition with one another for the same scarce resources. They compete for members, for donations, for media coverage, and so on. If one SMO is especially effective in mobilizing resources, rival organizations are likely to find resources harder to come by.

For example, the civil rights movement—now recalled as a grand, unified movement to end segregation—was characterized by internal competition and disagreements (Haines, 1984). Different civil rights organizations had different frames that led them to favor different strategies. For many years the NAACP had pursued a legal strategy, mounting court challenges to the constitutionality of segregationist practices. Dr. King's SCLC (Southern Christian Leadership Conference) favored high-visibility protests in communities such as Birmingham and Selma, Alabama. More radical organizations, such as CORE and SNCC, adopted riskier, more confrontational tactics such as sit-ins and freedom rides. Because potential donors could choose which organizations they wanted to support, the various SMOs were rivals for those donors' dollars. The NAACP, for instance, believed that it made sense to invest in a long-term legal campaign, and it opposed spending donors' money to bail out SNCC's demonstrators who engaged in protests that were certain to lead to their arrests. SNCC, on the other hand, argued that the NAACP's approach was too slow, and tried to rally support for its riskier activities.

In contemporary America, much social movement activity revolves not around convincing individuals to dedicate their lives to activism, or even around organizing thousands of people to march in the streets, but around fundraising. Although activists do sometimes organize large demonstrations, much of their activity focuses on seeking media coverage for their cause, lobbying policymakers, and so on. These activities cost money, and activists spend considerable time soliciting contributions from people who support the movement's cause (but may not feel they have the time or energy to work directly on movement activities). Note that we can distinguish between **beneficiaries** (who stand to benefit directly if a movement is successful) and **constituents** (who support the movement) (McCarthy & Zald, 1977). Some people belong to both categories, but many movement supporters are **conscience constituents**—that is, people who contribute money or even join demonstrations because they believe in the cause, although they do not expect to be direct beneficiaries (think of northern whites who donated to civil rights SMOs).

The growing importance of contributions has led to the emergence of sophisticated fundraising efforts using, for instance, direct-mail techniques. Mailing lists of people who are known to have contributed to previous fundraising campaigns are used to raise additional funds (see Box 3.3). Fundraising efforts become more sophisticated as new technologies become available; in recent years, SMOs have begun raising funds via the Internet, using Web sites and e-mail to solicit donations. Of course, this emphasis on bringing in money means that fundraising turns into yet another occasion when troubling conditions must be reconstructed with compelling rhetoric—in this case, arguments that funds are needed urgently to respond to an important opportunity or, more often, to a looming threat. Both pro-life and pro-choice activists, for instance, raise money by warning that, unless supporters rally to their cause (by donating money to support its activities), the opponents are likely to win.

Increasingly, then, successful activism requires sophisticated skills—organizing, fundraising, media relations, lobbying, and the like. These skills tend to be portable: individuals who learn skills in one SMO can move on and apply what they've learned at another SMO, or even in another movement. Just as some veterans of the civil rights movement took what they had learned in that campaign and used their new skills to help organize antiwar protests, the women's liberation movement, and the gay liberation movement,

Box 3.3 Mobilization through Direct Mail

By the end of the twentieth century, many social movements had shifted their goals. Instead of trying to directly mobilize large numbers of people to demonstrate, march, or take other action, they sought to raise funds to support lobbying and other activities. Direct mail played a key role in this fundraising.

Direct mail involves sending thousands of letters to individuals, requesting their support in the form of donations. The key to successful fundraising is to develop and maintain mailing lists of individuals who have previously contributed to the cause, because people who have given money in the past are far more likely to contribute in the future than are those who have not given previously.

The political conservatives who led developments in this sort of fundraising for social movements discovered the value of exchanging mailing lists (for example, fundraisers for conservative political candidates might generate donations using a mailing list of NRA supporters, and the NRA might solicit members using the lists of donors to conservative candidates). Once the potential of direct mail became apparent, all sorts of social movements began adopting similar fundraising methods (Viguerie & Franke, 2004).

More recently, of course, social movements have begun to direct their attention to the Internet as a means of keeping their sympathizers informed and soliciting donations to support further activities. Increasingly, mobilizing movement resources involves raising money from people whose most direct involvement with the cause is making a contribution.

people today pursue careers as activists, sometimes working for different causes over the course of their careers. Typically, these individuals do have ideological commitments, so they tend to move among social movements with which they are sympathetic: one individual may work for several liberal SMOs, while another becomes active in various conservative causes.

Resource mobilization is important because it reflects an SMO's ability to promote its claims. Organizations with more members and a bigger budget are better able to afford the services of skilled activists (who may in turn be attracted to working in campaigns that have plentiful resources and better chances of success). SMOs with money can afford further fundraising efforts, so they have better prospects for garnering future resources. Moreover, SMOs with greater resources find it easier to draw attention to their message: they are better able to gain coverage in the media; and, other things being equal, they are more likely to influence policymakers. Mobilizing resources is not glamorous, but it provides an essential base for would-be activist claimsmakers.

OPPORTUNITY STRUCTURES

Activists must worry about more than devising a persuasive frame and mobilizing necessary resources. Timing also matters. All too often, social movements face great obstacles. After all, movements seek to change existing social arrangements, and those arrangements work to the benefit of powerful people who can be expected to use their considerable resources to resist changes that might be to their disadvantage. On occasion, however, these obstacles to change are reduced, and activists must be alert for and ready to take advantage of such opportune moments. Various cultural and political circumstances can create opportunities to promote activists' claims.

Cultural Opportunities

Cultural opportunities arise when people become more willing to listen to the movement's claims (McAdam, 1994). Perhaps the most obvious cultural opportunity is the occurrence of a newsworthy event that focuses attention on a troubling condition. The September 11, 2001, terrorist attacks, for instance, suddenly moved terrorism from a peripheral concern to the central focus of national attention. Other, less dramatic events—a natural disaster, a brutal crime, and such—can have similar effects. They lead to a widespread sense that a particular troubling condition, previously neglected, must now be addressed. Activists who have been struggling to have their claims heard may suddenly find themselves in demand—reporters seek them out for interviews, legislators invite them to testify at hearings, and so on—because they are the ones who understand and have ideas for what to do about the troubling condition that is now the focus of concern.

Another sort of cultural opportunity emerges when a **master frame** becomes familiar (Snow & Benford, 1992). A master frame articulates a broad orientation that can be easily adapted for application to many issues. For instance, after the civil rights movement first drew national attention to blacks' struggle for equal rights and then succeeded in dismantling the system of institutionalized segregation in the South, the idea that demanding equal rights might be an effective way of framing social issues spread to other social movements. Within about ten years, activists were campaigning for women's rights, gay rights, children's rights, and the rights of the disabled, prisoners, and the elderly. This master frame remains influential: the abortion issue has been framed in terms of fetuses' *right to life* and women's *right to choose*; divorced men campaign for *fathers' rights*; an active animal rights movement has emerged; and so on. Like dramatic events, the availability of master frames creates cultural opportunities that can make it easier for activists to promote their claims.

Political Opportunities

Political opportunities to promote activists' claims arise when the distribution of power among different groups shifts, so that changes that previously would have been successfully resisted can now be implemented. Political opportunities may derive from shifting priorities, when formerly irrelevant concerns are redefined as relevant. One reason the civil rights movement gained momentum in the early 1960s was that former colonies—particularly the African colonies of Britain and France—were gaining independence. The Cold War was at its height, and the United States wanted to minimize the Soviet Union's influence in these newly independent nations. The concern that African nations might be repelled by the treatment of African Americans in the United States created a new pressure to do something about the system of segregation found in the southern states. In this case, shifting foreign policy concerns created new opportunities for civil rights activists trying to change domestic policies.

Another form of political opportunity emerges when, for some reason, opposition to a movement becomes weaker. Those who might be expected to resist the activists' claims may be losing influence, or they may be distracted by other concerns. Perhaps more important for the social problems process is the fact that support for claimsmakers may become stronger. Successful claims lead to sympathetic media coverage, public opinion polls that reveal growing support, and political leaders joining the cause. Support for "an idea whose time has come" can grow to the point that opponents may decide to drop their opposition. For instance, the basic principles of equal rights for African Americans and for both men and women advocated by the civil rights and the feminist movements, respectively—principles once considered quite controversial—have achieved broad acceptance.

Activists need to assess political opportunities and devise appropriate tactics for exploiting them. A tactic that is effective at one moment may be less effective at another. For instance, McAdam (1983) traces the history of tactical choices in the civil rights movement. The movement's activists devised a variety of protest tactics—sit-ins, large-scale demonstrations, and so on. Some of these tactics proved ineffective: they failed to attract media attention or to weaken the system of segregation. But others worked better, and news of these successes spread, leading activists in other communities to copy the effective tactics. Still, these successes were temporary; a tactic remained effective only for a time. News of the new tactic also inspired opposition; the movement's segregationist opponents searched for tactics of their own—responses that could minimize the movement's impact—and news of these successful opposition tactics also spread. In addition, each time civil rights activists used a particular tactic, it became more familiar and less newsworthy, so the media coverage dwindled. These processes created a cycle of tactical innovation in which a novel tactic would emerge, work for a while, then grow less effective, causing the activists to invent a new form of protest to keep the movement advancing.

Just as some circumstances can improve political opportunities, others create obstacles, occasions when claimsmaking probably can't succeed. Public attention is finite; if the media are devoting their attention to other newsworthy events, they aren't likely to cover a particular social movement's claims (see Chapter 5 for a more thorough discussion of how the media choose what they will cover). In the weeks immediately following September 11, 2001, media attention concentrated on terrorism, so there was almost no chance that claims about other issues could receive much attention. Similarly, when rival claimsmakers—activists for another social movement, or even for another SMO within the same movement—are occupying center stage and hogging the limelight, opportunities for promoting one's own claims are reduced. Rather than struggling to be heard under such adverse circumstances, it may be wiser to conserve resources and wait for a more promising opportunity.

Similarly, opportunities are unfavorable when opposition to a cause seems to be growing stronger, or when support for that cause seems to be growing weaker. Under such circumstances, activists need to consider what's wrong and make the necessary changes.

Perhaps the existing frame is losing its appeal; perhaps more resources need to be assembled. At these times it is better to back off and wait for a better opportunity, rather than forcing the issue and facing certain defeat.

For example, Taylor (1989) traces the history of the National Women's Party (NWP), which long promoted an Equal Rights Amendment (ERA) to the Constitution that would guarantee women full equality under the law. During much of its history, and particularly during the years following World War II, the NWP confronted poor political opportunities for success. This was a period of **abeyance**; that is, the NWP maintained a modest organizational structure, continued monitoring political developments, and waited for brighter opportunities. A good opportunity arose in the late 1960s, after the civil rights movement had captured Americans' attention, making the equal rights master frame more familiar and more acceptable (see Box 3.4). In particular, new calls for women's liberation began to gain notice, and as a new wave of feminist activism began to emerge, the NWP joined the new feminists (such as the newly formed National Organization of Women, or NOW) and encouraged them to campaign for the ERA (although that particular campaign was again narrowly defeated). By tending the feminist flame during the decades of abeyance, the NWP had conserved its resources until more promising opportunities developed to use them.

Summary

Social movements can experience decades of frustration, periods when activists cannot seem to interest anyone in their cause—when they face indifference, ridicule, even repression. It helps to be patient, to wait until cultural and political opportunities develop that offer more favorable conditions for claimsmaking. For instance, the civil rights movement and the feminist movement have had long histories featuring both periods of frustration and periods of

Box 3.4 Opportunities, Opposition, and Gay and Lesbian Activists

The modern movement for gay and lesbian rights began with the 1969 Stonewall rebellion, a spontaneous protest against a police raid on a gay bar in New York. Initially the gay liberation movement adopted classic outsider claimsmaking tactics, such as protest marches, designed to draw attention to the cause. Although political opportunities might not have seemed promising (Republican Richard Nixon was president), many people were advocating sexual freedom, which created cultural opportunities. The early movement favored an equal rights master frame, arguing that, just as blacks and women deserved equal rights under the law, so, too, did homosexuals.

Over time, gay and lesbian activists evolved into insider claimsmakers. Activists campaigned in many arenas: to get the American Psychiatric Association to stop classifying homosexuality as a mental disorder, to have gay and lesbian student organizations approved on college campuses, and so on. State fragmentation (the fact that there are many government arenas—federal/state/local, executive/legislative/judicial) meant that activists could search for particular arenas where political opportunities seemed promising. Although many gay rights campaigns failed, each success improved the prospects for future efforts and gave the activists better contacts and more insider credentials (Werum & Winders, 2001).

Meanwhile, the gay and lesbian rights movement inspired opposition, often from religious claimsmakers who insisted that homosexuality was immoral and warned that gays and lesbians sought to recruit children to homosexuality. Like gay and lesbian activists, these opponents also searched for arenas where they saw political opportunities. Opponents have been more likely to mount referenda (which usually defeat gay rights proposals); gay and lesbian activists have favored approaching legislative bodies and courts (which have proved more likely to support their cause).

Moreover, opposition alters activists' frames. Fetner (2001) studied gay and lesbian activists' rhetoric both before and after the countermovement emerged. Some of the activists' claims, such as complaints about police harassment and demands for more visibility in the media, had been ignored by the countermovement, and the rhetoric that activists used to address these issues was not affected. The countermovement focused its efforts on opposing calls for equal rights, and particularly for antidiscrimination protections. In response, gay and lesbian claims about discrimination and equal rights were reframed:

- Whereas precountermovement claims had adopted a calm, educational tone, the activists' rhetoric now became much more likely to express anger.
- Where earlier claims had declared that society had a shared interest in gay rights, postcountermovement claims were more likely to present the issue as us versus them.
- Whereas earlier claims had emphasized the values of justice and equality, later claims depicted gays and lesbians as a threatened minority.

When activists confront opposition, they are likely to rework their claims to incorporate the fact that their movement faces opposition into their rhetoric.

progress. These familiar examples teach other activists the importance of continuing the struggle, of hanging on until opportune moments arise.

THE ADVANTAGES OF OWNERSHIP

Activists whose efforts are particularly successful can gain **ownership** of a social problem (Gusfield, 1981). Ownership is established when particular claims or frames become generally recognized and acknowledged as the best way to understand a particular issue. The proponents of these claims become the recognized, go-to authorities on a troubling condition. If a dramatic event brings that problem back into the news, it is the owners who are asked by reporters to provide commentary and who are consulted by policymakers. Ownership relates to framing, resource mobilization, and political opportunities. The owners' frames become influential in shaping how others approach the problem and its solution; the owners' perspective may not be the only possible way of thinking about the troubling condition, but it becomes familiar, almost taken for granted by the press, the public, and policymakers. Precisely because they are well known, owners find it much easier to mobilize resources. People who want to contribute or otherwise become involved in a cause tend to know about and turn to a problem's owners, just as reporters looking for sources to comment on an issue are likely to think first of approaching the owners. And, of course, precisely because owners find it easier to garner resources, they have an easier time maintaining their ownership in the face of competing activists. As a result, owners are well placed to take advantage of opportunity structures. When, for instance, current events draw attention to a troubling condition, owners tend to be far better prepared to exploit whatever opportunities develop: they have contacts with the media and with policymakers; they are probably better placed to assess political opportunities; and they may even be integrated into the social problems process well enough to act as insider claimsmakers.

A social problem can have multiple owners. Position issues marked by intractable disagreements often feature SMOs that own the opposing sides in the debate. For example, the NRA long ago established itself as the leading SMO speaking on behalf of the rights of gun owners and in opposition to gun control. For a long time, proponents of gun control lacked a comparably influential SMO; in recent years, however, Handgun Control, Inc. (recently renamed the Brady Center to Prevent Gun Violence) has emerged as the most visible antigun SMO—the owner of gun control advocacy. And, as noted earlier, social movements often encompass a range of frames, from more moderate groups advocating modest reforms, to more radical SMOs pushing for more significant changes. Owners may emerge at different points along this spectrum. Within the 1960s civil rights movement, for example, the well-established NAACP favored deliberate pressure to gain favorable court decisions; while more radical SMOs, such as SNCC and CORE, became well known for organizing more confrontational activities, such as sit-ins and freedom rides. A few highly visible SMOs shared ownership of the large, broad-based civil rights movement.

Some SMOs own particular issues for extended periods. The NRA has led the fight against gun control for decades, and the NAACP has been a leading voice in the movement for African Americans' civil rights since its founding in 1909. Such owners must constantly strive to keep their issue—and their ownership—visible to the press, the public, and policymakers. Maintaining such a presence serves two purposes. First, of course, it keeps the owners' particular claims—their frame—for interpreting the issue visible and familiar, so that others find it easy to continue to think about the topic in the owners' terms. Second, it helps preserve the owners' status *as owners*. Attention—and contributions—tend to go to the most familiar advocates. Although ownership is harder to achieve in the first place than it is to maintain after being gained, it must always be nurtured.

Long-term ownership requires flexibility. Narrowly focused, single-issue movements are at a long-term disadvantage; it is too easy for public attention to drift away from an issue, and once that happens, supporters, media coverage, and access to policymakers may also dwindle. It helps to develop a broader set of interrelated concerns. The NAACP, for instance, has addressed a wide array of issues related to racial discrimination during its long history. In its early years, for example, the NAACP devoted considerable attention to its campaign against lynching. But as lynching declined and then disappeared, the NAACP turned to constructing other race relations issues, such as campaigns against discrimination in education and employment, opposition to hate crimes, and so on. As political opportunities shift, it can become easier or harder to promote particular claims, but to the degree that the NAACP maintains ownership over the full spectrum of issues related to African Americans, it can remain actively involved in the social problems process.

In contrast, narrowly focused SMOs run the risk of succeeding— and thereby losing their reason for existing. Consider the March of Dimes—a charitable organization originally launched to fight the problem of polio, a disease that left children severely disabled. Once polio vaccines were developed, the threat of polio virtually disappeared, and the organization faced a crisis. It could, of course, declare victory and disband. But why dismantle a successful fundraising apparatus? Instead, the March of Dimes redefined its purpose, declaring that it would continue to operate but would now dedicate its efforts to fighting birth defects. This was not just a new, but a broader, definition of the SMO's purpose: there are many different birth defects, so although further successes might result in eliminating some of these problems, the organization would continue to be needed to address the problems that remained.

When claimsmakers begin drawing attention to a troubling, previously neglected condition, there are three ways ownership of the issue might evolve:

1. *No one assumes ownership.* This situation is most likely when a newsworthy event, such as a dramatic crime, catapults an issue into the public eye. A variety of commentators may offer their takes on this troubling condition, perhaps suggesting different ways of thinking about the issue. However, it may be that none of these claimsmakers will assume ownership of the topic, work to keep the issue visible, manage a prolonged campaign to change public policy, and so on. Under these circumstances, even topics that receive a burst of intense publicity can shift away from public attention, forgotten as soon as

the next, different dramatic event commands notice. Without owners to remind people of a problem's importance, issues can fade (this possibility is discussed further in Chapter 5).

2. *Activists establish a new SMO that can assume ownership.* A familiar example is the emergence of Mothers Against Drunk Driving (MADD). Although drunk driving had a long history, MADD gave the issue not just new visibility, but a new frame as a threat to children menaced by drunk drivers. MADD lobbied legislators, observed courtroom proceedings, established local chapters around the country, and generally took control over what had been an ownerless issue.

3. *Existing SMOs assume ownership of the new issue.* This is what happened when stalking emerged as a new crime problem and the battered women's movement adopted the issue as its own (see Box 3.5). Over time, SMOs can become a familiar part of the landscape and run the risk of being taken for granted. Stalking gave the battered women's movement a fresh focus—an expanded domain—so that the movement found itself back in the spotlight. In turn, the movement was able to use its resources to successfully campaign for antistalking policies. This meant that the antistalking cause benefited from more prolonged attention than it would have received if it had not been adopted by new owners, even as the new owners also benefited through their association with a hot issue.

Ownership, then, affects the prospects of both an issue and the activists who promote it. Unless someone assumes ownership, it is hard for the social problems process to proceed; it is too easy for public attention to shift away as soon as the next new issue arrives on the scene. Owners are needed to tend the topic, to remind people of its importance, to revise their claims so that the topic remains fresh and interesting. But ownership also benefits the owners: their claims seem better established; their authority seems more legitimate; and as they become familiar figures with a larger network of

Box 3.5 Owning the Stalking Problem

In the late 1980s, several heavily publicized episodes occurred in which fans annoyed, attacked, or even killed celebrities. In response, some commentators constructed a new crime problem: "star stalking." In California, the Screen Actors Guild supported the first antistalking law, which was passed in 1990 (Lowney & Best, 1995).

By 1993, virtually all states had passed their own antistalking laws, and the federal government had begun trying to coordinate a national campaign against stalking. But these new actions had little to do with protecting celebrities. Within just a few years, stalking had been redefined as a crime against women (even though several of the best-known celebrity victims had been male). Stalking was now understood to occur when former boyfriends or ex-husbands—often men who had been physically abusive—harassed their former partners.

This redefinition reflected a shift in ownership of the stalking problem. The battered women's movement framed stalking as a serious, potentially fatal form of domestic violence. Stalking offered a way of rejuvenating interest in violence against women. The movement's activists led the campaigns to persuade state legislatures to pass antistalking laws. In the process, they established themselves as the authorities on the stalking issue—an arrangement that benefited both the cause (the activists kept stalking in the public eye until the laws were passed) and the movement (which was seen as engaged in a vital new form of advocacy).

social contacts, they can begin to transform themselves from outsider to insider claimsmakers.

ACTIVISTS: PRINCIPLES AND PRACTICALITIES

Discussions of social movements often emphasize their principled character. That is, they depict activists as individuals committed to

Figure 3.2 ACTIVISTS CONCERNS IN MAKING EFFECTIVE CLAIMS

a particular cause, seeking to promote a higher good. But sincerity is not enough. As claimsmakers who seek to influence the social problems process, activists need to convey their message to, and influence the behavior of, the media, the public, and policymakers. That is, they need to confront the practical problems posed by social movements.

This chapter has explored four such problems (see Figure 3.2). First, activists must develop effective frames; that is, they must construct their claims so that others will find them convincing, so that people will support the activists' SMOs. Principled statements that cannot persuade others threaten to stall the social problems process before it has really begun.

Second, activists must mobilize sufficient resources to promote their movement's goals. Activists who prove unable to attract and manage members, money, and other necessary resources probably will not be able to keep their SMOs functioning long enough for their cause to succeed.

Third, activists need to be able to recognize and figure out ways to take advantage of opportunities. Current events and the shifting political landscape can aid—or hinder—social movements. Activists need to be careful not to miss promising opportunities, just as they should avoid expending their resources when they have no chance to advance their cause.

Finally, activists can acquire and maintain ownership over an issue. Owning a social problem allows enduring influence, a means of keeping an issue—and the activists' leadership—visible, so that the activists' frames remain familiar and widely accepted, resources are easier to mobilize, and the activists stay in position to take advantage of whatever opportunities develop.

Although they are the most obvious examples of claimsmakers, activists are not the only people who promote social problems claims. They often acquire allies—claimsmakers who, in addition to their commitment to principles, bring special knowledge or expertise to the social problems process. These expert claimsmakers are discussed in Chapter 4.

MAKING CONNECTIONS

- *Through framing, resource mobilization, and taking advantage of opportunities, activists attract attention to their claims in order to establish ownership over a problem and its proposed solutions.*

- *As you read Chapter 5 on the media, you will learn why ownership of a problem helps win attention from media organizations.*

- *To establish effective frames, activists rely on focus groups, polls, and other tools to measure public reactions. You will learn more about public reactions in the social problems process in Chapter 6.*

CASE STUDY
Activists Concerned with Globalization

Globalization refers to the spread of stronger economic and social connections linking people around the globe. Such links are not new; people have long traveled and traded over great distances. However, today's speedier transportation and communication make this sort of long-distance interaction easier—and a more important aspect of life—than ever before. The Internet allows people all over the world to make contact with one another, and there is the sense that movies, music, and other cultural products can now gain global audiences. Increasingly, globalization has economic consequences, as manufacturing shifts to countries where labor costs are very low, even as corporations span international boundaries and seem to be above any particular nation's laws. And, of course, some environmental issues, such as overpopulation, resource depletion, and global warming, seem to reflect what's occurring around the globe.

Globalization has its defenders, who argue for its overall benefits: average life expectancies and standards of living have improved by most measures, disease and hunger have been reduced, and so on. Globalization's proponents would not deny that the process harms some people in some places; when an American textile mill closes, for example, its workers may find it difficult to find other jobs that pay as well. But, they argue, there is an overall benefit: those American workers may lose, but the workers at the Asian factory that now fills the orders benefit, as do customers (including Americans) who pay low prices for textile goods.

Still, it is very easy to construct globalization as a social problem—or, actually, as a host of social problems. Various claimsmakers indict globalization for, among other things: harming ecosystems, destroying local cultures and ways of life, damaging human rights, impoverishing the world's poorest and least powerful people while enriching giant corporations, and so on. Globalization's critics tend to oppose international economic agreements (which they see as promoting the interests of large corporations while harming the world's poorest peoples), although they also tend to support international political agreements (such as the Kyoto Protocol to address the problem of global warming, or international campaigns against the sex trade) (Langman, 2005).

In short, opposition to globalization offers a very broad banner beneath which advocates, promoting many different claims about a diverse set of troubling conditions, can declare a common cause. Globalization's critics come from the labor movement, the feminist movement, the environmental movement, the peace movement, and many other movements. Each of these groups has its own take on why globalization should be considered troubling. U.S. labor leaders, for instance, worry that globalization tends to keep wages low (because workers in less developed countries earn much lower wages than their counterparts in the industrialized West, so manufacturing has been shifting overseas, and the threat of further job losses gives American workers very little leverage in bargaining with their employers); they also call for more protections of workers' rights around the world. Environmentalists focus on the ecological impact of globalization: as living standards rise among the huge populations of China and India, for example, there is more pollution, as well as greater demand for scarce resources. Other advocates have their own concerns.

Precisely because globalization is criticized from so many different directions, it is possible to detect, if not contradictions, at least strains within the movement. Environmentalists, for example, view rising living standards in less developed nations as one source of strain on the planetary ecosystem; labor advocates, in contrast, are likely to call for better living standards for workers throughout the world. The resulting alliance is something much larger, but also more amorphous than a traditional social movement. Activists are by no means opposed to all forms of globalization; their movement itself is an effort to develop a global coalition opposing the dominant economic order, and its very existence depends on the Internet and other forms of electronic communication that allow millions of activists and concerned citizens to communicate, so that ideas spread widely and rapidly.

Concern about globalization issues links hundreds of SMOs, NGOs (nongovernmental organizations), and other entities in a fluid, flexible alliance. Not every group need be concerned with every issue, and there may be no issue that elicits universal concern, let alone agreement. Groups within the larger movement promote different frames, hold different values, command very different resources, and disagree about strategies and tactics. Some focus on local issues; others, on global topics. Sociologists struggle to conceptualize this new form of activism, speaking of "transnational social movements," "internetworked social movements," "reflexive framing," and so on (Chesters & Welsh, 2005; Fisher, Stanley, Berman, & Neff, 2005; Langman, 2005).

Still, research suggests that theoretical concepts devised to study more traditional social movements can be applied to specific globalization protests. One study of participants at five large protests held in three countries found that SMOs played two key roles: they mobilized a large share of the nonlocal participants (that is, those who had to travel to get to the event); and they coordinated travel to the protest for many of those participants (Fisher et al., 2005). Overall, the largest share of participants learned about the protests from SMOs, although substantial numbers also heard about them from people they knew, or from the media, the Internet, or e-mail messages. Traditional SMOs continue to play an important role in shaping specific movement actions, but overall campaigns related to globalization have a very diffuse structure.

Globalization, then, is best understood as an umbrella term that covers a diverse array of claims about different troubling conditions. The globalization movement encompasses a multitude of frames, mobilizes resources using both traditional and new methods, and finds all manner of opportunities to address different issues. In size, scope, and structure, it is unlike all previous social movements.

QUESTIONS

1. What are some of the frames that antiglobalization activists use to attract supporters?

2. What are SMOs, and how does the antiglobalization movement rely on them?

3. How do different movements within the antiglobalization movement compete for ownership?

4

Experts as Claimsmakers

Colonial Massachusetts was established by Puritans, and ministers were key figures in that society. They saw evidence of God's hand everywhere in the world, and their sermons sometimes commented on current events, interpreting them in religious terms. A bad harvest might be evidence of God's wrath, and problems among people were caused by sin, by individuals breaking God's commandments. Virtually any event could be interpreted within this religious framework. Ministers, then, were colonial New England's principal experts; their theological training qualified them to explain and evaluate most aspects of life. Their religious frame was seen as authoritative because it was promoted by professionals representing the society's leading institution.

The ministers' religious perspective seems less authoritative today. In at least public discussions of social problems, modern Americans rarely speak of *sin* (and when politicians or even religious leaders do invoke such language, they often come under criticism). Rather, contemporary Americans are more comfortable with a kind of medical vocabulary; when talking about social problems, we are more likely to speak of *diseases, syndromes, disorders,* or *addictions*—words that seem grounded in medical, scientific classifications. Consider how contemporary discussions of Aquinas's classical list of the seven deadly sins often redefine these behaviors as medical problems; for example, lust might be characterized as *sexual addiction*, gluttony as *food addiction* or *compulsive eating*, anger as an *anger management* problem, and sloth as *chronic fatigue syndrome*. (At the same time, modern medicine sometimes seems to promote those same deadly sins by treating their absence as medical problems that also may require treatment; consider drugs to enhance sexual performance [lust], cosmetic surgery [pride, envy], liposuction [gluttony], or concerns about workaholism and type A personalities [sloth] or low self-esteem [pride].) At least when they talk about social issues, contemporary Americans are less likely to accept the judgments of religious leaders, and more likely to defer to doctors.

The declining influence of ministers and growing clout of doctors illustrate how constructions of social problems reflect shifting patterns of institutional influence. In societies where religious authorities hold sway, social problems often are discussed in religious language; where medical authorities are more influential, social problems tend to be understood in medical terms. At different times and in different places, ideas about which people with which sorts of knowledge ought to be considered experts vary. *Experts* are presumed to possess especially authoritative knowledge, and other people—including activists, the media, and policymakers—may defer to this expertise.

In short, experts rank among the most influential claimsmakers because they are thought to have special knowledge that qualifies them to interpret social problems. Some experts are what Chapter 3 referred to as *insider claimsmakers*; their status as experts can give them easier access to policymakers, so that they are part of the polity. This chapter examines the role of experts as claimsmakers in the contemporary social problems process. It begins by exploring the central place of medical authorities in constructing social problems, then turns to other sorts of experts.

MEDICALIZATION

Sociologists who have noted the increased use of medical language to characterize social problems speak of **medicalization** (Conrad, 1992), the process of defining troubling conditions as medical problems. A century ago, it was generally recognized that some people drank too much; that is, their drinking was blamed for causing problems at work, in their homes, and so on. The common label for these people was *drunkards* (Gusfield, 1967). Being a drunkard was seen as, if not a sin, at least a moral failing; drunkards were doing something they shouldn't do, and they needed to reform (the solution to being a drunkard often involved making a pledge to practice temperance; that is, the drunkard would promise to stop drinking).

Today, the term *drunkard* has virtually disappeared from our vocabulary. Of course, there are still people who drink too much, and whose drinking is thought to cause job problems, family problems, and so on. But we call these people *alcoholics*, and we speak of the *disease* of *alcoholism*. Alcoholics may receive *treatment*, often at *clinics*, where some of the costs are reimbursed by health insurance. In short, alcoholism has been medicalized, in that we now view it as a medical problem that should be addressed through medical solutions.

Consider another example: some students do not do well in school. Traditionally, those students were blamed for their poor performance: perhaps they were of lower intelligence, or perhaps they weren't trying hard enough. Today, claims suggest that poor performance at school may be caused by medicalized conditions, that these students have *learning disabilities* or *attention deficit hyperactivity disorder* (ADHD) (Conrad & Potter, 2000; Erchak & Rosenfeld, 1989). Medical language—words such as *diagnosis, symptom,* or *therapy*—increasingly frames discussions of students' difficulties, and doctors now prescribe drugs to large numbers of children to help them become more attentive.

Why is medicalization important? There are two obvious ways it makes a difference. The first is that medicalization seems to shift responsibility away from the individual. In our culture, we routinely hold individuals responsible for what we view as deliberate behavior—acts that people choose to perform. Drunkards were once seen as weak because they gave in to drink, and poor students used to be viewed as lazy; in both cases, the individuals were held responsible for their own problems. In contrast, we generally do not hold people responsible for their illnesses; we don't blame them for becoming sick. Therefore, saying that people have the disease of alcoholism or a learning disability means that they shouldn't be blamed for their problems, that they merit sympathy and support, rather than criticism.

A second consequence of medicalizing a problem is that it provides a familiar frame—sometimes called the **medical model**—for thinking about the issue. Medical problems are described as diseases, disorders, syndromes, or disabilities. The people with these problems are ill; they display symptoms. They need to become patients, who can receive treatment from medical personnel— doctors, nurses, therapists—who often work in hospitals or clinics, and who can be reimbursed through the patient's health insurance. In other words, medicalization is a claim arguing that some problem should be owned and controlled by medical experts and organizations.

Medicalization, then, frames troubling conditions in particular ways. At first glance, our culture seems to construct sins or crimes differently from illness: sinners and criminals are held responsible, blamed for their actions, and punished; people who are ill are not blamed and receive treatment instead. However, the medical model also focuses on the individual rather than the larger society. In a medicalized view, people have diseases or syndromes that lead them to drink too much, to eat too much, and so on; and they must confront and overcome these problems through healthy behavior. Medicalization shifts attention away from the ways in which larger social

Box 4.1 MEDICALIZING DRINKING DURING PREGNANCY

Medical authorities have long argued that children whose mothers drank heavily during their pregnancy often have serious health problems. During the 1970s, physicians began using the term *fetal alcohol syndrome* (FAS) to describe a specific set of serious birth defects associated with chronic maternal alcoholism. The new diagnosis had some critics, who argued that the cause may have been poverty and poor nutrition, rather than alcoholism. These critiques have continued, and there is considerable evidence of a link between FAS and poverty, yet criticisms challenging the diagnosis proved less influential than efforts to expand it (Armstrong, 2003).

Medical researchers began arguing that, just as alcoholism during pregnancy might damage the fetus, so, too, might social drinking. The set of possible medical consequences of maternal drinking expanded to include, for example, such diffuse results as "failure to thrive." In addition, whereas FAS was originally characterized as a set of serious birth defects, it was argued that many children suffered from less obvious harms. The evidence for these claims was not particularly strong, yet warnings that there was no safe level of alcohol consumption during pregnancy, and that pregnant women simply should not drink, became increasingly common.

Medicalizing FAS as a product of drinking, rather than of poverty, places responsibility on mothers while letting the larger social structure off the hook. It is also worth contrasting the active campaign to regulate pregnant women's drinking with the evidence that males tend to be more heavily implicated in other alcohol-related problems—problems that receive much less attention. Medicalization, like all claims about troubling conditions, draws attention to some features while downplaying others.

arrangements, such as poverty, shape these troubling conditions (see Box 4.1).

Medicalization grew markedly during the twentieth century. In part, this shift reflected dramatic changes in the practice of medicine: doctors and hospitals became subject to tighter professional standards, so the quality of care rose; at the same time, advances in medical science led to new medications and treatments. All this meant that the chances of medical care actually helping patients rose sharply; people began to expect more of medical authorities, and the prestige and authority of physicians rose.

The rising stature of medicine encouraged the expansion of medical authority into a broader domain of social problems. In particular, psychiatrists (who were trained as physicians) began to claim that many troubling behaviors—including juvenile delinquency, unconventional sexual activity, drug addiction, and crime—should be recognized as symptoms of psychiatric problems. After World War II, the American Psychiatric Association began developing its *Diagnostic and Statistical Manual of Mental Disorders* (the so-called *DSM*), a huge catalog of all recognized mental disorders, which has continued to expand with each new edition (Kirk & Kutchins, 1992). The growing number of available diagnoses means that more and more behaviors can be understood in medical terms.

In addition to psychiatrists, whose medical training clearly placed them within medicine, practitioners in a variety of other quasi-medical professions adopted the language of *disease, symptom,* and *treatment.* Among these were clinical psychologists, licensed clinical social workers, and many others, including some with little or no professional training. Drug treatment, for instance, increasingly was provided by "professional ex-s [sic]"—recovered drug users who did not necessarily have professional credentials, but who were employed by drug treatment centers to lead therapeutic groups and who used medical language to describe what they did (J. D. Brown, 1991).

Often medicalization consists of little more than adopting a medical vocabulary. Take what is called the disease of *alcoholism*: its symptoms are drinking and getting into trouble at work, at home, and so on; there are no clear biological symptoms that distinguish alcoholics from nonalcoholic drinkers (Appleton, 1995). Similarly, treatment for alcoholism is to get people with drinking problems to choose to drink less (most often, total abstinence is recommended). The leading program for dealing with alcoholism, Alcoholics Anonymous (AA), is a resolutely amateur operation. There are no professionals; all of AA's members are people who identify themselves as recovering alcoholics. Individuals attend meetings with fellow alcoholics and discuss AA's twelve-step program for achieving sobriety.

AA insists that alcoholism is a disease, but that the cure is to stop drinking, continue attending AA meetings, and follow the Twelve Steps. Note that AA's solution for alcoholism—that is, helping the individual with a drinking problem to make a commitment to stop drinking—is not all that different from the way drunkards were expected to reform by taking a pledge of sobriety, although the language of medicine seems to impart special authority to treatment as a solution. The twelve-step model has been adapted to help people deal with a variety of troubling behaviors—including drug abuse, overeating, and gambling—that have also been characterized as addictions or diseases.

In short, various medical authorities, with very different sorts of credentials, claim ownership of many contemporary social problems. As noted in Chapter 3, ownership can bring important benefits. Experts who gain ownership of a social problem usually gain a good deal: their social visibility and prestige rises, they become more powerful, and typically they stand to benefit financially from the increased business that people afflicted with the problem bring to them. This means that experts often have a vested interest in promoting claims that depict social problems from their perspective.

In a classic constructionist case study, for example, Stephen Pfohl (1977) argued that pediatric radiologists played a leading role in bringing attention to battered child syndrome—what would later be called *child abuse*. Initially this problem was typified in terms of physical injuries to children too young to explain how they had been hurt. Pediatric radiologists—specialists in interpreting children's X-rays—argued that they could distinguish fractures caused by accidents from those caused by abuse. These claims not only promised to improve the protection of vulnerable children, but also gave pediatric radiologists—who represented a small, relatively low-prestige medical specialty—ownership of a life-threatening disease, so the specialty's status rose. Expert claimsmakers often experience such gains, and thus wind up doing well by doing good.

Experts often seek to defend their professional turf and even expand their domain of ownership. The process may be gradual. Consider the changing scope of pediatrics (Pawluch, 1996). When this medical specialty emerged in the early twentieth century, pediatricians focused their efforts on problems associated with infant feeding; the milk supply was often tainted, causing many infants to become seriously ill. However, improved techniques for managing the purity of the milk supply soon made infant feeding much safer, so the major service that pediatricians had been providing was becoming less needed. In response, pediatricians began to expand their domain to emphasize the treatment of, first, other childhood diseases, and then normal, healthy childhood development. As birth rates fell, of course, there were fewer children for pediatricians to treat, but the specialists began to extend their services to treating patients in adolescence and even early adulthood.

These efforts need not be seen as cynical and self-serving. Experts generally believe that they have valuable knowledge and offer useful services, and they are continually looking for new opportunities to apply their expertise. In periods when their services are already in high demand, they have less time to extend their domain, but when business is slack, the prospect of attacking new problems becomes much more attractive. In this way, professional domains expand and the professionals' interests are advanced.

Ideally, experts' gains can be consolidated into institutionalized ownership. For instance, rising health care costs increasingly require patients to have medical insurance. But what sorts of treatments should health insurance cover? Professionals who provide different treatments want medical insurance to cover their services, so that more patients will seek those services. Thus, the federal government's decision to define alcohol and drug problems as medical problems, and to require health insurance programs to cover some of the costs of their treatment, institutionalized these experts as owners of the alcohol problem (Weisner & Room, 1984). As Chapter 3 noted, owners have advantages in promoting their constructions of social problems; when ownership is coupled with such experts' institutionalized arrangements, experts' authority becomes entrenched.

In recent years, medicalization has taken a new direction, with troubling conditions becoming subjects of **biomedicalization** (Clarke, Shim, Mamo, Fosket, & Fishman, 2003). Experts argue that biological processes are the root cause of many troubling conditions, which means that effective solutions must then address biology. For instance, the scientific revolution in genetics has led to claims that it will soon be possible to identify particular genes that cause various troubling conditions. Clearly, genetic anomalies cause some medical disorders, such as Down syndrome. But biomedical proponents argue that it will soon be possible to identify the genetic roots of all manner of behaviors, such as homosexuality or alcoholism, and research funding increasingly supports biomedical studies (see Box 4.2). Some of these claims may be borne out; others may prove false. At least for the foreseeable future, however, medicalization is likely to remain our society's leading form of expert claimsmaking.

THE ROLE OF SCIENCE

Medical authority may be seen as a subcategory of a broader form of expertise: science. As with medicine, the advances made possible by the expansion of science, particularly during the last two centuries, have given scientists considerable authority in our cul-

Box 4.2 ALCOHOL ABUSE RESEARCH AND BIOMEDICALIZATION

In 1992 a reorganization of federal agencies shifted the National Institute on Alcohol Abuse and Alcoholism (NIAAA) from its original location within the U.S. Public Health Service (USPHS) to a new home within the National Institutes of Health (NIH). Although this might seem to be an inconsequential bit of bureaucratic shuffling, it had significant implications for research on alcohol abuse (Midanik, 2006).

Within the USPHS, alcohol abuse was understood as a public health problem, and the NIAAA funded a broad range of research on treatment programs, alcohol control policies, and other topics. Shifting the NIAAA to the NIH signaled that the federal government had decided to adopt a biomedical approach for understanding alcohol problems. President George H. W. Bush had declared that the 1990s would be the "Decade of the Brain" and, as part of that emphasis, alcohol research would focus on genes and neuroadaptation mechanisms. Funding would be directed toward research studying biological processes related to alcohol abuse. Research that focused on social or behavioral issues, such as the role of environmental factors, prevention, or treatment of alcohol abuse, would find it much more difficult to gain government support.

Note that experts can be rivals for scarce resources, such as research funding. The ascendancy of one group of professionals, such as those promoting biomedical research on alcohol problems, may cause experts holding different points of view to lose influence, so that they find themselves at a disadvantage in attracting attention to their claims.

ture. Society has been transformed by the growth in scientific knowledge; think of the Industrial Revolution, the exploitation of new forms of energy (steam, electricity, petroleum), faster transportation, speedier communication, and so on. Increased scientific knowledge made these changes possible.

Science depends on an appreciation of evidence. A scientific theory must generate falsifiable predictions; that is, those predictions must be able to be tested, and if they are proven wrong, the theory is rejected. Scientists do research to produce evidence that can support or challenge their theories' predictions; the more supportive evidence they find, the more confidence scientists have in their theories. This system of reasoning has proved very powerful and has provided the foundation for all sorts of technological and medical advances, and in our society scientists are considered to have considerable authority when speaking about matters for which they have gathered evidence.

This is not to say that scientific evidence is infallible. Science is socially constructed; it is one of the ways people make sense of the world. To be sure, we have considerable confidence in well-established scientific findings, but it takes time for findings to become well established. Research can be flawed, and evidence can be incomplete or incorrectly interpreted. Scientists may debate issues among themselves, questioning one another's reasoning and evidence. Scientific progress can be a slow process; such debates can continue for years, even decades, until the evidence compiled becomes sufficiently compelling for a consensus to emerge among scientists.

Unfortunately, the deliberate pace of science is not well suited to news media eager to report on dramatic scientific breakthroughs. For instance, the media may publicize reports of the initial study on a particular topic, even though that research may eventually prove to have been flawed. A dramatic example was the media's reaction to a 1989 report by two researchers who said that they had observed a cold-fusion reaction in their laboratory. The implications were staggering—harnessing cold fusion would provide limitless, inexpensive energy—and the media began to speculate about the social changes this discovery would bring. Alas, other scientists soon concluded that the researchers had misinterpreted their results—that they had not found a way to produce cold fusion—and the media quickly dropped the topic.

Scientific experts' claims derive much of their rhetorical power from the understanding that scientists have special knowledge and access to particularly strong evidence, so their views deserve respect. The media's tendency to treat the results of a single piece of research as definitive leads to confusion in the case of ongoing scientific debates. Until sufficient evidence becomes available, scientists—like other experts—do not necessarily agree. Their evidence and interpretations may differ, even conflict. The press, the general public, and policymakers often find such disagreements frustrating, because they tend to look to scientists for not just authoritative, but correct, information. Apparent contradictions call scientists' authority into question (see Box 4.3).

For example, one week the media might report that a medical journal has published a research report concluding that drinking alcohol increases the risk of contracting a particular disease. The following week the media might announce that another group of researchers has concluded that moderate drinking improves one's health. What should people think? It is possible that both reports are correct—that is, that drinking raises the risk of contracting a particular disease but generally improves health. Or perhaps one of the studies is flawed (or even both are flawed). Over time, additional research is likely to lead to an eventual scientific consensus, but it is important to recognize that disagreements are normal within science and many other expert communities. Experts may disagree about which are the important questions to ask, about the best way to arrive at answers to those questions, about how to interpret the available evidence, and so on.

In general, research questions and answers are most clear-cut in the physical sciences (such as physics and chemistry), less so in the biological sciences (such as medicine), and the least so in the social sciences. The physical sciences have fewer disagreements about what constitutes compelling evidence, and debates among physi-

BOX 4.3 CREATING AN EXPERT DISPUTE OVER GLOBAL WARMING

Global warming first came to public attention through the claims-making of climate scientists supported by the environmental movement. Policymakers in many countries became concerned, and a 1997 international conference led to the Kyoto Protocol, an agreement to try to control greenhouse gas emissions (and thereby slow global warming).

U.S. political conservatives mounted a countermovement to challenge claims about global warming and prevent the United States from officially adopting the Kyoto Protocol (McCright & Dunlap, 2003). In particular, conservatives helped publicize the views of scientists who were skeptical of global warming claims. The views of these skeptics (who represented a minority within the scientific community) were brought to the attention of the media, congressional investigations, and other forums where the claims might attract notice. Whereas early global warming claims had conveyed a sense of scientific consensus, the topic now seemed to be the subject of intense debate. Reporters increasingly felt the need to balance their coverage by quoting representatives of both points of view.

Nonscientists have a difficult time assessing scientific evidence. The press, members of the public, and policymakers become frustrated by competing scientific claims. By conveying the sense that global warming claims were disputed within the scientific community, opponents were able to garner support for American opposition to the Kyoto Protocol.

cal scientists often can be settled decisively; in contrast, social scientists often cannot agree about what constitutes convincing evidence. In addition, it is important to appreciate that disagreements among scientists can center around very different sorts of questions, and that the authority of science depends on the sort of question being asked.

Consider, for instance, the debate over global warming. At the most basic level is the question of whether the planet's temperature is indeed rising. Scientists have devised various ways of measuring temperatures going back through time. Although there may be some disputes about the accuracy of particular measurements, or about which methods of measuring temperature changes are most accurate, these are relatively technical matters, and there is considerable scientific consensus that there have been cycles of global warming and global cooling in the past, and that temperatures have been risen about 0.6°C over the last 150 years or so (Cline, 2004). Accurately measuring changes in temperature presents a relatively clear-cut research challenge—the sort of question that scientists are clearly qualified to answer. It is, of course, more difficult to predict what will happen in the future, although again there is fairly widespread consensus that temperatures are likely to continue to rise over the next century (but considerable disagreement about how much they are likely to rise, with estimates ranging from 1.8°C to 4.0°C).

A second issue—over which there is more debate—concerns the causes of global warming. Although some argue that the current global warming may be a natural process—just part of the long-term cycle of planetary heating and cooling—most scientists agree that at least some of the warming is due to humans' impact on the planet. Most commonly these claims focus on the role of greenhouse gases (for instance, emissions of carbon dioxide from vehicles and smokestacks) in retaining heat in the atmosphere. Note that these explanations are not mutually exclusive; perhaps the planet would be warming naturally in any case, but human activities are exacerbating the trend. At this level, the scientific issues are not as straightforward, and even experts who agree that global warming is occurring may disagree over the extent to which people's activities contribute to this process.

The debate's third level is far more contentious. Even if we assume for the moment that everyone agrees that human activity plays a substantial role in causing global warming, what should be done? Here, debates can address many different issues, including what the consequences of global warming might be, what sorts of policies might reduce global warming, what the costs of those policies might be, whether the prospective benefits justify those costs, who should bear the costs, and so on. At this stage, purely scientific issues are less central; science may offer fairly compelling evidence about the extent and causes of global warming, but scientific knowledge cannot specify the correct course of policy. Consider nuclear weapons, for example: scientists were able to design and build nuclear weapons, but the decisions to use—or not use—those weapons were made by political leaders, not scientists. Scientific knowledge ordinarily is not sufficient to set social policy.

In short, we need to understand that, when scientists participate in debates over social issues, the relevance of their expertise varies, depending on the particular questions being considered. In addressing a question such as how much the planet's temperature has increased during the past century, scientific expertise is likely to play the central role. However, many commentators would argue that science cannot provide authoritative answers to questions such as whether the prospective benefits of implementing a particular policy to reduce greenhouse gases will justify the policy's costs, or how the costs of controlling emissions should be distributed among richer and poorer countries. The willingness of audiences to grant authority to scientists is likely to depend on how relevant they believe the experts' knowledge to be.

Contemporary debates over scientific authority often focus on constructions of risk. The modern fascination with risk can be dated to the 1960s, when the surgeon general announced that smoking was hazardous to health, activist Ralph Nader drew attention to unsafe automobiles, and author Rachel Carson warned that pesticides were causing significant environmental damage (Gunter, 2005). These highly visible claims led to concerns about other risks, which in turn produced all manner of warnings—about the dangers of cholesterol, secondhand smoke, toxic wastes, and so on. Such claims often couple scientific evidence (suggesting, for example, that a particular chemical may be carcinogenic) with warnings that the danger is widespread and the issue urgent. Increasingly, the media covers scientists' warnings that this or that condition poses risks to individuals' health, to environmental safety, and so on. Although the evidence regarding some risks—such as the link between smoking and lung cancer—is overwhelming, scientists disagree about the extent and significance of other risks (see Box 4.4).

It can take time for scientists to agree on assessments of risk. The most compelling scientific evidence comes from experiments, but it is usually impossible to design experiments to study risk. We cannot take identical groups of infants and make sure that they have identical experiences going through life—except that we can expose the experimental group to a particular risk and keep the control group from being exposed to that risk. Such a study might produce very strong evidence, but it would be time-consuming, expensive, and unethical. In practice, researchers must settle for much weaker evidence; they might, for example, identify people exposed to a particular risk, try to match them with similar folks who have not been exposed to that risk, and then study whether the two groups have different rates of particular diseases. It is always possible to challenge the results of such studies—for instance, were the two groups matched on every relevant variable?—and it takes a great deal of evidence (such as the countless studies on smokers' health) to make a convincing case.

It is difficult for nonscientists—a category that includes most activists, members of the media, the general public, and policymakers—to assess claims about risk that refer to scientific evidence. Debates over social problems often ignore such issues as comparative risks (for instance, the number of people at risk, the number of people likely to be harmed, and so on). All kinds of activities (for example, driving to work) carry risks. Often we take these risks for granted and ignore them, even though they may be far greater than are the heavily publicized dangers of, say, exposure to secondhand smoke. Scientific evidence—particularly calculations

Box 4.4 Is It Safe to Drink Ontario's Water?

During the 1990s, Canadians debated safety standards for tritium (a radioactive waste product from nuclear power plants) in Ontario's drinking water. Earlier policies had declared the maximum acceptable level of radioactivity to be 40,000 becquerels (a measure of radioactivity) per liter of water (40,000 Bq/L). A government agency recommended a tougher standard (7,000 Bq/L), and an advisory committee called for an even more stringent standard (100 Bq/L, to be reduced to 20 Bq/L within five years). Both groups cited scientific calculations to justify their standards (McMullan & Eyles, 1999).

The government agency's recommendation was endorsed by a "pro-economic coalition" (including the firm that operated the nuclear reactors) that was worried about the economic costs of trying to meet the 100 Bq/L standard (actual levels of radioactivity rarely exceeded 100 Bq/L in any case, but meeting the eventual 20 Bq/L goal would have required expensive improvements). This group noted that people receive only a tiny fraction of their exposure to radioactivity from drinking water, and they calculated that one year's exposure to drinking water at the 7,000 Bq/L level might lead to five additional fatal cases of cancer per million people—which they deemed an acceptable risk.

In contrast, the advisory committee's recommendation was supported by a "pro-environmental coalition" that warned that the 7,000 Bq/L limit was insufficient to protect public health. The coalition's calculations were based on lifetime—rather than one-year—exposure, which would produce 340 additional fatal cancer cases per million over 70 years, whereas a lifetime of 20 Bq/L exposure would lead to only one additional cancer death. In the coalition's view, the public health benefits of maintaining this strict standard outweighed the economic costs.

Scientific findings usually cannot, in themselves, dictate social policy. In most cases, the key policy decisions are based on more than purely scientific considerations, such as weighing estimated economic costs against projections of risk.

of risk—are not well understood, and such issues often lead to confusion in the face of what is thought to be expert claimsmaking.

EVIDENCE, INTERESTS, AND ADVOCACY

A major reason why people defer to experts is their presumption that experts command knowledge that other people don't have. Although all knowledge is socially constructed, we consider experts' knowledge to be more likely to be accurate than gossip, rumor, or other less authoritative sorts of knowledge that, we know from experience, often prove to be wrong. Thus, we tend to consider expert knowledge to be relatively correct. We defer to medical authorities because we assume that they know how to diagnose diseases, are able to understand the causes and workings of those diseases, and can recommend the best possible treatments. Similarly, we presume that scientists have done careful research and compiled evidence that offers the best available information about how the world works.

In other words, we turn to experts for sound information based on high-quality evidence, and experts' status as relatively authoritative claimsmakers depends on such understanding. Experts are commonly assumed to be impartial judges—their medical diagnoses or scientific findings grounded in facts rather than opinions. Yet experts often have an interest in promoting claims, and when they become advocates for particular positions or policies, they are not necessarily guided solely by their expert knowledge.

We have already noted that experts stand to benefit from the ownership of social problems; recall how the status of pediatric radiologists rose after they drew attention to battered child syndrome. Experts also may have social ties to parties with interests in social issues. Scientific research can be extremely expensive, and many scientists derive funding from corporations, government agencies, and so on. These funders may have an interest in the researchers' findings. For example, both medical researchers and their pharmaceutical-company sponsors may have financial stakes in a new drug, and they may hope that the drug proves safe and effective, just as scientists employed by a corporation may be under pressure to affirm that the firm's waste disposal practices are safe. Other scientists may be closely associated with particular social movements, such as environmentalism.

Even though we tend to idealize scientists as objective, impartial observers, they may have allegiances that help shape their conclusions. Some legal trials feature psychiatrists hired as expert witnesses by the prosecution and the defense, who testify, respectively, that the defendant's mental state was such that the trials should or should not proceed. The point is not that social ties make science illegitimate—a very large share of scientists have such commitments—but that scientific knowledge is not produced or disseminated in a social vacuum.

In some cases, scientists' allegiances may be to the particular perspectives or approaches that characterize their disciplines. For instance, sociologists and other social scientists also act as expert claimsmakers. Just as medical authorities bring their professional training to bear when they medicalize troubling conditions by characterizing them using the language of diseases, symptoms, and other medical concepts, social scientists have their own orientations and conceptual tools. Economists, for example, argue that people can be understood as rational actors who make choices to maximize their own satisfaction. This proves to be a powerful underlying assumption, in that it can be extended to analyze all manner of choices. Thus, economists tend to see social problems as the products of particular choices, and to promote policies that will encourage people to make particular choices. For example, one way to discourage smoking is to raise tobacco taxes; if tobacco is more expensive, at least some people may choose to stop smoking.

Sociologists, too, apply their discipline's perspective to the analysis of social problems in their works (including this book). Sociologists argue that people shape one another's actions, and that social problems are products of particular social arrangements. Thus, where a psychiatrist may approach a social problem in terms of individuals whose thinking is disordered because they suffer from a syndrome of some sort, or an economist may see it in terms of arrangements that reward some choices more than others, sociologists are more likely to point to the way culture and social structure constrain and shape people's activities. C. Wright Mills (1959) called this mode of thinking the *sociological imagination* (discussed further in Chapter 5). This book, for instance, emphasizes understanding the social problems process through which actors socially construct social problems.

In other cases, experts may have allegiances to particular ideological positions. Liberal and conservative experts can approach social problems in very different ways: they focus on different causes, and they recommend different solutions. So-called think tanks—private nonprofit organizations dedicated to policy analysis and advocacy—often have an ideology that shapes their experts' recommendations (see Box 4.5). These experts maintain connections with media outlets and politicians that share their ideological orientations, so advocates from different positions have access to expert knowledge that can be used to buttress their claims.

Although we might like to imagine that experts are completely independent, impartial authorities, without interests or ideological commitments, this perfect objectivity is, in practice, impossible to achieve. Experts are part of the larger social order. At a minimum, they believe in the value of their professions: psychiatrists consider psychiatry a valuable perspective, just as sociologists promote the value of the sociological imagination. Experts can further be expected to believe that the problems they have chosen to study are important, worthy of their attention, and that the solutions they have been working on are promising. They may also have more obvious interests (such as a financial stake in the outcome of their research) or ideological preferences. Such social connections do not

Box 4.5 Thinking about Think Tanks

Think tanks are independent, nonprofit organizations that offer expertise designed to influence the press, the public, and especially policymakers. Many of the most familiar think tanks are located in Washington, DC, including the American Enterprise Institute for Public Policy Research (founded in 1943), the Brookings Institution (1916), and the Heritage Foundation (1973). Think tanks host conferences, issue reports, maintain elaborate Web sites, and use other methods to promote claims about different policy issues. Experts at major Washington-based think tanks are insider claimsmakers, with access to all manner of government officials (Rich, 2004).

Think tanks pay experts to develop and promote claims. Traditionally, these experts conducted careful research designed to weigh the effectiveness of alternative policies, in order to recommend the most promising approaches. Increasingly, however, think tanks reflect overt ideological stances; for example, whereas the Cato Institute and the Heritage Foundation have conservative agendas, the Worldwatch Institute and the Center on Budget and Policy Priorities promote liberal positions. The information coming from these more ideological think tanks can be discounted by observers who are familiar with these organizations, and who may suspect that their recommendations are shaped less by research than by the experts' political agendas.

Think tanks, then, display a familiar tension. Although they want to trade on the authority of expertise, their claims are often predictable, given their ideological goals of advocating for particular positions.

necessarily mean that the experts are wrong, but they do suggest that experts may be less than perfectly objective, and may think less critically when they confront ideas that fit their prejudices, so their claims should not be automatically accepted.

Expert knowledge is imperfect because it is produced by scientists, physicians, and other experts who are themselves actors in the larger society. It should be no surprise that experts' ideas evolve as new information becomes available. But it takes time for novel ideas to emerge and gain acceptance. As evidence accumulates, consensus is likely to develop, but this process cannot occur overnight. This is why expert knowledge is best understood as a special type of claim, part of the larger social problems process.

OFFICIALS AS EXPERT CLAIMSMAKERS

Another important category of expert claimsmakers consists of officials, particularly those employed by government agencies, such as the Centers for Disease Control and Prevention (CDC) or the Environmental Protection Agency (EPA). Such agencies have various responsibilities: they may compile information (collecting data to measure the crime rate, the unemployment rate, and so on); they may administer regulations (regarding workplace safety, pollution, or other issues); they may fund research through grants to experts outside the government; they may disseminate information to the citizenry; and so on. The work of many agencies bears upon one or more social problems. Because the federal government spends billions on the budgets of its various agencies, these officials can draw upon substantial resources. Usually they are able to compile more and better information about troubling conditions than unofficial claimsmakers can, giving officials' claims special authority in many social problems debates. Official agencies often achieve a level of ownership for social problems.

Agencies compete with one another for budget allocations and other scarce resources. Often multiple agencies have an interest in the same social problem. For instance, alcohol issues are the concern of several federal agencies: the Bureau of Alcohol, Tobacco, Firearms and Explosives (ATF); the National Institute on Alcohol Abuse and Alcoholism (NIAAA); the National Highway Traffic Safety Administration (NHTSA), which is concerned with alcohol-related traffic fatalities; and on and on. Imagine how many federal agencies must be concerned with any particular aspect of racial inequality. Just as social movement organizations find themselves competing with one another, officials—at least some of the time— view other agencies as competitors, both for resources and for ownership of particular social issues.

Protecting and, if possible, expanding an agency's turf becomes a central concern for officials, and claimsmaking provides one weapon for bureaucratic infighting. That is, drawing attention to a particular troubling condition, devising a program to deal with the problem, and then administering that program can serve two ends. On the one hand, it is easy to imagine that most officials are sincere, that they have joined an agency because they believe that it does important, valuable work. Like other claimsmakers, officials probably believe their own rhetoric and adopt the frames they promote. At the same time, officials have instrumental reasons to promote claims: successful claimsmaking is likely to serve the agency's interests, to increase its power, influence, and budget. Whatever their convictions, officials often have an interest in the claims they promote. For example, officials of the U.S. Bureau of Narcotics undoubtedly saw marijuana as a dangerous drug when they first called for a federal law against it in the 1930s, but that law also helped protect the bureau from further budget cuts (see Box 4.6).

Officials may recognize that their agencies could address certain additional troubling conditions if they could help launch the social problems process. Happily, agencies often control significant, flexible resources that can be used to jump-start the claimsmaking process. In the 1960s, for instance, the U.S. Children's Bureau (CB) was under fire from critics and losing control of some programs that were being shifted to other agencies (Nelson, 1984). At the same time, CB officials had long been in contact with the American Humane Association, an organization that had historically been concerned with the physical abuse of children. The CB began funding the research that drew national attention to what was initially

---

Box 4.6 The U.S. Bureau of Narcotics Discovers the Marijuana Menace

Passed by Congress in 1937, the Marijuana Tax Act was the first federal antimarijuana law. Although we might imagine this law to have been a product of activists' claimsmaking that raised public concern and pressured lawmakers to act, this was not the case. Marijuana use was not an especially visible social issue prior to the passage of this law. (Remember that the country's attention was concentrated on the Great Depression and the signs that there would soon be another world war.)

The leading claimsmaker warning about marijuana was Harry Anslinger, the commissioner of the U.S. Bureau of Narcotics. Anslinger was a vocal opponent of drug use, but his calls for a federal law against marijuana seem to have reflected bureaucratic interests. The bureau's budget allocations fell by 26 percent between 1932 and 1936, as the federal government shifted funding into New Deal programs. Adding marijuana to the list of illegal drugs expanded the bureau's responsibilities and helped Anslinger defend his agency against further budget cuts. The bureau instituted a public relations campaign to warn of marijuana's dangers—but only after the drug had been banned (Dickson, 1968).

Government agency officials such as Anslinger usually believe that their work is important, but they are also engaged in political struggles for funding and other resources. Because successful claimsmaking campaigns can expand an agency's turf, officials stand to benefit directly from promoting social problems.

---

called *battered child syndrome*, soon to be renamed *child abuse* (Pfohl, 1977). Child abuse became a visible, dramatic subject of considerable public concern, and in the process helped restore the CB as an important agency of the federal government. As an owner of the child abuse problem, the CB could extend its programs—funding further research, helping develop legislation requiring doctors and other professionals to report child abuse, and so on.

Although the expert claimsmakers in these examples were federal officials, analogous processes can occur in state or local governments, wherever officials become involved in drawing attention to troubling conditions. In some cases, national attention on a problem may lead local officials to call for action in their communities; in other locales, officials may be slower to acknowledge that the problem exists in—and requires action in—their jurisdictions. The policies of different cities toward homelessness, for instance, depend on how local officials respond to the issue (Bogard, 2003). In other cases, claimsmaking by officials may focus on purely local issues—such as whether an old building should be demolished to permit new development, or be preserved as part of the community's historical heritage (Lofland, 2003).

Officials working in government agencies usually have special knowledge or expertise that justifies their participation in claimsmaking. They are insiders, and their activities often occur behind the scenes, out of the public view. In sharp contrast are the claimsmaking activities of elected officials—presidents, senators, and the like—who may seize upon an issue and become active claimsmakers. These officials may lack special expertise, but their visible positions make it much easier for them to attract media attention and help publicize a cause.

EXPERT CLAIMSMAKERS IN THE
SOCIAL PROBLEMS PROCESS

Chapter 3 explored the role of activists and social movements in claimsmaking; this chapter has concentrated on the claimsmaking of experts—particularly medical authorities, scientists, and public officials. In many cases, claimsmaking campaigns feature alliances between activists and experts. Activists often contribute enthusiasm, passion, and whatever organizational resources their movements may control, whereas experts provide authoritative knowledge.

(This is obviously an oversimplification: many activists become quite knowledgeable, and experts can become highly dedicated to claimsmaking campaigns.)

Knowledge is an important commodity in claimsmaking. Remember that social problems claims begin with grounds statements—that is, statements about the facts concerning the troubling condition. When claimsmakers are trying to draw attention to a neglected condition—one that hasn't attracted much attention—often they discover that little information is available and no experts are studying the problem yet. One solution is for activists to begin to collect their own information. For instance, it was only after gay and lesbian activists in some cities tried to gather reports of homosexuals who had been assaulted that official efforts to collect hate crime statistics started (Jenness, 1995). Similarly, residents living near toxic waste sites may begin to collect their own evidence of health problems as a way of arousing concern about the risks they face (P. Brown, 1992). In such cases, amateurs try to generate the sort of knowledge that experts have failed to collect, in order to fill what would otherwise be a gap in their claims. Figure 4.1 illustrates how both trained professionals and those without formal training as experts can make use of professional knowledge when making claims.

Just as activist claimsmakers must be alert to the responses of others—particularly the media, the public, and policymakers—so, too, must experts be concerned with feedback from other actors in the social problems process. Because experts are likely to consider the knowledge that they contribute to the social problems process especially valuable, they may be disappointed that their statements are not more influential. Audiences may have trouble interpreting what experts have to say, particularly when the experts present their findings using a professional, technical vocabulary. To bridge the gap, experts may discover that they need to popularize their work, to translate their findings into lay language.

Figure 4.1 Experts' Role in the Social Problems Process

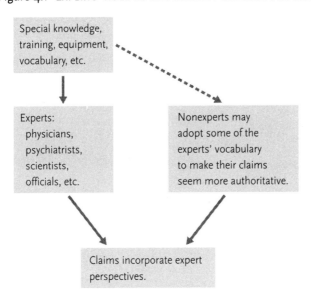

Another problem is that audiences may have impossibly high expectations for experts' contributions; as we have suggested, experts may add to our understanding of a troubling social condition, but their knowledge usually is not sufficient to identify policies that can make the problem disappear. Ultimately, whether experts' claims—or, for that matter, the claims of activists—are widely understood depends on the treatment they receive in the media.

Making Connections

- *The role of experts in the policymaking process is discussed further in Chapter 7.*

- *The media relies on experts to make claims about social problems. In the next chapter you will learn how experts and the media collaborate in the social problems process.*

- *In Chapter 9, the role of experts in evaluating the outcomes of social problems and making new claims about problems will be discussed.*

CASE STUDY
MEDICAL EXPERTS CONSTRUCT THE
OBESITY EPIDEMIC

Claims that the United States was experiencing an obesity epidemic emerged in the late 1990s and surged dramatically beginning around 2002. Many of these claims were promoted by medical authorities, particularly specialists in public health. They argued that Americans were gaining weight, that a growing proportion of the population was obese, and that this trend posed a serious medical problem because obese individuals are more likely to experience a broad range of serious medical problems and die at earlier ages, and because those medical problems consume expensive health care services and thus place a burden on the larger society.

Obesity is defined in terms of an individual's body mass index (BMI), calculated from a person's height and weight. According to current standards, those with a BMI of 18.5 to less than 25 are designated as being of *normal weight*; a BMI under 18.5 is considered *underweight*; a BMI of 25 to under 30 is labeled *overweight*; and those with higher BMIs are classified as *obese*. The BMI is a crude measure (even some lean, heavily muscled athletes, for example, can qualify as obese). In 1998 the federal government redefined *overweight*: previously, men with BMIs below 28 had been considered of normal weight, but the upper limit for normal weight was lowered to 25 (Squires, 1998). This meant that an additional twenty-nine million Americans with BMIs between 25 and 28—who had been considered of normal weight—suddenly were reclassified as overweight.

In 1991, 23 percent of Americans were obese; by 2004, that figure had climbed to 31 percent (Kolata, 2004). Although this might seem to be a dramatic increase, the average individual weight gain was only 7 to 10 pounds. Weights did not change for everyone; rather, most of the increase was at the heavier end of the weight distribution—the portion of the population with the lowest BMIs did not gain much weight, and those who were heavier gained the most. Although it is generally agreed that Americans' weights have risen, how to interpret this change remains a topic of debate.

Explanations for the increase in obesity vary a good deal. Is it caused by Americans getting less exercise and becoming more sedentary? Is it exacerbated by the growing proportion of meals eaten in restaurants (especially fast-food restaurants that serve large portions of relatively high-calorie foods), or by the growth in convenience foods (because foods packaged to be microwaved tend to be higher in fat)? Or is weight governed primarily by genetics? Some blame bad eating habits; others, the food industry; and still others, biological processes.

Although there remain all manner of competing claims, including those from "fat acceptance" activists, obesity has been medicalized, and medical experts have assumed ownership of the problem. In particular, public health officials, led by the federal Centers for Disease Control and Prevention, have promoted the idea that obesity constitutes an epidemic. In 2004, the CDC publicized research estimating that overweight and obesity caused 400,000 deaths annually: "America's weight problem is rapidly overtaking cigarette smoking as the leading cause of preventable deaths. . . . If current trends continue, obesity will become the leading cause by next year, with the toll surpassing 500,000 deaths annually" (Stein, 2004). Just as public health officials had assumed ownership of the smoking problem and led the campaign to reduce smoking (and thereby improve the nation's health), they sought to frame obesity as another serious problem that they were best qualified to address.

Barely one year later, however, another group of CDC researchers challenged those findings (Kolata, 2005). Their more accurate statistical measures offered a new, much lower estimate for the number of annual excess deaths attributable to overweight or obese individuals. This study found that obese individuals accounted for about 112,000 extra deaths, but that individuals classified as overweight were actually *less* likely to die than might be expected (an estimated 86,000 deaths were prevented in this group, so the overall figure for deaths among overweight and obese individuals was only 26,000 [112,000 minus 86,000]). In fact, the study showed that those classified as being of normal weight ran higher risks of death than those who were merely overweight (as opposed to obese). In other words, the new research suggested that the health risks of being overweight—as opposed to obese—had been exaggerated.

The conflicting reports by different teams of CDC researchers—was excess weight killing 400,000 or only 26,000 Americans every year?—inspired a good deal of frustrated media commentary. What were medical findings worth, if experts could not agree on an answer to the apparently simple question of whether being overweight (but not, remember, obese) increases a person's risk of death? The CDC continues to characterize the problem using the term *overweight and obesity*. Others, including the Center for Consumer Freedom (funded by the food industry), continue to charge that the CDC exaggerates the risks of being overweight.

Why not simply exclude the overweight category and restrict claimsmaking to obesity? Including overweight has rhetorical advantages, if only because overweight people outnumber obese people. Remember: about 31 percent of Americans are defined as obese, but 65 percent are considered either overweight or obese. Defining the overweight as part of the obesity epidemic makes the problem seem larger, more urgent. It makes the work of the problem's expert owners—public health officials in particular—seem more important. And although sectors of the food industry may worry (particularly about the possibility of lawsuits analogous to those faced by the tobacco industry charging that they knowingly promoted a hazardous product), it is worth noting that others stand to profit from concern about being overweight. Included in this group are the diet industry; the pharmaceutical industry (which designs not just medications to encourage weight loss, but also many other products designed to reduce health risks thought to be brought on by being overweight); and, for that matter, the food industry itself, which markets a vast array of products designed to encourage weight loss (such as low-fat or reduced-calorie versions of popular foods). Thus, the validation by medical experts of claims about an obesity epidemic supports many different interests.

QUESTIONS

1. In the debate over obesity, who has assumed ownership of the problem and what are their claims?

2. How might certain industries benefit from claims that obesity is a major social problem?

3. What are the counterclaims against the experts who say that obesity is a problem?

5

The Media and Claims

Analyses of the mass media's role in the social problems process often focus on the issue of **bias**. Conservative critics charge that the media systematically present a liberal point of view:

> The argument over whether the national press is dominated by liberals is over. Since 1962, there have been 11 surveys of the media that sought the political views of hundreds of journalists. . . . And the proportion of liberals to conservatives in the press, either 3-to-1 or 4-to-1, has stayed the same. That liberals are dominant is now beyond dispute. (Barnes, 2004)

Meanwhile, liberals counter that the media have a conservative bias:

> Even the genuine liberal media . . . [are] no match—either in size, ferocity, or commitment—for the massive conservative media structure that, more than ever, determines the shape and scope of our political agenda. (Alterman, 2003, p. 11)

These critiques address the news media that report information (such as newspapers, newsmagazines, and radio and television news broadcasts), but also the entertainment media (such as television dramas, novels, or movies) and so-called infotainment that uses entertaining formats to discuss social issues (such as television talk shows, or "reality" shows that depict police at work).

All forms of **media coverage** tend to alter how social problems are constructed, although not necessarily in the ways that critics of media bias imagine. The social problems process typically begins with claimsmaking that precedes the media's involvement; usually activists or experts present the initial, or **primary, claims** (Best, 1990). Unless these claimsmakers are insiders who have ready access to policymakers (see Chapters 3 and 4), they probably hope that the media will cover their claims, thereby bringing those claims before a larger audience than the claimsmakers could hope to reach on their own. Newspaper stories, talk show episodes, or made-for-TV disease-of-the-week movies can bring claims to the attention of millions of people in the general public, as well as policymakers. However, media coverage almost inevitably alters the claims that it presents.

Media workers face their own constraints: they work under deadlines, so they rarely have time to become thoroughly familiar with the claims they cover; their presentations are usually constricted (for example, newspapers can print only so many inches of news per day [journalists call this the *newshole*], and television news programs have only so many broadcast minutes available); and they need to make their coverage interesting enough that the audience won't stop reading or watching. The media, then, translate and transform claimsmakers' messages into what we will call **secondary claims**, typically by making them shorter, more dramatic, and less ideological than the original primary claims.

Because there are many claimsmakers and the media can cover only a limited number of stories, claimsmakers find themselves competing for media attention. Savvy claimsmakers realize that they need to package their claims so as to interest the media in covering them. The media prefer to cover new, seemingly fresh material, so it is important to present claims in novel ways (the first sit-in or peace march may get a lot of coverage, but each additional sit-in or march is likely to get less, unless it offers an interesting new angle). The media like to be able to plan their coverage in advance, so it helps to issue press releases and schedule press conferences so that reporters know when and where they can find someone willing to talk with them. The media favor claims presented by interesting people, so claimsmakers need to find spokespersons who seem engaging (note how often claimsmaking campaigns use either celebrities—interesting in their own right—or highly dramatic figures, such as parents who have suffered the loss of a child, to present the claims). Television seeks visually interesting material that can accompany a story, so claimsmakers favor marches, demonstrations, and other easy-to-film ways of presenting their claims. In the competition for media attention, claimsmakers who take the media's needs into account have an advantage.

Hilgartner and Bosk (1988) suggest that the marketplace for social problems can be understood as composed of multiple **arenas**. Each arena is a venue where social problems claims can be presented; the pages of a newsmagazine, a TV talk show, or the hearings of a congressional subcommittee are all arenas. Each arena has a limited **carrying capacity** for presenting claims: magazines have only so many pages per issue, talk shows schedule a set number of episodes per season, subcommittees hold only a limited number of hearings, and so on. In Chapters 3 and 4, we considered the perspective of claimsmakers, who understand that they are competing for attention in various arenas. In this chapter we will adopt the perspective of those who work in the media. We can think of them as managing different arenas and having the job of sorting through all the competing claims and choosing which ones will receive attention in their arena.

In general, sociologists who have observed how news reporters and editors decide which stories to cover and how to cover them conclude that bias—in the sense of an underlying political ideology—is less important in shaping how the news is covered than the nature of the work that reporters and editors do. This chapter begins by considering the nature of those jobs—and the parallel considerations that shape how social problems are treated in entertainment media—before examining the forms that secondary claims tend to take. The chapter ends with a caution against exaggerating the media's influence.

WHAT'S THE NEWS?

The term **news work** draws our attention to the fact that reporters and editors have the job of locating and presenting news to the larger public. Like all other occupations, news work has constraints (Gans, 1979; Schudson, 2003; Tuchman, 1978). Some constraints are economic: it costs money to collect and produce news, and news workers operate within budgets, so newspapers and television news operations can afford only so many employees; the newshole (that is, the number of available column inches or broadcast minutes) can contain only so many stories; and so on. Other constraints are cultural. News workers have their own understanding of what they should do; that is, their sense of professionalism also shapes their coverage.

News workers operate under pressure. They have schedules and deadlines; newspapers and magazines need to reach the printer on schedule, just as radio and television programs need to be ready in time for their broadcasts. News workers cannot simply sit back and wait for news to happen and come to their attention; rather, they must try to plan ahead, to anticipate what might be and ought to be covered. Many news organizations assign reporters to beats—types of news that are expected to generate suitable stories; for example, a reporter on the police beat covers stories about crimes. News workers also are drawn to predictable events; a scheduled demonstration or even a press conference can be attractive precisely because reporters and editors have some sense in advance of what sorts of stories those events might generate.

News workers also judge some stories as being more deserving of coverage than others. Most obviously, they consider some stories to be more important or, as they say, more newsworthy. Important stories involve consequential events, things about which people need to know. But importance depends on the news workers' audience. Imagine a passenger jet crashing and killing, say, 150 people. How much attention should a newspaper give that story? If the crash occurred in the city where the newspaper is published, we can imagine this dramatic local story consuming most of the front page. If it occurred, say, in a city a thousand miles away, and if there were other compelling stories competing for the paper's attention, the crash story might well be pushed off the front page. If the crash occurred in a foreign country (and especially if no Americans were killed), it is likely to receive no more than a paragraph or two, somewhere well inside the paper. In other words, it is not just the death toll that makes a story seem important, but also the story's perceived relevance to the paper's readers.

In addition to being of varying importance, stories strike news workers as being more or less interesting to their audience. Television news, for example, favors stories that can be accompanied by videotaped footage showing something happening. The earliest television news broadcasts featured newscasters facing the camera and reading stories to the audience. Television workers soon realized, however, that theirs was a visual medium, and that audiences found these "talking heads" boring. There is, then, a strong preference for having some sort of videotaped action to illustrate the story, even if the activity shown is mundane; this explains why stories about ongoing trials—where cameras are often forbidden in the courtroom—are often accompanied by footage of trial participants walking into the courthouse, so that viewers have something to watch, to accompany the sound of a reporter describing what happened in court that day. There are, of course, other ways of making stories interesting. Like claims generally, news stories often begin with typifying examples. For example, a story on homelessness might begin by describing the experiences of one or two particular homeless individuals; such an introduction puts a human face on the story and gives the problem "human interest." Stories that seem less interesting can easily lose out in the competition for media attention; news workers will favor covering stories that can be presented in an interesting manner.

Another quality of an attractive story is novelty. Notice the very word *news*—that is, "what's new." In general, news workers prefer stories that are current (especially "breaking news") and that seem different. "Fresh" news is preferred to stories that seem too familiar, that have grown "stale." After all, if there isn't something new to report, why should news workers expect the audience to pay any attention? This means that familiar, troubling conditions that affect many people—such as world hunger—may not attract nearly as much media attention as the latest sex scandal or lurid murder.

In assembling the stories they report, news workers apply other professional standards as well. For example, when the story's subject is clearly an issue about which people disagree, many news workers consider themselves obliged to *balance* their coverage by reporting the views of "both sides." This expression reveals an assumption that most issues have only two sides—pro and con, liberal and conservative, or whatever. The news media often resist reporting complex stories in which there are more than two competing positions; they prefer to construct the issue as a straightforward, two-party disagreement. Note, too, that news workers do not feel the need to balance coverage when they perceive a general unanimity of opinion (concerning what Chapter 2 called *valence issues*). If there is general, widespread agreement that, say, child pornography is bad, then reporters will not consider themselves obliged to balance their coverage by reporting the views of child pornographers. Considerations such as importance, interest, novelty, and balance shape how news workers construct the news. These are inevitably matters of judgment, with editors making choices—deciding which stories deserve more attention, which deserve less, and which can be ignored. In some cases, news workers may act as primary claimsmakers; that is, they might originate the claims-making through their coverage. "Crime waves," for instance, often represent waves in media coverage rather than changes in the incidence of crime. In such cases, the media link unrelated crimes and depict them as evidence of a disturbing trend, identifying a troubling condition that no other claimsmakers are promoting (see Box 5.1).

For social problems claimsmakers, the challenge is to construct claims that will strike news workers as sufficiently important and interesting to merit news coverage. Sophisticated claimsmakers learn to take the news workers' concerns into account: they make it easy to cover their claims by, for example, staging demonstrations and other events that will seem interesting and therefore newsworthy; they schedule these events and press conferences in advance so that news workers will know when and where to go to get their stories; they designate articulate spokespersons who can present the claims, answer reporters' questions, and help them identify suitable typifying examples; they devise novel, visually interesting ways of presenting their claims—new forms of demonstrations, new evidence, and such—so that their message seems fresh and the story well suited for television; and so on. For instance, a small San Francisco prostitutes' rights movement managed to attract a great deal of media attention by organizing the "First Annual Hookers' Ball" (Jenness, 1993). Understanding the news media's concerns allows claimsmakers to package their claims in ways that will appeal to news workers, and thereby makes it

Box 5.1 Waves of Freeway Violence

During the summer of 1987, a reporter at the *Los Angeles Times* wrote a short article noting that two people had been shot in unrelated incidents on southern California freeways. A few days later, a *Times* columnist speculated that freeway shootings seemed to be on the rise. Within a month, national newsmagazines and network newscasts were speculating that LA's wave of freeway violence might spread nationwide. Yet by summer's end, the problem was nearly forgotten (Best, 1991).

This example illustrates that crime waves are usually nothing more than waves in media coverage: a reporter claims to notice an increase in a particular crime, and other media begin covering the story until it begins to seem stale, at which point coverage shifts to a fresh topic. In his autobiography, Lincoln Steffens (1931), a great muckraking reporter from the Progressive Era, described the same process in his chapter "I Make a Crime Wave." There are many other examples; Los Angeles media, for instance, reported on other waves of freeway violence in 1977 and 2005 (Garvey & Lin, 2005).

The media need not wait for others to make claims; media coverage can launch the social problems process. However, because the media are constantly looking for new topics to cover, they rarely assume ownership of the problems they construct, and without long-term owners willing to continue promoting an issue so that it remains in the public eye, concern—however intense—is likely to be short-lived. Crime waves and other social problems for which the media act as primary claimsmakers tend to be brief episodes.

more likely that those claims will, in fact, become the subjects of news coverage.

News workers are not naive; they understand that experienced claimsmakers tailor their campaigns to attract news coverage. On the one hand, news workers may be wary of being manipulated; they particularly want to avoid wasting time covering a story that will strike themselves and their audiences as familiar and boring. They want to be convinced that the information they're being given is fresh, accurate, and interesting; they have no interest in attending yet another press conference where the same speakers make the same old claims. Still, depending on what rival stories are under consideration, it may be easier to cover a well-packaged story. There are, after all, "slow news days" when there seems to be a shortage of newsworthy stories, just as summer has long been known among journalists as the "dog days" or the "silly season"—months when the federal government and other news-generating institutions are less active, so that competition for coverage is less intense and it is easier for offbeat stories to attract news coverage. A well-assembled claim can become very attractive to news workers if there aren't strong alternative stories competing for attention.

Geography also plays a role in this process. News workers are not evenly distributed across the country; rather they are concentrated in larger cities (Best, 1999). In particular, three cities have exceptionally large concentrations of news workers: New York is the nation's largest city, and it remains the traditional base for such important news media as the *New York Times*, the *Wall Street Journal*, and the three major television network news broadcasts; Los Angeles is the second largest city, and as the center of the entertainment industry, it has its own concentration of news media; and Washington, D.C., is, of course, the center of the federal government and attracts a vast army of news workers devoted to covering the government's actions. Events that occur near such concentrations of news workers are more likely to attract coverage (see Box 5.2).

Such geographic concentrations of news workers are important because where there are more reporters, there are more opportunities for claimsmakers to get their claims covered. There is nothing to keep people from making claims in a small town in a remote rural location, but it is more difficult to get news workers to travel there to cover the story. It is far easier for a claim to gain wide-

Box 5.2 News Media and the Shootings at Columbine High School

On April 20, 1999, two heavily armed students entered Columbine High School in Colorado and killed twelve fellow students and a teacher before killing themselves. The previous year, well-publicized incidents in Kentucky, Arkansas, and Oregon had helped construct school shootings as a social problem. But the Columbine shootings became a focus for especially intense media coverage. Why?

In part, of course, Columbine's death toll, which exceeded the combined total of the three major incidents in 1998, made it newsworthy. But additional factors also proved relevant:

- Columbine High School was located in an affluent, largely white suburb of Denver, a major city with many news workers. These facts not only made it easy for reporters to reach the scene but invited claims that, if violence could happen at a school like Columbine, no school was safe.

- Because it took several hours for police to enter the school and locate the victims, there was an extended opportunity for live, on-the-scene television coverage, and the result was some dramatic footage of students fleeing the school.

- Because the two juvenile killers died at the scene, the press was free to identify them by name, explore their lives, and speculate on their motives.

- Twenty-four-hour cable news networks carried live coverage of several memorial services, which also served to keep the story in the foreground for some days.

If these circumstances had been different, coverage of the Columbine shootings might have been less intense.

Source: Filler, 2000.

spread attention if the claimsmakers bring their case to a major media center, to a location where many news workers will have convenient access to the story. Thus, even claimsmakers who begin in distant places tend to migrate to larger media centers.

All of this is to say that the news is a social construction, produced by news workers operating under various constraints that force them to make choices—to prefer stories that can be covered in ways that fit their sense of what good news ought to be. Claimsmakers who ignore these considerations do so at their own peril.

CHANGING NEWS MEDIA

Note that the news media's forms shift over time. During television's first thirty years, the great majority of Americans relied on broadcast signals; even those living in fairly large urban centers might receive signals from only half a dozen stations. The three major networks (ABC, CBS, and NBC) originally ran fifteen-minute news broadcasts on weekdays, which were expanded to thirty minutes in the early 1960s, then later to six days per week; in addition, local stations offered their own news broadcasts a couple times a day.

Today, most households receive either cable or satellite television signals offering access to dozens, if not hundreds, of channels. Several channels offer round-the-clock news coverage. This shift has had all manner of consequences: the audience for the networks' evening news broadcasts has grown smaller as viewers turn to all-news channels at more convenient times; the audience for print journalism—both newspapers and weekly newsmagazines—has also declined as more people rely on electronic media for their news; and some cable networks have begun to adopt overt editorial stances (as the emergence of FOX News as an unabashedly conservative network illustrates).

For claimsmakers, one important consequence of these changes in the media is that competing twenty-four-hour news channels have a colossal appetite for fresh stories. In television's early years, when the networks broadcast five fifteen-minute shows per week, it was far tougher to get an issue covered on national television than it is today. Television's carrying capacity for news has increased vastly. (On the other hand, as their advertising has declined, newspapers and newsmagazines have been shrinking in size, so their carrying capacity has grown smaller.)

As television channels have increased in number, they have increasingly aimed at targeted audiences. Theorists once worried about the "mass media" that would turn society into an undifferentiated mass receiving the same media messages (Turow, 1997). In practice, the media find it more profitable to practice **audience segmentation**, to aim at particular demographic groups; because people fitting a particular demographic profile (defined by age, sex, income, and so on) are more likely to watch programs aimed directly at their interests, the audience for those programs will be relatively homogeneous, and advertisers who believe that their customers will be concentrated in that segment of the larger audience will prefer—and even pay a premium—to place their ads on those programs. Thus, there are cable channels aimed at women, Spanish speakers, people in particular age groups, and so on. (A similar process changed magazine publishing: general-interest magazines such as *Life* that once sought to appeal to huge mass audiences have folded, yet a visit to a newsstand reveals hundreds of titles aimed at people with particular interests.)

Audience segmentation affects the media's role in the social problems process. Because different television channels or magazines seek to appeal to demographically distinct audiences, their coverage of claimsmaking will reflect their sense of which issues will strike their viewers or readers as interesting and relevant. Because advertisers often favor more affluent customers who can afford their products, the news media are less likely to target poorer audiences, which means that social problems coverage tends to downplay claims of greater concern to the poor and the powerless. Newspapers' economic reporting, for instance, tends to devote far more attention to the concerns of corporations than to those of workers or the unemployed (Kollmeyer, 2004). The consequence of audience segmentation for social problems claimsmaking is that, although it is becoming easier to gain media coverage for claims, that coverage often is tailored for the particular audience that follows the television programs or magazines that choose to cover the claims.

The obvious example of changing media is the emergence of the Internet. The Internet is a boon to claimsmakers in that Web sites, discussion groups, and blogs can be established quite easily, and at minimal cost. Claims of all sorts can be posted and made accessible to anyone who knows how to use a search engine; in effect, the Internet has an unlimited carrying capacity. Because there is little in the way of filtering, however, it becomes difficult to evaluate the various claims that wind up posted in cyberspace. (In contrast, note that news workers in print and broadcast journalism routinely sort through prospective stories and have standards for rejecting some claims.) Moreover, posting a claim does not guarantee that it will gain a large audience; bloggers have learned to encourage traffic to their sites by providing mutual links to other sites. Still, it seems likely that the Internet will have a long-term effect on claimsmaking. In some instances already, Web sites or bloggers have forced more established news media to cover particular issues by breaking stories about those issues.

Thus, the news media's structure is changing: Some media, such as newspapers and magazines, seem to be losing part of their audience, shrinking their coverage, and becoming less influential. Others, such as television news, are expanding their coverage and shifting forms (by, for example, becoming more openly ideological). At the same time, new, Internet-based forms, such as blogs, Web sites, and electronic discussion groups, are emerging. Thus far, these changes seem to make it easier to gain some sort of media coverage of claims, although, because the target audiences for different media tend to be smaller and more homogeneous, it is not necessarily easier to bring claims to the attention of a broad, general audience.

PACKAGING SOCIAL PROBLEMS IN THE NEWS

In short, the nature of news work and the structure of the news industry shape which stories are covered and the form that coverage takes. In particular, news about claimsmaking tends to display some fairly clear patterns.

The Advantages of Issue Ownership

First, remember that particular claimsmakers sometimes assume ownership of their social problems. That is, they become widely recognized as *the* authorities on the problem, as especially knowledgeable. One of the principal benefits of such ownership is that, when news workers find themselves covering a story related to a certain social problem, they routinely turn to the problem's owners for comments. This status is self-reinforcing; once the media have used particular activists or experts as sources for one story, they are more likely to seek out the same sources for future, related stories.

Of course, achieving ownership is easier for some people than for others. The news media frequently turn to government officials as sources for their stories, and other experts have credentials that make their comments seem particularly authoritative. The news media also favor covering people who are already well known; thus, when movie stars or other celebrities enlist in claimsmaking campaigns, they often draw press attention. In short, the news media prefer to collect their information from those who already have high status.

The flip side of ownership arises when the media define some claimsmakers as lacking the legitimacy to deserve coverage. We might call these *dispossessed* claimsmakers (that is, they are the opposite of owners). News workers may view people who are poorer—who lack power, wealth, or high status—as less newsworthy, and claimsmakers representing these people find it hard to get their claims covered. Similarly, those with views considered too far outside the mainstream—too unpopular or too radical—find it much harder to gain media coverage for their claims. Remember, the media often try to balance their coverage by presenting "both sides" of an issue—typically understood to mean liberals and conservatives, or Democrats and Republicans. Those who adopt other, very different positions—who are too radical or too reactionary, who hold unpopular beliefs or values—usually find it difficult to break into the news media that have the largest audiences. As a result, claimsmakers whose rhetoric strikes news workers as too far outside the mainstream—think of vegans, hate groups, or unfamiliar new religions—may find themselves ignored by the major media. Those newspapers, newsmagazines, and television networks with the largest audiences tend to concentrate their coverage on less controversial claims.

Dispossession also reflects the news media's efforts to appeal to their target audiences. Although we might imagine that newspapers or television news broadcasts want to gain the largest possible audience, audience segmentation leads them, in practice, to be more concerned with reaching some people than others (Hamilton, 2004). Advertisers are more likely to place their ads in media that reach particular types of consumers, and editors may favor stories that will appeal to their target audience. To the degree that social problems claims address troubling conditions thought to be of concern to that target audience, it is easier to get coverage; however, claims that may be of more concern to people outside the target

audience have a tougher time getting covered. Again, advertisers—
and therefore the news media—tend to be especially interested in
reaching more affluent audience members, and less interested in
attracting poorer readers and viewers; therefore, claims about problems that face the poor may have a harder time gaining news
coverage.

Not all social problems come to have owners, because claimsmakers must themselves choose which issues are most important
(Best, 1999). Consider the media coverage of school shootings that
began in 1998; there were several heavily publicized incidents
(most notably, of course, at Columbine High School in 1999). Various claimsmakers sought to explain these episodes, but the cacophony of explanations was remarkable. School shootings were blamed
on insufficient gun control laws, violent video games, the Goth sub-
culture, bullying, theaters admitting those under seventeen into
R-rated movies, the gun culture, and so on.

This is a common pattern: reports of novel sorts of violent crime
often lead to all sorts of commentators offering competing explanations and solutions. In the case of school shootings, none of these
explanations emerged as dominant; that is, no single set of claimsmakers assumed ownership. Why not? Probably because school
shootings were not central to the causes of any of the commentators who spoke out on the issue. Gun control activists, for example, saw school shootings as just one small part of the larger gun
problem; they wanted to continue to draw attention to all of the
aspects of that problem, rather than to focus on school shootings.
The emergence of ownership requires claimsmakers who are motivated to continue promoting an issue, as well as news workers who
treat those claimsmakers as authoritative.

The Dominance of Landmark Narratives

Second, particular typifying examples—what are called **landmark
narratives**—often come to dominate news coverage of particular

problems (L. T. Nichols, 1997). That is, a particular case may become the central focus of media coverage of a social problem—the subject of more newspaper and magazine articles than other, similar cases, or represented in more of the video clips that accompany numerous TV news stories on the topic. Just as the typifying examples chosen by claimsmakers are often quite atypical—more serious, dramatic, or troubling than most cases—so news workers choose landmark narratives not because they accurately reflect the larger problem, but because they are the stuff of compelling news (see Box 5.3). These cases serve as landmarks in two senses: they guide news workers' thinking about the nature of the problem and how it should be covered, and they shape the terms by which the news audience understands the problem.

Constructing Packages

Third, landmark cases often fall within larger constructions called **packages** (Beckett, 1996; Gamson, 1992; Gamson & Modigliani, 1989; Sasson, 1995b). A package is a familiar, more or less coherent view of a social issue, including its causes and what ought to be done about it. A package has a core idea, or frame; for example, arguments that global warming is substantially caused by humans' activities, that it poses a serious threat, and that steps need to be taken to minimize the problem are at the core of one familiar package. Similarly, arguments that global warming is not necessarily caused by humans' activities and may not constitute a serious threat are the frame for a rival package. Within a package, there is room for disagreement: people may accept the same basic frame yet disagree about specifics, such as the exact processes causing the problem or what needs to be done. Not everyone who shares the basic concern about global warming has to agree on every aspect of the package.

In addition, packages offer **condensing symbols**, shorthand elements—landmark narratives, typifying examples, slogans, visual

---

Box 5.3   Turning the Bank of Boston into a Landmark Narrative

During the 1980s, federal authorities cracked down on money laundering at financial institutions (they charged that, by not reporting deposits made by drug dealers and people in organized crime, banks allowed ill-gotten gains to be transformed into apparently legitimate bank accounts). Media attention focused on charges that the Bank of Boston had laundered money for a local organized crime family. Interestingly, although the Bank of Boston became the typifying example in many press reports about the money-laundering problem, it was neither the first institution to be charged nor the worst offender. Why, then, did it attract so much attention?

Several factors seem to have made it an attractive subject for media coverage. Boston's popular image emphasizes the city's propriety, so the idea that a leading Bostonian institution was implicated in criminal activity made the story seem more interesting. In addition, press reports emphasized the story's dramatic elements, such as reports that people involved in organized crime had brought paper bags filled with cash to the bank. Government authorities sought to make an example of the Bank of Boston by bringing criminal charges against it, whereas other banks faced only civil penalties. The federal government had attracted much criticism when many savings and loan firms proved to be financially unstable during the 1980s, and it used its prosecution of the Bank of Boston as proof that it was being effective. In other words, the Bank of Boston's landmark status had less to do with what the bank had done than with the goals of the press and government officials.

Source: L. T. Nichols, 1997.

---

images, and so on—that evoke the package. Editorial cartoons in newspapers depend on the fact that readers will understand such symbols; a figure in a Klansman's robe and hood denotes racism, a smokestack belching smoke symbolizes pollution, and so on. Similarly, a bumper sticker's slogan—"When Guns Are Outlawed, Only Outlaws Will Have Guns"—can encapsulate a larger package of ideas about guns and gun control. Condensing signals remind people of the larger package, which presents claims that define the nature of the problem, its causes, and a vision of what ought to be done about it.

Note that packages draw upon the larger stock of cultural resources. Like primary claimsmakers designing their claims, news workers want to assemble coverage that seems sensible to themselves, and that also will seem sensible to their audiences. Their stories, then, incorporate the culture that they take for granted— values, symbols, worldviews, and so on. These underlying assumptions are invisible to those who share them, although they may seem quite glaring to others. Consider Americans' shock when they discovered that, during the hostage crisis of 1980 (perhaps the first time serious tensions with the Muslim world became apparent), Iranian media had described the United States as the "Great Satan." In most cases, however, the way news coverage draws upon cultural resources that are taken for granted goes unnoticed.

Media packages help organize people's thinking about social problems. News workers sort through many, if not all, of the available claims, select some as worthy of coverage, and give that coverage shape. The packages they choose may change over time (see Box 5.4). News workers' choices are influenced by the nature of the claims they encounter, but also by other considerations, including the need to produce news under the pressures of news work, the range of available stories competing for coverage, the desirability of tailoring coverage to the target audience, and so on. Social problems packages are one outcome of this process; they give the news media's secondary claims a sense of coherence: among all the things that might be said about race or crime or anything else, these become the most visible positions. It is relatively easy for the public to become familiar with the packages presented by the news

Box 5.4 Changing Media Packages for Welfare

Often the media present alternative packages of claims about a particular social issue. For example, a study of the coverage of welfare by popular magazines identified four major packages of ideas (Misra, Moller, & Karides, 2003):

1. *Welfare causes dependency.* People who receive welfare benefits become dependent, incapable of supporting themselves.

2. *Welfare undermines families.* Welfare programs make it easier for existing families to break up, and they discourage the formation of new families.

3. *Welfare helps the needy.* Welfare programs assist those in need to get back on their feet.

4. *Welfare supports families.* Welfare programs support families by allowing them to balance care and work.

Note that the first two packages criticize welfare programs, while the latter two endorse them. The media do not speak with a single voice; on most issues they present more than one package. Moreover, the relative prominence of particular packages varies over time. Magazine stories presented the two critical packages more often during the 1960s and '70s than in earlier or later decades. In addition, use of the "helping the needy" package tended to increase over time, while arguments that welfare supported families appeared less often.

Most social issues can be packaged in many different ways. At particular times, particular packages receive more media attention—depending on current events, the claims currently in circulation, and the media's own practices.

media, and considerably harder for people to learn other ways to think about social problems.

It is possible to exaggerate the media's role in packaging social problems; they do not have a completely free hand. News workers have to derive and present packages that they believe will make sense to their audiences. American culture, for example, places great weight on the idea of individual responsibility; this idea runs through much commonsense thinking about life. We tend to hold individuals responsible for their circumstances; people who are poor, overweight, or addicted to drugs bear, most Americans agree, at least part of the blame for their troubles. It is, then, relatively easy to devise frames and packages in which individual responsibility plays a key role, but much harder, for instance, to present explanations that argue for the influence of social forces.

IS IT JUST ENTERTAINMENT?

We assume that the news media will cover social problems; after all, it is their job to report on serious matters. But social problems claims are also picked up by a wide range of entertainment media and are portrayed in what is called **popular culture**. Television talk shows, for instance, often present episodes focused on particular sorts of relationship problems, addictions, and the like. But even fictional genres, such as mystery novels, adopt topics from the news: when missing children became a national concern, fictional detective heroes tried to find missing kids; once stalking attracted notice, some of those same heroes confronted stalkers; and so on. And just as the demands of news work shape how the news media cover social problems, entertainment media are constrained by conventions that affect how they construct social problems.

Consider the format for a typical TV talk show: the host moderates a discussion among several guests, a group typically including several "ordinary people" who have firsthand experience with the problem at issue. For instance, a show on compulsive gambling might feature two or three gamblers who can tell tales of being unable to control their gambling, as well as a couple of spouses or other relatives who can describe the frustration and despair of dealing with a compulsive gambler. Toward the end of the show, the host often turns to an expert, perhaps a psychologist who medicalizes the problem by explaining that gambling is a disease, and that the solution lies in the twelve-step program of Gamblers Anonymous. This formula resembles a religious revival, in which sinners confess, repent, and are shown the path to salvation (Lowney, 1999).

Every popular-culture genre has its own conventions and constraints—a formula that it follows. Television situation comedies need joke-filled scripts that will last about twenty-three minutes (thirty minutes less time for the commercials and the opening and closing credits), in romance novels the main characters fall in love, and comic-book superheroes confront and defeat supervillains. The people who produce popular culture follow these formulas because they are known to work; that is, they appeal to each genre's respective audience. Romance authors, editors, and publishers, for instance, doubt that their readers want stories about people who can't find love.

These formulas shape how entertainment media deal with social problems claims. Although popular culture often reflects current social problems claims, with stories "ripped from the headlines," its depictions of those claims must conform to the different formulas' requirements (Gitlin, 1983). For example, to be dramatic, a confrontation requires an uncertain outcome; this means that the hero must face a villain who seems capable of winning. For instance, detective heroes—whether on television or in mystery novels—must be matched with powerful lawbreakers. As a result, fictional criminals tend to be far more powerful than their real-world counterparts: fictional child molesters belong to organized rings of wealthy abusers, drug dealers are millionaire industrialists, or gang leaders command hundreds of highly trained, well-armed followers. In comparison, real-life offenders, often people with very limited resources, offer poor material for entertaining plots.

Sociologists often complain that popular culture's conventions focus on individuals rather than on social forces. Novels, movies, and television series tend to match good people with heroic virtues against bad people with villainous vices, instead of exploring how social problems emerge from social arrangements. Thus, when racism appears in popular culture, it is often treated as a sort of personality defect: villains and other unsympathetic characters express racist sentiments, thereby affirming their poor character. Where sociologists view racism as a widespread problem with roots in social arrangements and consequences for the larger society, popular culture often treats racism as a personal characteristic of flawed individuals, because the formula requires a hero triumphing over a particular villain. Similarly, talk shows and other genres that mix elements of news and entertainment feature the same emphasis on flawed individuals. They present problem gambling as a psychological compulsion that affects some individuals, rather than emphasizing how social institutions, such as government and the gaming industry, exacerbate the problem by promoting gambling.

In other words, the formulas used in entertainment media highlight stories about individuals. This individual focus is found in both fictional popular-culture genres (such as mystery novels) and the quasi news of infotainment (such as talk shows). Entertainment media may address social problems claims, but regardless of whether primary claimsmakers view a problem as widespread and systemic (think of claims about racism, environmental degradation, or global warming), entertainment tends to translate those claims into stories about the struggles and successes of particular people. This focus on telling compelling stories about individuals is central to the formulas for many entertainment genres, and the people who work as creators and producers within the media understand the need to focus on typifying individuals (see Box 5.5).

This means that entertainment media have an especially difficult time adopting what C. Wright Mills (1959) called a **sociological imagination**—that is, viewing the world in terms of social arrange-

Box 5.5 How to Write a Magazine Story about Domestic Violence

Sociologist Nancy Berns (2004) asked editors at several major women's magazines (such as *Seventeen* and *Good Housekeeping*) to explain what they were looking for in stories about domestic violence. She found that there is a formula for writing such stories, consisting of the following elements:

- *Providing a service.* The editors saw their magazines as offering information that readers could use as "caretakers for their families."

- *Empowerment.* The editors wanted articles to encourage women to make decisions and take control of their lives.

- *Keeping it personal.* The editors favored stories that focused on the problems of particular individuals rather than on larger social forces.

- *Upbeat and positive endings.* The editors preferred articles describing cases in which women had gotten out of bad relationships or the abuse had ended.

Women's magazines thus depict domestic violence—and all sorts of other social problems—in terms of individual stories with positive outcomes. Editors believe that their readers find such articles appealing, and that their audience doesn't want to read stories that seem depressing either because they don't have happy endings or because they suggest that individuals can't cope with the larger problem. Fearing that dissatisfied readers will turn to other magazines, editors insist that their writers stick to the familiar formula.

This is just one example. Every entertainment genre has its own conventions that shape how it depicts social problems; these conventions often direct attention to individuals rather than to larger social forces.

ments and social forces. Mills noted that, in everyday life, people focus on their private troubles, such as not having a job. Adopting a sociological imagination requires seeing those private troubles in terms of larger public issues; for example, whereas an individual may have trouble finding a job, the larger society confronts the more general problem of unemployment. Sociologists, then, tend to downplay the experiences of individuals and focus on larger, social patterns. (To use concepts from Chapters 3 and 4, the sociological imagination can be understood as the frame that sociologists as experts use to construct social problems.) No wonder sociologists—as well as many primary claimsmakers—often criticize the entertainment media's portrayal of social problems; by translating claims into dramatic tales about individual suffering and redemption, the media favor constructions that run counter to more sociological interpretations.

Critics worry that media constructions—whether in news or entertainment genres—are important because they are influential. That is, it seems obvious that people who follow the news or consume entertainment must be affected by how these media portray social problems. But is this true?

THE MEDIA'S IMPACT

Commentators often assume that the media are extremely powerful and influential, that members of the audience are regularly affected by media messages. To be sure, most of us would deny that we, personally, are easily manipulated by the media. We are made of stronger stuff; we take an attitude of healthy skepticism toward the messages in news, entertainment, and especially advertising. But others, we worry, must be easily bamboozled by the media and may require protection.

The media's powerful influence may seem obvious, but it turns out to be fairly difficult to document. Consider claims that televised violence leads to violent behavior. Television is nearly universal in our society (which makes it difficult to construct experimental studies of its effects, since there is no natural control group lacking exposure to television), yet most people do not engage in violent acts. Similarly, most people who view commercials do not rush out to purchase the advertised products. Although claimsmakers often insist that media exposure has damaging effects, it is hard to observe and measure these consequences. Clearly, the media don't have the same effects on everyone.

If we are to understand the media's role in the social problems process, we need to specify what forms its influence might take. One thing we might mean is that the media can bring a social problem to public attention. As we have already noted, this is a central goal of many claimsmakers. When claimsmakers are calling attention to a new problem—that is, to a troubling condition that has been generally neglected or ignored, one that is unfamiliar to many people—getting media coverage can bring the topic out in the open. Media attention can make the public aware that the issue exists or encourage the public to think that something ought to be done to remedy the problem. This is sometimes called **agenda setting** (McCombs, 2004).

Just as a meeting may be guided by an agenda—a list of topics to be addressed, usually in order of importance—we can envision a society's members as needing to prioritize their concerns. All people have countless topics competing for their attention. Many of these concern the individuals' personal lives—routine errands, conversations with friends and relatives, and on and on. The media—particularly the news media—provide some sense of what's occurring in the larger world, suggesting what else deserves people's notice. Media coverage, then, can make people aware of a social problem—get it on society's agenda. Agenda setting can affect both public awareness (as will be discussed in Chapter 6) and policymakers' sense of what deserves their attention (a topic covered in Chapter 7).

Note that the media do not have a free hand in agenda setting. They are constrained. First, some events—say, a major disaster—may demand media coverage. Second, the media can be influenced to cover particular topics—by claimsmakers who convince the media that a problem is worthy of their attention, by officials who herald a particular new policy, even by other media outlets whose coverage suggests that a topic must be worthy of coverage. Third, as we have already noted, people working in the news and entertainment media are limited by the resources available to them, by their sense of the sort of coverage they ought to produce, and so on.

Nevertheless, in one sense the media make choices that are consequential. We have already noted that the media translate and transform social problems claims. In the case of contentious issues, topics (such as abortion) about which claimsmakers may advance contradictory claims, media coverage can structure the debate by assembling a small set of claimsmaking packages. Although the media cannot force people to adopt particular ideas, they make some constructions readily available, so it is easier to come to understand social problems in particular ways. In some cases, media coverage may give individuals a new perspective on their personal lives, to help them redefine their personal troubles as part of larger social problems (see. Box 5.6).

The public and policymakers pay attention to what the media cover for a couple of reasons. First, they use the media as a source of information: media coverage may be how the public and policymakers first learn about particular social problems. Second, policymakers may begin to hear from members of the general public who, having learned about the problem via the media, may call for action. Although the media are by no means all-powerful, they do help shape the social problems process.

Box 5.6 Self-Help Books Promote Fibromyalgia Syndrome

Fibromyalgia syndrome (FMS) is a diagnosis given to people—usually women—who report experiencing widespread pain and a variety of other symptoms. There is disagreement about whether its causes are physiological or psychological; FMS has no objective indicators, and there are no consistently effective medical treatments. Both patients and doctors find the disease frustrating; people in distress often cannot be helped.

FMS has spawned several self-help books that are intended to help readers recognize its symptoms, and that recommend various courses of treatment (Barker, 2002). These books sell tens, even hundreds, of thousands of copies, mostly to people who suspect that they—or someone they know—might have FMS. The books offer lengthy lists of symptoms that might be indicative of FMS; many of these are widely shared experiences (for example, feeling nauseated). They help some readers to assign a label to their problems; as one put it, "There was a lot of stuff in there that I could identify about myself. Like, oh yes! I have this, and I have that, this symptom, and that problem, and so forth" (p. 291).

The FMS literature illustrates the way in which media can help construct a troubling condition, not only for the general public, but also for those directly affected by it. All manner of Internet sites, as well as more traditional media coverage, are intended to help individuals recognize that they are directly affected by—part of—a particular social problem. This is an important form of feedback in the social problems process: media coverage can lead more people to join claimsmaking efforts.

THE MEDIA IN THE SOCIAL PROBLEMS PROCESS

Part of the reason why commentators exaggerate the media's power is that the media play an especially visible role in the social prob-

Figure 5.1 THE MEDIA'S ROLE IN THE SOCIAL PROBLEMS PROCESS

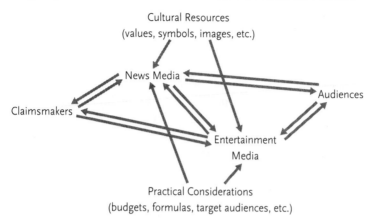

lems process. Outsider claimsmakers view media coverage as almost essential for making the public and policymakers aware of their claims. More powerful people use press conferences and other public relations techniques to attract and shape coverage for their activities. Meanwhile, much lobbying and other insider claimsmaking is hidden from the public (unless an enterprising reporter draws attention to it). Media coverage remains the easiest way for most people to learn about social problems.

This chapter has argued that the media must also be understood in terms of their social arrangements. Figure 5.1 illustrates some of the key features of these arrangements. First, note the distinction between news and entertainment media; the figure portrays news coverage as occurring first and often shaping the entertainment media's coverage of social problems. Second, the figure draws attention to the role of cultural resources. News workers' sense of what is newsworthy, as well as how news stories should be assembled and reported, depends in part on their understanding of how the larger culture will make sense of claims; a parallel set of considerations will shape what will be considered entertaining. Finally, note that both news and entertainment media have their own organizational constraints—operating budgets, production schedules, established conventions and formulas, and so on—that also influence what the media produce.

In addition, the media constantly receive feedback. Most obviously they worry about the reactions of their audiences: Are people interested in the news or entertainment they produce? If not, the media are likely to modify what they're doing. But also the media may hear from claimsmakers who offer congratulations or complaints about coverage, from segments of the general public who are not in their target audiences (and who often have their own criticisms), and from policymakers who may endorse or challenge what the media have done. The people who work in the media, then, should not be seen as all-powerful, as able to dictate what others think. Rather, they are connected to—and influenced by—the other actors in the social problems process. And just as the media transform and translate primary claims into the secondary claims presented in news coverage or entertainment, the media's audience—the public—reworks those messages for its own purposes.

MAKING CONNECTIONS

- *The media are eager for new claims and fresh ways of framing problems. Chapters 3 and 4 explain how activists and experts frame their claims to attract the most media attention.*

- *Claimsmakers use the news media to encourage recognition of a problem. In Chapter 7 you will learn about the essential role that the media play in introducing a social problem into the policymaking process.*

- *In the next chapter you will learn how the public responds to media coverage of social problems.*

CASE STUDY
The Media Debate Whether Wal-Mart
Is a Social Problem

Wal-Mart is not just America's largest retailer; it has grown to have more employees and larger revenues than any other corporation in the world. It is relentlessly efficient at holding down costs so that it can offer the low prices that attract the customers who propel its continuing growth.

Wal-Mart's emergence as a retail giant has attracted claims-makers who argue that the company and its policies constitute a social problem, that holding down prices carries social costs. Many of these claims focus on the company's treatment of its employees. For instance, critics note that Wal-Mart's employees earn relatively low wages, that many are not covered by health insurance, and that even some full-time employees earn so little that they qualify for social assistance programs such as food stamps and Medicaid. Wal-Mart also stands accused of vigorously fighting campaigns to union-ize its workforce, of violating child labor laws (by requiring adolescent employees to work excessive hours), and of sexual discrimination in its employment practices (Lichtenstein, 2006).

In addition to claims that the company abuses its workers, crit-ics charge Wal-Mart with damaging the larger society. To the degree that Wal-Mart's workers depend on government social services, these critics say, the taxpaying public is subsidizing the company. Critics also argue that Wal-Mart harms other businesses—not just mom-and-pop retailers whose firms fail because they cannot match the giant firm's low prices, but also the suppliers who, in order to capture Wal-Mart's huge orders, must sell at very low profit mar-gins, as well as manufacturers who have to close their doors when Wal-Mart chooses to buy goods from foreign suppliers who pay their workers a fraction of U.S. wages. Wal-Mart's impact grows as the company becomes larger; Wal-Mart is the largest retailer for all manner of goods, so what and how it chooses to buy can determine what happens in many industries (Head, 2004).

The U.S. press has been somewhat cautious about criticizing Wal-Mart. In part, the doings of a discount retailer might not seem newsworthy; in part, the caution may stem from fears that Wal-Mart might choose to withdraw its ads from newspapers or television stations perceived as hostile to its interests. However, claimsmakers have found other media outlets. Publishers have produced books critical of Wal-Mart, such as *The United States of Wal-Mart* (Dicker, 2005) and *The Bully of Bentonville: How the High Cost of Wal-Mart's Everyday Low Prices Is Hurting America* (Bianco, 2006). The corporation has also become the subject of documentary films focusing on the social damage caused by Wal-Mart, such as a PBS *FRONTLINE* episode, "Is Wal-Mart Good for America?" (2004), and Robert Greenwald's film titled *Wal-Mart: The High Cost of Low Price* (2005). In addition, certain Web sites are dedicated to Wal-Mart critiques, such as Wal-Mart Watch (www.walmartwatch.com).

Documentary films have emerged as an important new vehicle for claimsmaking. Traditionally, documentaries rarely played in theaters, and they have had trouble attracting a large audience. However, Michael Moore has had several successes, most notably his 2004 critique of the war on terrorism, *Fahrenheit 9/11*, which grossed well over a hundred million dollars. Morgan Spurlock's film about McDonald's, *Super Size Me* (2004), is another example of a documentary that gained considerable exposure in theaters. These documentaries do not pretend to be evenhanded records of events; they are polemical and adopt a variety of entertaining elements, such as Spurlock's premise—following him for a full month while he ate only high-calorie foods from McDonald's, cut back on exercise, and gained weight. The size of the audience for such films is enhanced by DVD sales and rentals: a film that attracts even modest attention may not play in all that many theaters, but people are aware of its existence and may pay to watch the DVD. Other films begin as DVDs and, if they attract interest (as was the case with *Wal-Mart:*

The High Cost of Low Price), later play in theaters. Because documentaries tend to be relatively inexpensive to make, claimsmakers may use films to promote their messages. And Web sites, which cost vastly less to establish and maintain, are another useful vehicle for claimsmakers.

Wal-Mart even inspired a documentary based on counterclaims: *Why Wal-Mart Works (and Why That Makes Some People C-r-a-z-y)* (2005), which defended the company by arguing that Wal-Mart represents free markets at work. News media, in turn, were attracted by the spectacle of dueling documentaries, bringing more attention to the debate about the company (Featherstone, 2006).

The attention given to Wal-Mart's critics led the corporation to respond with its own publicity campaign. For example, after the *New York Review of Books* ran a lengthy essay endorsing many anti-Wal-Mart claims, the corporation responded by taking out an ad in the form of a letter from Lee Scott (2005), Wal-Mart's CEO. The corporation also operates a Web site promoting Wal-Mart's positive role in society (www.walmartfacts.com). Wal-Mart's defense centers on claims that it benefits poor Americans. Wal-Mart's customers tend to have lower incomes, and they are attracted by the retailer's low prices. Some economists have calculated that, although Wal-Mart does cost the company's workers many millions of dollars in lower wages and benefits, those costs are exceeded by the savings that Wal-Mart's customers receive when they pay lower prices. According to studies cited by the company, by holding down prices, Wal-Mart saves consumers thousands of dollars per household per year and actually has reduced the rate of inflation.

Perhaps because Wal-Mart seems too mundane to be newsworthy, or perhaps because news media are reluctant to offend a major advertiser, Wal-Mart's impact on society has not received intensive news coverage. However, the debate over whether Wal-Mart should be considered a social problem or a social benefit—launched in such specialized media as books, documentary films, and Web sites—has attracted attention and, in the process, brought claims about the company to wider notice. This case illustrates how the media environment is changing the social problems process.

QUESTIONS

1. What are the claims leveled against Wal-Mart by activists?

2. Why have films become one of the major media outlets for criticizing Wal-Mart?

3. How has Wal-Mart responded to the claims made against it in the media?

6

■

Public Reaction

■

Discussions of the social problems process usually assume that, at some point, claims reach and influence members of the general public. Sometimes there's a direct connection between the primary claimsmakers and the public; sometimes people hear a claimsmaker give a speech, or find themselves listening to a claim during a conversation. More often, of course, claims reach the public via the media; people encounter secondary claims on television or radio, or through reading newspapers, magazines, Web pages, or books. All this simply reflects the media's ability to reach very large audiences; claimsmakers who receive media coverage can be exposed to a far larger segment of the general public than they can hope to reach through face-to-face contacts.

As part of the audience for claims, members of the public are not completely passive; they can react in various ways. They may be energized and moved to action by some claims, deciding to contribute to a social movement organization, participate in a demonstration, write their legislators, or relay the claims to others they know. Some may treat a claim as interesting information—something to talk over with friends and acquaintances. Others may be indifferent, apathetic; they may find the claim boring and ignore it. Still others may react negatively, disagreeing with the claim and opposing its conclusions. Probably all claims elicit all of these possible reactions in different people.

Because the public is both large and diverse, because people can respond to claims in different ways, and because many of those responses are relatively private (in that people may keep their opinions to themselves or share them only with others they know well), interpreting the public's role in the social problems process poses special problems. Nonetheless, the other actors in the process want to understand the public's reactions. Claimsmakers use the feedback they receive from the public to modify their claims, in hopes of making them more persuasive; the media also attend to feedback from the public, in order to better devise news and entertainment that will capture the audience's attention; and policymakers may respond to public pressure to do something about a particular social problem. Thus, many people want to learn what the public is thinking, in spite of the difficulties in doing so.

This chapter will focus on the methods that claimsmakers, the media, and others involved in the social problems process—as well as sociologists—use to assess public reactions. It will consider several of these, beginning with the most familiar method—public opinion polls or surveys.

MEASURING PUBLIC OPINION

Public opinion polls have become a part of our political landscape that we take for granted. We are used to hearing news reports that polls show one candidate favored to win the upcoming election, that the president's approval rating has risen higher or fallen lower, that the public is more or less concerned about particular issues, and so on. Before considering how public opinion figures into the social problems process, we need to consider how the very methods of polling can affect a survey's results.

The Impact of Polling Methods

Efforts to measure public opinion through polling came of age during the early twentieth century. Usually this research involves conducting a **sample survey**. Because it would be prohibitively expensive to contact, say, all voters or all citizens (what statisticians call the **population**), the poll approaches a **sample** of people within that population and asks them questions. The responses to the poll can be tallied to reveal, for instance, the proportion of sampled voters favoring Candidate A in an election; in turn, the sample's results provide a basis for generalizing about the population by projecting the likely outcome of the election.

Many people are suspicious of sample surveys because the samples seem too small to promise accurate results. National surveys often use samples of 1,000 to 1,500 respondents. How, critics ask, can such a small number of people accurately represent the huge U.S. population (approaching 300 million)? However reasonable this question might seem, it emphasizes the wrong issue. A relatively small sample—say, 1,000 people—can produce fairly accurate results, as long as it is a **representative sample**—that is, as long as the sample is not selected in ways that make it more likely that some sorts of people will be chosen than others. (Statisticians calculate that, for a population of 300 million, a poll with a representative sample of 1,000 will produce results accurate within about 3 percent, 95 percent of the time. Thus, if a survey shows that 54 percent of voters favor Candidate A, there is a 95 percent probability that between 51 and 57 percent of the population favors A's candidacy. Moreover, larger samples aren't that much more accurate: a 10,000-person sample—for which collecting the data would cost about ten times as much—will produce only slightly more accurate results: accuracy within 1 percent, 95 percent of the time [de Vaus, 1986].)

However, statistical theory's assumptions about representative samples often have to give way to the realities of survey research. It is both difficult and expensive to design perfectly representative samples, and unrepresentative samples can lead to inaccurate results. Consider some sampling problems that affect today's pollsters: an increasing number of households screen calls using answering machines or Caller ID, and some of those people may choose not to answer the pollsters' calls; in addition, a growing proportion of the population has only cell phones (which pollsters are forbidden by law from calling) (Link & Oldendick, 1999). Can we assume that people who refuse to answer—or who can't be reached via land lines—have the same distribution of opinions as those who pick up the phone, or should we suspect that those who don't respond or can't be reached may have somewhat different opinions from those of the respondents? Refusal to take the pollsters' calls or having only a cell phone—like any other factor that may make the sample less representative—can damage the accuracy of a survey's results.

In addition, survey results are sensitive to many other influences. Pollsters know that the wording of a question can affect the results. Polling is expensive, and often the costs are covered by claimsmakers who hope to use the results to support their campaigns. As a result, many polls ask questions worded in ways that encourage people to produce the answers that the poll's sponsors favor (see Box 6.1). Of course, when the claimsmakers or sponsors release the poll results to the press, they tend to ignore the questions' wording, while emphasizing the favorable results.

Another important problem is that surveys usually try to distill people's thoughts about complex, multifaceted issues into one or two questions. The result is inevitably crude and oversimplified. For example, many discussions of abortion attitudes imply that people can be classified as either pro-life (opposed to abortion under any circumstances) or pro-choice (in favor of women having complete freedom to choose whether to have abortions) (Best, 2001a). But the largest proportion of Americans' attitudes fall somewhere between those extremes: these people favor permitting abortion for "good" reasons (such as pregnancies resulting from rape or incest,

Box 6.1 How a Question Is Phrased Makes a Difference

Even apparently minor differences in the wording of survey questions can make a big difference in how people respond. For example, one experimenter told different groups of respondents, "I'm going to name some . . . problems, and for each one I'd like you to tell me whether you think we're spending too much money on it, too little money, or the right amount." If the problem was stated as "assistance to the poor," 63 percent said they thought too little was being spent; but if the problem was described as "welfare," that number dropped to 23 percent.

The Gallup Poll recently asked one-half of its respondents, "Are you in favor of the death penalty for a person convicted of murder?" The results seemed to indicate strong support for the death penalty: 67 percent of those responding to that question favored the death penalty, and only 28 percent were opposed. However, the other half of the respondents were asked a different question: "If you could choose between the following two approaches, which do you think is the better penalty for murder—the death penalty, or life imprisonment with absolutely no possibility of parole?" The responses to that question were about evenly divided: 49 percent chose the death penalty, and 47 favored life imprisonment without parole.

In short, the words chosen for survey questions and the way the questions are framed can make big differences in the responses to polls. It is quite possible to word a survey's questions so that public opinion will seem to favor whatever position the people designing the poll want to promote.

Source: Bishop, 2005.

or cases in which continuing the pregnancy might endanger the woman's life), but they have reservations about allowing abortions for less compelling reasons. A simple question asking whether the respondent favors or opposes abortion cannot hope to accurately measure these complicated attitudes.

We should also remember that answering a survey is a social situation. That is, respondents who are interacting with a pollster usually want to make a good impression, to be a good respondent. This means that some respondents may try to say whatever they believe the pollster might think they ought to say. For example, if a pollster asks whether X should be considered a serious problem, the very fact that the question is being asked suggests that at least some people consider X a problem, and some respondents may feel that they ought to agree that, yes, X should be considered a serious problem. But responding in that way to a question does not mean that the respondent actually spends much time thinking about—let alone worrying about—X.

In short, a variety of methodological issues—who is polled, how the questions are phrased, and so on—can affect the results of survey research. Every survey's results have been shaped by the choices that the people conducting the surveys have made, and those people may have designed their poll to produce particular results. This doesn't mean that all survey results are meaningless, but they need to be viewed with some caution. After all, media coverage of poll results is fairly common, and this measure of public opinion often becomes a factor in the social problems process.

Constructing the Meaning of Public Opinion

Typically, discussions of the role of public opinion in the social problems process have two distinct themes. First, analysts argue that public opinion is a product of claimsmaking and media coverage of social problems, that effective claims can make the public aware of and concerned about some social problem. Second, policymakers are assumed to be responsive to public opinion; that is, it is assumed that high public concern about a social problem will in turn lead policymakers to try to do something about that problem.

Factors Affecting Public Opinion. Some evidence suggests that public opinion can be affected by media coverage. However, it is important not to exaggerate the media's influence; people are not passive recipients of media messages who automatically must accept whatever the media tells them. The media are probably more effective at agenda setting than at communicating particular messages. That is, they may be better able to influence what topics people are thinking about than what exactly people think about those topics.

For example, one study (Beckett, 1994) found that the proportion of people who expressed concern about crime in polls did not correlate well with official crime rates—concern for crime might rise even when the crime rate was falling; similarly, public concern about illegal drug use did not correlate closely with official measures of drug use. In other words, the shifts in public concern about crime and drug use revealed in surveys do not seem to have been responses to changes in the actual levels of those conditions. However, public opinion did correspond fairly closely with media coverage of crime and drug use, and particularly with officials' announcements about anticrime and antidrug policies (which were, of course, covered by the press). The media coverage tended to rise first, with public opinion following somewhat later; that is, opinions lagged behind media coverage. Thus, increased media coverage of crime and drug problems led to higher proportions of poll respondents expressing concerns about crime and drugs.

This example suggests that the public can be influenced to at least pay attention to heavily publicized social problems. And naturally the perception that this is true affects the behavior of claimsmakers, who work hard to promote their constructions of social problems by gaining media coverage, in hopes of arousing public concern. Of course, concern is not spread evenly throughout the population. On most issues, opinions vary with the respondents' characteristics: differences in race, social class (as measured by education or income), age, gender, and region often influence people's opinions. The media cannot affect everyone equally, but they can sometimes arouse fairly broad public concern about a particular troubling condition.

The Impact of Public Opinion. Survey results contribute to the social problems process in two major ways. First, polls offer feedback at earlier stages in the process. Claimsmakers use polls to determine whether their claims are effective or ineffective, hoping that their efforts—particularly if they have received a reasonable amount of media coverage—will cause public opinion to shift in the direction the claimsmakers favor. For instance, imagine that gun control advocates mount a campaign to promote a new law restricting guns. They may organize demonstrations, testify before legislators, appear on talk shows, and so on, in an effort to make the public aware of the issue. If polls taken following this effort suggest that a growing portion of the public is aware of and favors the proposed gun control law, the claimsmakers will view this result as evidence that their campaign has been effective. But, of course, if the poll results do not reveal a substantial shift in public opinion in support of their position, the advocates may look for ways to alter their claims, in hopes of making them more effective. Polls, then, provide feedback to claimsmakers.

The second major way polls affect the social problems process is that policymakers often follow poll results. In particular, elected officials may view evidence of widespread concern about a troubling condition as an indication that they need to take action, to develop a new policy to address the problem. This is not an automatic response. Poll results are one of the considerations that may influence officials, but they are by no means the only one. Still, it is possible to track poll results as "the voice of the people," and to justify policymaking as a response to what the public wants. Polls become one element in the construction of policymaking—a topic that will receive further attention in Chapter 7.

FOCUS GROUPS AND OTHER INTERVIEWS

Survey questionnaires are limited by the questions asked. Sampling does allow analysts to measure the relative distribution of opinions in large populations, but each respondent's views tend to be reduced to relatively simplistic responses to particular questions; moreover, as we have noted, those responses can be affected by precisely how the questions are worded, the order in which questions are asked, and so on.

Sometimes researchers try to circumvent these problems by organizing **focus groups**. Focus groups are sets of people to which a moderator poses questions that stimulate discussion on a particular topic. Group members may be chosen so that the group has a particular racial composition, level of education, and so on. Sometimes the members are acquaintances, who presumably will feel comfortable talking with one another about controversial social issues. Focus groups have several advantages over surveys. Individuals have more freedom to express their ideas about the topic, to qualify their remarks and explain what they really mean. In addition, the group is a social setting in which people can respond to one another's comments.

Focus groups often reveal that the public's views about social problems are more complex than the simple pro/con disagreements revealed by many surveys. Analysts tend to imagine that the public's views are internally consistent, and that they reflect the sorts of ideological consistency that claimsmakers often bring to the social problems process. Compared to these expectations, the views of members of the public often seem confused, ambivalent, or uncertain. These apparent inconsistencies can become evident in focus group discussions.

Studies of focus groups reveal that individuals tend to draw upon at least three sorts of information when discussing social problems (Gamson, 1992; Sasson, 1995b): First, they use popular wisdom—

"commonsense" understandings about how the world works as expressed in aphorisms, stereotypes, and so on. Second, people refer to personal experiences—things that have happened to them or others they know. Third, they may adopt various information and ideas derived from media messages about the larger world, including not just news reports, but also the various forms of infotainment and popular culture that depict the workings of the world beyond our personal experience. Popular wisdom, personal experiences, and media discourse are resources that can be used to construct public definitions of social problems, and focus group conversations reveal how people weave these elements together (see Box 6.2). In general, groups that are able to integrate all three sorts of information—to combine their personal beliefs and experiences with information about the larger world—are more confident that their constructions are correct and more willing to defend their views.

Given the importance of experiential knowledge in focus groups, it should be no surprise that people with different backgrounds construct issues differently. Such background characteristics as race, social class, gender, age, and education affect how people think about social problems. For example, among groups given the task of discussing crime, references to racism in the criminal justice system were relatively common in all-black groups, but relatively rare in all-white groups (Sasson, 1995b). In some cases, African American group members presented conspiracy theories, arguing that powerful whites supplied guns and drugs to poor black neighborhoods as a means of keeping them disadvantaged (Sasson, 1995a). Such findings illustrate a strength of focus groups; survey researchers might not even think to ask questions that could reveal whether their respondents hold such views.

The results of focus groups can, in turn, influence claimsmakers. Like political consultants trying to understand voters' views during election campaigns and firms seeking to market their products to consumers, activists sometimes use focus groups to better

Box 6.2 Constructing the Crime Problem in
Focus Groups

The sociologist Theodore Sasson (1995b) organized focus groups
to discuss crime problems. The following quotes taken from tran-
scripts of the conversations indicate the sorts of knowledge that the
participants used to construct crime and justice issues.

- *Popular wisdom* (using familiar ideas about how the world
  works):

  It comes down to these—teach the child right from wrong
  and what they should do and what they can't do. From
  when they're very young. . . . In other words, the Golden
  Rule: "Do Unto Others." You have to start when they're
  very young. (p. 143)

- *Experiential knowledge* (drawing on events that the speaker
  knows about):

  The young man whose trial I sat in on . . . this young man
  was sentenced to three years and [the judge] *suspended* the
  sentence. . . . Now he was caught with the gun and bul-
  lets. . . . It's the judges! It's the judiciary system! (pp.
  135–136)

- *Media discourse* (referring to information learned via news or
  entertainment media):

  They're too light with [prison inmates]. They . . . even give
  them weekends to have a little get-together with their
  wives and girlfriends. They have a private room and every
  doggone thing. . . . Seen it on TV. It was on one of the
  talk shows, you know? They had their little private time.
  (pp. 138–139)

understand what the public is thinking. Identification of the frames
that emerge within focus groups can be used to revise claims so
that they are tailored to influence the public more effectively. For
example, when opponents of abortion successfully campaigned

against public funding for abortions during the 1980s, abortion rights advocates organized focus groups that revealed that people who opposed such funding also objected to government intrusion in their lives (Saletan, 2003). Abortion rights advocates used this knowledge to craft a new argument—that the right to have an abortion was tied to a broader right to privacy; in this view, restrictions against abortion became another form of government interference in people's private lives. This new pro-choice campaign proved relatively effective.

As a source of information about public reactions, focus groups obviously have limitations. They are relatively costly in terms of time and money, and it is impossible to know how representative particular groups may be. Much depends on the moderator's skill in directing the conversation, making sure that the various participants have their say, and so on. Still, focus groups can be an important way of discovering what ordinary people think about social problems.

LEGENDS, JOKES, AND OTHER FOLKLORE

Public opinion polls and even focus groups involve somewhat artificial, formalized situations in which people know that their opinions are being solicited for analysis, and this knowledge may affect what the people who participate are willing to say. But talk about social problems also is the stuff of everyday conversations. It would be nice to know how members of the public construct social problems when they are not self-conscious about being observed. Studying folklore offers one way of examining such everyday constructions.

The term *folklore* refers to information that is disseminated informally, among the *folk*—that is, among ordinary people. Traditionally folklore was transmitted orally, rather than through writing: people told one another folktales, or taught each other folk songs, folk dancing, or folk crafts. You may have a mental image of a folklorist seeking out old folks living in remote corners of society, hoping to capture traditional folk wisdom that is in danger of disappearing as the last generation to have this knowledge fades. This common image equates folklore with an elderly person perched in a rocking chair on a rickety, unpainted front porch, talking about the old days.

This is a mistaken image because it is far too narrow. *All* people have folklore—young people, people living in cities, everyone. Contemporary folklore spreads in new ways—in photocopied bits of humor posted in offices (Dundes & Pagter, 2000) or through faxes ("faxlore") and e-mail messages—as well as by the traditional means of word of mouth. And some of the time, this folklore expresses ordinary people's reactions to social problems claims. Let's consider two common folklore genres: contemporary legends and joke cycles.

Contemporary Legends

Sometimes called *urban legends*, **contemporary legends** are stories that people tell one another (Ellis, 2001; Fine, 1992). In general, contemporary legends lack supernatural elements; they are far more likely to feature criminals than, say, ghosts. Typically the teller claims—and the listener believes—that the story is true, that the events in the story really happened. Often the teller offers evidence of the story's truth, such as identifying the place where it happened (perhaps a nearby shopping mall), or explaining the teller's connection to a person who witnessed or experienced the events: "This really happened to my roommate's cousin's neighbor." Folklorists refer to this sort of attribution as a *FOAF* (for Friend Of A Friend). Efforts to trace the story back to the FOAF inevitably fail; the roommate's cousin's neighbor may agree that the story is true but explain that "it actually happened to my mother-in-law's brother's friend."

As legends spread, the details tend to shift. A story about a horrible crime at a shopping mall may be revised so that it is relocated at the local mall; the shocking thing that someone said on a TV talk show may be said to have occurred on several different programs, and so on. Folklorists call the differing versions of the same tale **variants**. Variants often make the story more interesting to the audience; for example, the story is better if, instead of having occurred at an unknown mall somewhere, the events actually occurred at a nearby mall.

Contemporary legends must be good stories—good enough for people to remember them and want to repeat them—in order to spread. Thus, effective legends tend to evoke strong emotional reactions, such as fear or disgust (Heath, Bell, & Sternberg, 2001). People are more likely to recall—and repeat—stories that pack a punch. Often legends warn that the world is far more dangerous than we might imagine: that gang members lurk beneath our parked cars or in our backseats, that terrible crimes occur in the mall where we shop, that having a drink with an attractive stranger may lead to having a kidney stolen, and so on.

What is the difference between a rumor and a legend? The distinction is somewhat blurry. Basically, *rumors* tend to be specific, confined to a particular time and place. They spread in conditions of uncertainty; they report "improvised news" when more authoritative information is not available, and they tend to be short-lived, one-of-a-kind stories (Fine, Campion-Vincent, & Heath, 2005; Shibutani, 1966). Rumors tend to have local relevance: they refer to a case of corruption by a local official, a local business in trouble, and so on.

In contrast, *legends* can survive over decades—they may lie dormant for a time, only to be revived. A story may pass through a city, disappear for years, but then reappear. Though a legend may include local references ("It happened at our mall"), the same story may be told as having occurred in many places. Legends often invoke familiar **motifs**; that is, the same elements recur in many legends. For example, many contemporary legends involve maniacs with sharp objects—the escaped killer with a hook replacing his missing hand, the man (disguised as an old lady) with a hatchet, Halloween apples laced with razor blades, and such—just as a surprising number of contemporary legends involve terrible crimes at shopping malls (see Box 6.3). Legends can supply raw material for rumors; that is, familiar legendary elements, such as villainous conspiracies, can easily be reworked to become the stuff of a new rumor.

What do rumors and contemporary legends have to do with social problems? They often reflect contemporary claimsmaking: when the media report on the dangers of drugs, stories circulate about drug dealers giving small children LSD-laced lick-on tattoos; when gangs become a hot news story, tales of vicious gang initiation rites circulate; and so on. Many contemporary legends respond to current claims, but they also reconstruct those claims to fit the constraints of legend. Their need to be memorable means that legends tend to be melodramatic; these stories feature innocent, vulnerable victims preyed upon by villains whose evil nature explains their crimes. Why would drug dealers distribute LSD to preschoolers? That's just the sort of bad thing those bad people do. Just as news and entertainment media reshape primary claims to fit the demands of their respective genres, legends rework the topics of the media's secondary claims to make them disturbing, dramatic, memorable—the qualities of successful legends.

Rumors and legends often revolve around social conflicts. Many tales, for example, center around racial or ethnic conflict (Fine & Turner, 2001). Typically, these stories circulate within one ethnic group and describe the nefarious activities of people of another ethnicity. In the United States, for instance, there is a long history of both whites spreading tales about blacks, and blacks telling stories about whites. Sometimes these stories are mirror images of one another—the same story, only with the races reversed. A major race riot in Detroit in 1943 featuring open conflict between blacks and whites, for example, was inspired by rumors that a woman and her baby had been thrown off a local bridge (Langlois, 1983). But the

Box 6.3 Legendary Dangers at Shopping Malls

The traditional stories about Goldilocks, Little Red Riding Hood, and Hansel and Gretel share a motif: the forest as a place where strange things can happen. In contrast, consider how often contemporary legends are set in shopping malls: gang members lie beneath parked cars, waiting to grab ankles and attack shoppers leaving the mall; a woman leaving the mall discovers a hatchet-wielding man dressed as a little old lady waiting in her car; a baby is stolen in a mall department store (and recovered only after having been disguised); a young boy is castrated in a mall restroom by gang members of another race; or a young woman enters a mall restroom and is drugged by people intending to force her into prostitution.

Here is an excerpt from an e-mail mall legend circulating in 2005:

A woman had finished shopping, went out to her car, and discovered she had a flat. She got the jack out of the trunk. . . . A nice man in a business suit and carrying a briefcase walked up to her and said, "I noticed you're changing a flat tire. Would you like me to take care of it for you?"

The woman . . . accepted his help. They chatted amiably while the man changed the flat, and then put the flat tire and the jack in the trunk, shut it and dusted his hands off. The woman thanked him profusely, and as she was about to get in her car, the man told her that he left his car around on the other side of the mall, and asked if she would mind giving him a lift to his car. She was a little surprised and she asked him why his car was on the other side.

He explained that he . . . got turned around in the mall and left through the wrong exit, and now he was running late. The woman hated to tell him "no" because he had just rescued her from having to change her flat tire . . . but she was uneasy. Then she remembered seeing the man put his briefcase in her trunk before shutting it. . . .

She told him that she'd be happy to drive him around to his car, but she just remembered one last thing she needed to buy. She said she would only be a few minutes; he could sit down in her car and wait. . . . She hurried to the mall and told a security guard what had happened. [They] came out to her car . . . but the man had left. They opened the trunk, took out the locked briefcase and took it down to the police station. The police opened it . . . [and] found rope, duct tape, and knives. When the police checked her flat tire, there was nothing wrong with it; the air had simply been let out.

Malls may be the locale where we most often encounter lots of strangers, and these stories warn us not to trust people we don't know. Malls often assure customers that the mall is a safe place; for instance, many malls invite children to go trick-or-treating safely there (so as to avoid the legendary maniacs who poison Halloween treats). But the crime-at-the-mall motif serves as a warning that malls are never completely safe (Donovan, 2004).

story whites told one another featured a white woman and baby thrown off the bridge by blacks, while blacks shared a story of a black woman and baby thrown off the bridge by whites. In either case, the incident was apparently imaginary; there was no evidence that anyone had been thrown off a bridge.

Stories based on ethnic tensions do not necessarily have such precise counterparts. Several stories circulating among African Americans, for instance, warn that particular companies have connections to racist groups (for example, that a fried-chicken franchise is owned by the Ku Klux Klan); or report that a popular clothing designer appeared on a TV talk show and stated that he (or she—the story is told about different designers) did not want black people wearing the designer's clothes, so he (or she) deliberately designed clothing lines that would not fit blacks (Fine & Turner, 2001). Such stories share an underlying theme that African Americans have a subordinate place in a largely white-controlled economy. Not surprisingly, whites do not have many such tales about black-controlled firms (although they have circulated warnings that some businesses are controlled by other conspiratorial elements, such as satanists).

Other contemporary legends explore gender conflict. For example, women pass along warnings about methods that gang members, rapists, and other criminals use to prey on women, just as men share stories about seductive women who intend to harm males. Any social fault line—between ethnic groups, the sexes, bosses and employees, students and professors, and so on—can inspire rumors or legends.

Several other contemporary legends reveal concerns about immigration. These include: "The Mexican Pet" (tourists bring home a little stray dog they discovered while vacationing in Mexico—only to learn that it is a "Mexican sewer rat"); a Mexican-raised yucca plant purchased at a garden store explodes and showers baby poisonous spiders around the new owners' home; clothing, rugs, or other items imported from Asia contain poisonous snakes or spiders; or a popular Mexican beer contains urine (Fine, 1992). Note that all of these tales specify that the danger has been imported from either Mexico or Asia—two sources of recent immigrants who seem culturally and ethnically different from America's traditional white majority. Although linking these legends to immigration may strike some as forced, note that some of the same stories also circulate in some European countries, but there the dangers, such as the spider-infested plant, come from North Africa—an important source of recent immigrants in those countries.

Other social changes also inspire contemporary legends. For instance, numerous legends warn about the risks of AIDS, including the widespread story of a person who awakens after a sexual encounter to discover the message "Welcome to the World of AIDS" written on the bathroom mirror, and warnings that AIDS-infected IV-drug users leave used needles in the coin return slots of pay phones (Goldstein, 2004). Similarly, stories of organ thefts—that is, of stolen eyes, kidneys, and other human organs—have global popularity (Campion-Vincent, 2005). In less developed countries, these stories warn about westerners who only pretend to adopt children but actually harvest their organs to be used for transplants in the United States; Americans and Europeans tell one another about people awakening after sexual encounters only to discover that a kidney has been removed. The morals of these stories—warnings about imperialistic exploitation or the risks of casual sex—reflect issues that are themselves the subject of claimsmaking.

As these examples illustrate, the larger significance of rumors and contemporary legends is that they are, in a sense, ripped from the headlines. They translate topics of claimsmakers' concern—racial and ethnic tensions, the impact of immigration, the spread of AIDS, and so on—into melodramatic, disturbing stories, however unlikely, that people tell one another, assuring their listeners that the tales are really true, that the events happened nearby, to someone who knows someone they know. To be sure, many of those who pass along these stories do not think of themselves as participating in the social problems process. Rather, they consider these merely memorable stories, troubling and worth repeating. They probably don't view themselves as claimsmakers, or these stories about social problems as claims.

Note, however, that many rumors and contemporary legends do share a worldview. They generally warn that the world is a dangerous place, bedeviled by dangerous villains, and that one can't be too careful. Ordinary activities, such as driving in a car, visiting the shopping mall, and striking up a conversation with a stranger turn out to be portals into a world of violence and victimization. Thus, there is a sort of conservatism underlying most contemporary legends, a worldview characterized by the suspicion that change is dangerous and needs to be approached with great caution.

Joke Cycles

A second form of contemporary folklore that builds on social problems claimsmaking is the **joke cycle**. Joke cycles are sets of jokes that share a form ("knock knock" jokes) or a topic (jokes about blondes); a cycle often becomes quite popular for a time, before losing favor. Some folklorists seek to explain the emergence of particular joke cycles as reactions to awareness of social problems; Dundes (1987) argued that the popularity of elephant jokes in the 1960s reflected public attitudes toward the civil rights movement, and the dead-baby joke cycle of the 1970s was a reaction to concern about abortion and contraception.

At first glance, these interpretations may seem peculiar, but Dundes noted that elephant jokes (for instance, "Why do elephants paint their toenails red? To hide in cherry trees") often ridicule the elephant's efforts to fit into a particular setting, and they often portray elephants as sexually dangerous. The timing of this joke cycle—it emerged in the 1960s, when the civil rights movement was at its height—suggests that this may have been an indirect means of expressing resistance to the cause of integration.

Similarly, the dead-baby joke cycle (for example, "What's red and sits in a corner? A baby chewing razor blades") presented various disturbing images and emerged during the early 1970s, shortly after the contraceptive pill became widespread and around the time that abortion was being legalized. It is not impossibly far-fetched to view joking about dead babies as linked to ambivalence about these changes. Although not everyone finds them convincing, such interpretations suggest that even the silliest-seeming joke cycles may be part of the social problems process.

Many joke cycles pose much less difficult interpretive problems. There is a long tradition of joke cycles that play on and reinforce racial, religious, or ethnic stereotypes (Dundes, 1987). Similarly, other joke cycles are grounded in stereotypes regarding gender or sexual orientation. Various joke cycles depict different target groups as being lazy, stupid, dirty, sexually promiscuous, or having other undesirable qualities. Repeating such jokes can be seen as a sort of claim about different sorts of people, although of course it is always possible for those telling the jokes to deny this, to insist that they're just joking. The links between joking and claimsmaking are especially apparent with joke cycles inspired by dramatic current events—such as the explosion of the space shuttle *Challenger* in 1986; the deaths at the Branch Davidian compound in Waco, Texas, in 1993; or the terrorist attacks on the World Trade Center on September 11, 2001 (Oring, 1987; Lowney & Best, 1996; Ellis, 2003). One important quality of such **topical joke cycles** is that we know the date they started spreading. Obviously there were no *Challenger* jokes before January 28, 1986 (the day the explosion occurred).

Studies of topical joke cycles reveal that such jokes spread widely and very rapidly through informal channels. Media commentators, for instance, noted the existence of jokes about the *Challenger* within a few days after the catastrophe, although the jokes themselves were not circulated by the media (which viewed the jokes as in very bad taste and therefore unrepeatable). In these cases, both the number of jokes told and the number of people who reported having heard them increased rapidly in the days and weeks following the event that inspired the jokes (Ellis, 1991; Lowney & Best, 1996). Of course, after a few weeks people stopped telling these jokes, presumably because those who might have enjoyed them had, by that time, already heard them, but also because the subject no longer seemed topical.

Topical jokes tend to spread where they have relevance. Local scandals may become the subject of local joke cycles, but they are unlikely to spread beyond that locality. For example, the on-camera suicide of Pennsylvania's state treasurer in 1987 inspired a joke cycle in that state, but those jokes did not spread widely beyond the area where he was a familiar figure (Bronner, 1988). In much the same way, the 1986 Chernobyl nuclear reactor disaster—which released radiation—did not become the subject of extensive joking in the United States (which seemed geographically far removed from the danger), but it did become the subject of a substantial joke cycle in Europe (where people worried about their exposure to radioactive contamination) (Kurti, 1988).

Why do people tell jokes about disasters? It is easy to argue that there is nothing funny about these events, and that such jokes are inappropriate. The most popular explanations are psychological—either that such jokes are symptoms of a "sick" society, or that telling jokes is cathartic and eases people's psychological strain. Sociologists might argue, however, that topical jokes, like contemporary legends that address subjects of current claimsmaking, offer an indirect way of expressing public attitudes toward troubling social conditions. Jokes often reveal skepticism: the vast majority of jokes about the Branch Davidians characterized them as deviant, and jokes about other disasters often seem to question the authorities' wisdom (see Box 6.4).

Here it is worth noting one other form of folk humor: the photocopies of jokes, cartoons, mock memos, and such that are posted in offices and other workplaces (Dundes & Pagter, 2000). This "office folklore" has become much easier to reproduce and disseminate, thanks to improved technologies, such as photocopiers, fax machines, e-mail, and computer software, which allow people to create, modify, store, and transmit photos and other graphics very easily (Ellis, 2003). Often these bits of folklore suggest considerable skepticism about the workings of bureaucracies and the abilities of their leaders. Like legends and joke cycles, such office humor often addresses ethnicity, class, gender, and other familiar bases for social conflict. The fact that they are widespread suggests that their subversive reconstructions of different social problems are relatively popular, although—as is the case with all other types of folklore—it is always possible to shrug off objections by insisting that these postings aren't serious commentary, that they are just in fun. Still, such folklore remains one way in which ordinary people can express their thoughts and respond to more visible claimsmakers.

Box 6.4 JOKING ABOUT HURRICANE KATRINA

Heavily publicized events—especially scandals and disasters—often inspire joke cycles. For example, when Hurricane Katrina devastated New Orleans in 2005, an event that left thousands of mostly poor, mostly African American residents stranded in the flooded city for days before the federal government began to respond effectively, dozens of jokes began to circulate (especially via Internet joke sites):

> The mayor of New Orleans has denied canceling Mardi Gras this year; in fact, he said today, "I expect a record number of floats on Main Street this year!"

> KFC announced an addition to its menu in honor of Katrina's victims: New Orleans–style chicken, served in a Bucket of Water.

> What is George W. Bush's position on *Roe v. Wade*? He doesn't care how the blacks get out of New Orleans.

Katrina jokes varied; some were more pointed than others. Many were frankly racist; others, such as the third example here, seemed critical of the government's ineffective disaster planning and response.

Public opinion is not uniform; opinions—including opinions about what is funny and what are appropriate subjects for joking—vary. But many jokes are topical, and they offer one way that ordinary people can participate in the social problems process. Although we cannot assume that everyone who tells a joke endorses a particular point of view, jokes at least let people express views that they might be reluctant to voice in a more serious manner.

THE PUBLIC'S ROLE IN THE SOCIAL PROBLEMS PROCESS

Although opinion polls, focus groups, and contemporary folklore all offer ways of understanding something about how the general public responds to constructions of social problems made by claimsmakers and the media, none of these methods can hope to tell the whole story. After all, the general public is very large and very diverse. It includes people who virtually ignore social problems claims, but also people who follow claimsmaking with enthusiasm. It includes people from a wide range of social groupings—different occupations, different ethnicities, different social classes, different genders and sexual orientations, different political ideologies, and on and on. These various groups have, if not different values, at least different interpretations of which values are most important and how they ought to be realized. There are, then, all sorts of differences that can affect how people in the general public will respond to particular social problems claims.

Moreover, even people who seem to respond in the same way—who, for example, give the same response to a survey question—may, in fact, be quite different. Some people may be energized by particular claims—they may become committed, inspired to join the cause, to devote their time, money, and energy to bringing about change. Others may become interested enough to follow the issue, to read books and articles on the topic, watch TV coverage, and become well informed, although they may never actually enlist in the cause. Still others may be only dimly aware of the claims, knowing enough to tell a pollster that they think the problem is serious, but not moved to do anything more. In other words, what people mean when they respond to a survey question indicating their concern is not at all clear.

Similarly, people who hear and repeat contemporary legends or jokes may understand this folklore in very different ways. Some may indeed view themselves as participating in the social problems process, as expressing particular beliefs or attitudes; for example, probably many people who tell ethnic jokes understand that, in so doing, they are promoting particular stereotypes. But others may insist that this is just innocent fun, that it has no larger meaning.

Earlier chapters noted that claimsmakers often hope to affect public opinion, to make people aware of and concerned about a troubling condition, and that the media justify their own activities by referring to the importance of an informed public. Similarly, policymakers (discussed in Chapter 7) often argue that they are responsive to the "will of the people." Other actors in the social problems process, then, argue that public reactions play an important role. Claimsmakers, the media, and policymakers want to reach—and influence—the public, but those actors also pay attention to the public's reactions and try to adjust their own behavior in response (see Figure 6.1).

This book has emphasized the competitive nature of the social problems process: there are countless claims being promoted, and nearly as many media reports about troubling conditions. With all these bids for the public's attention, some claims inevitably must fail to attract the public's notice (see Box 6.5). This is why rhetoric— the way claims and media coverage are packaged—becomes important; the public is likely to ignore many claims and focus only on those that it finds particularly compelling.

This chapter has argued that all the ways in which social scientists measure public reactions, including public opinion surveys,

Figure 6.1 THE PUBLIC'S ROLE IN THE SOCIAL PROBLEMS PROCESS

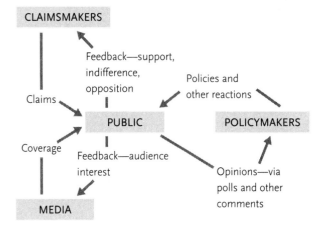

Box 6.5 The Compassion Fatigue Cycle

The term *compassion fatigue* (Moeller, 1999) refers to the effect of the many calls for public concern made by claimsmakers and the media. The news seems filled with reports of disasters and crises; it becomes difficult for the public to stay abreast of ongoing events, let alone care about all of them.

The need to make claims competitive, so that they will command the public's attention, encourages claimsmakers to devise compelling rhetoric—disturbing typifying examples, shocking statistics, and so on. Well-packaged claims fit the media's criteria for newsworthy stories; claims that can be covered in ways that incorporate striking visual images—dramatic photographs or heartrending video—will receive more media attention than other claims that do a poorer job of meeting the media's requirements. And, of course, the public is most likely to learn about—and care about—troubling, well-covered topics.

The process escalates. Members of the public confront one disturbing claim after another. And observing what has worked for others—which topics and coverage have attracted public concern—leads claimsmakers and the media to copy those successes, to present new claims and new coverage that are designed to be even more compelling, more competitive in the social problems marketplace, which of course seems to guarantee further compassion fatigue. Does a sense of overwhelming crisis encourage—or discourage—public involvement in the social problems process?

focus groups, and folklore, offer indirect, imprecise ways of interpreting what the public is thinking. We might wonder, then, whether we can hope to fully understand this stage in the social problems process.

However, there is other evidence of public reactions. Over time, we can also witness changes in people's behavior that reveal responses to claimsmaking. For instance, motorists have become more likely to use seat belts; some of this change is doubtless due to laws that subject people who fail to buckle up to fines, but it is also true that a growing proportion of the population now buckles up automatically, as a matter of habit. Over time, the proportion of the adult population that smokes has fallen—again, partly because of higher taxes and restrictions on where smoking is permitted, but also partly because a growing proportion of people see smoking as risky behavior. Although our ways of measuring these changes are imperfect, the incidence of child abuse and other family violence has probably fallen, people's willingness to express racist sentiments in surveys has dropped, and so on.

We can, in short, find evidence of actual changes in people's behavior motivated, at least in part, by the public's redefining what is wise, prudent, or appropriate. Although we cannot measure the public's reactions with precision, we can still recognize that the public is responsive to—and an active part of—the larger social problems process.

Making Connections

- *Claimsmakers study public reactions and reframe their claims on the basis of the feedback they receive from the public. See Chapters 2, 3, and 4 for more about the claimsmaking process.*

- *Public opinion polls that measure the reaction to claims about a social problem also help determine which issues garner attention from policymakers. In the next chapter, you will learn more about the policymaking process.*

- *Public reactions to social problems change over time. Chapter 10 discusses how reactions to social problems have evolved throughout history.*

CASE STUDY
The Public Responds to Terrorism after 9/11

The September 11, 2001, terrorist attacks on the World Trade Center and the Pentagon attracted intense media coverage. For several days, the major television networks broadcast commercial-free, around-the-clock news coverage. Political leaders declared "war on terrorism" and all manner of officials and experts pontificated on the terrorist threat. The days after 9/11 were marked by widespread collective displays of flags—a spontaneous demonstration of patriotic sentiment. But how did the public react to claims about terrorism?

Public opinion polls revealed a modest, relatively short-lived reaction. Although this might seem surprising—only a small reaction when we might imagine there would have been a major shift—we must remember that terrorism was neither new nor unfamiliar. There had been well-publicized terrorist attacks on Americans overseas, as well as two extremely prominent recent episodes within the United States—the 1993 truck bombing of the World Trade Center, and the 1995 bombing of a federal building in Oklahoma City. Terrorists had been stock villains in action movies throughout the 1990s. Thus the public already had a sense that terrorism was a real threat.

This may explain why opinion polls did not reveal more dramatic shifts. Consider, for example, the responses to questions about the likelihood of a major terrorist attack within the next few months (Huddy, Khatib, & Capelos, 2002, pp. 432–434). From mid-September through October 2001, polls found 36 to 53 percent of respondents judging that such an attack was "very likely." In contrast, several polls taken between 1986 and 1991 showed only 23 to 28 percent "very likely" responses (although one poll from 1995 [after the first World Trade Center attack and the Oklahoma City bombing] showed 48 percent). However, polls taken between December

2001 and February 2002 recorded 18 to 23 percent "very likely" responses, showing that fears had fallen back to pre-9/11 levels. Similarly, questions that sought to measure the public's confidence in the government's ability to prevent further attacks showed a brief rise in confidence immediately after 9/11, but confidence soon receded to pre-9/11 levels. All in all, 9/11's effects on responses to public opinion poll questions about terrorism tended to be modest.

However, terrorism did inspire a good deal of contemporary folklore. Rumors flourished, such as the claim that someone at the top of the World Trade Center had managed to survive by "surfing" down the collapsing tower atop a slab of debris. In particular, two widespread stories deserve special attention. First, in several U.S. cities with substantial Arab American communities, reports circulated that Arabs had been seen celebrating the news of 9/11. (This story may have conflated a widely circulated news photo said to show Palestinians celebrating news of 9/11 with immigrants' reactions in the United States; there was no evidence that any such celebrations occurred in this country.) Often these tales specified that the celebration had occurred at a particular restaurant (Fine & Khawaja, 2005; Langlois, 2005). In some cases, customers boycotted these establishments, and the owners found themselves displaying their 9/11 security camera tapes as proof that the alleged celebrations had not occurred. These tales, of course, reconstructed the 9/11 terrorist attacks in terms of ethnic tensions, by challenging the loyalty of Arab immigrants and even of Arab Americans whose families had been in the United States for generations.

If the story of Arabs celebrating 9/11 portrayed ethnic tensions as insurmountable, the second legend suggested that—at least on occasion—humans can make contact across ethnic and cultural divides. Folklorists call this the "grateful terrorist" story; it describes someone who performs a minor act of courtesy for a stranger who comes from the Middle East (Fine & Khawaja, 2005). In response, the benefactor is taken aside and given a warning—don't eat in this restaurant, stay away from that place, or the like—the implication being that this would soon be a site of a terrorist attack. Another version of this tale, widely circulated during October 2001, told of a woman who had been dating an Arab (or Afghani) man who had suddenly disappeared but left behind a note warning her not to fly on September 11 or visit a shopping mall on October 31. This story, of course, wove together three legendary motifs: the grateful terrorist, sinister doings at malls, and fears of Halloween threats.

Finally, even the worst tragedies can inspire joke cycles, and the 9/11 attacks were no exception. In the United States, jokes emphasized revenge against the terrorists' sponsors. For example, one graphic joke circulating on the Internet adapted a Weather Channel page for Kabul:

> Afghanistan weather forecast. [Tomorrow's predicted high—3000 degrees: image of a mushroom cloud.] (Ellis, 2003, p. 54)

In contrast, the most popular British joke involved wordplay:

> Osama bin Laden announced today that he will give up terrorism to become a TV chef. For his first programme he'll be showing us how to make a Big Apple Crumble. [Apple crumble is a British dessert.] (Ellis, 2003, p. 60)

Other European jokes imagined ineffective local terrorists: in England, the Irish Republican Army was reported to have hijacked a blimp and bounced it off Big Ben, while Hungarians exchanged e-mail attachments of a photo showing a small crop-dusting plane apparently heading toward a church steeple (Csaszi, 2003). These examples suggest that Europeans found it much easier to make fun of a tragedy that had occurred an ocean away.

Obviously the public did not have just one, unified reaction to claims about terrorism. However, by examining responses to public opinion polls, as well as rumors, contemporary legends, and jokes, we can at least get a sense of the range of public reactions to the terrorist menace.

QUESTIONS

1. What was the public reaction to the terrorist attacks on September 11, 2001?

2. Explain the shifts in public opinion about the likelihood of terrorist attacks.

3. How did the 9/11 attack inspire a new wave of urban legends?

7

Policymaking

Most claimsmakers hope to do more than simply draw attention to a troubling condition; they also want to change things, to improve social arrangements so that the problem can be, if not eliminated, at least made better. Toward this end, claimsmakers seek to change social policies, to alter how the society deals with the troubling condition; and this means that their claims must reach those who have the power to make policy changes—the **policymakers**.

The most obvious way to change policy is through the law. Laws define what is and is not legitimate within a particular jurisdiction; they specify what is required, what is permissible, and what is forbidden. So the study of policymaking turns first to the study of legislative bodies—Congress, state legislatures, city councils, and so on—that not only pass laws but also allocate funds and issue guidelines to the various official agencies that administer those laws.

We are used to seeing media coverage about legislative debates over proposed new laws; such debates can be a high-visibility arena for policymaking. Votes on controversial legislation—to fund or cancel a program, to criminalize or decriminalize a behavior, and so on—are dramatic, visible policymaking moments. But much policymaking is less visible. Many new laws attract little attention, and once passed by legislators, those laws must be implemented, which creates further opportunities for behind-the-scenes policymaking. All manner of government agencies enforce and implement laws. Though our thoughts may turn first to law enforcement agencies (such as the FBI or local police forces), we must recognize that all sorts of administrative agencies oversee how particular laws are applied (for example, the Environmental Protection Agency is charged with administering many federal environmental policies). Even local governments have specialized officials responsible for enforcing health ordinances and other local laws. And because laws usually cannot spell out how they should be applied in every possible circumstance, much of the work of interpreting how the law should be applied falls to such agencies, which therefore find themselves making policy.

In addition, in the United States, court rulings have the power to shape the law. Appellate courts, for example, can rule that legislators have exceeded their authority by passing laws that are unconstitutional, or they can rule that the way a particular law is being applied or enforced is not legal. In dramatic cases (such as the *Roe v. Wade* ruling, which dictated that states could not restrict a woman's access to abortion during the first trimester of pregnancy), Supreme Court rulings can shift fundamental perceptions of what is considered legal. Thus, sometimes government agencies and courts also act as policymakers.

However, we should not equate policy with law. A wide range of organized nongovernmental bodies—think of corporations, churches, professions, charities, and so on—set their own rules or policies. When a homeless shelter announces rules regarding who is qualified to seek admission or how people must behave if they are to be allowed to remain in the shelter, this, too, is a form of policymaking. Although this chapter will tend to concentrate on how legislatures and other government bodies establish laws, we should not forget that policymaking occurs in many different settings.

POLICY DOMAINS

One way sociologists think about how legislators and other policymakers organize policymaking revolves around the concept of **policy domains** (Burstein, 1991). A policy domain is that part of the political system that focuses on a particular social issue, such as family problems, criminal justice, or health policy. A given domain includes many people who are especially concerned with the issue addressed by that domain, including legislators, other officials, and people outside the government. For example, Congress has committees that deal with health issues; various federal agencies, such as the Centers for Disease Control and the National Institutes of Health, address those issues; and outside the government, there are interest groups, think tanks, medical professionals, and other experts especially concerned with health policy. In general, health policy is likely to be formulated by those who belong to that policy domain; after all, these are the people most knowledgeable about—and most willing to devote time and energy to—health policy issues. Although Congress as a whole must vote on health-related legislation, the legislation itself is shaped within the health policy domain.

The concept of a policy domain is akin to but not the same as the concept of an arena (see Chapter 5). An *arena* is a setting where claims can be presented (a congressional committee's hearings might be an example). A *policy domain* is a network of people who share an interest in a particular policy issue; those people may oversee several arenas in which claims about that issue can be presented (such as different committees' hearings, specialized newsletters, and so on).

We can begin thinking about policy domains by considering the social circumstances of legislators. Although analysts usually focus on the federal Congress, we can assume that similar considerations affect state and local legislative bodies. Imagine a social problems claim that has been attracting attention: the media have been covering the story, public opinion polls may indicate that people are expressing concern about this troubling condition, and claims-makers and constituents may contact legislators and ask them to take action. These circumstances might lead to a new law—to policymaking—but then again, they might not.

A new policy is by no means an automatic outcome. After all, there are lots of people who want legislators to do lots of different things, and legislators cannot possibly respond to all of these demands, because there are simply too many calls for action, it would cost too much to implement them all, and many of them call for legislators to take contradictory actions. Although some claims about valence issues enjoy nearly unanimous agreement (see Chapter 2), people disagree about many position issues, so there may be both people who favor and people who oppose passing a particular law. How can legislators sort out all of these demands?

Recall that Chapter 5 spoke of the media's role in agenda set-ting. It helps to think of legislators as having an agenda—a prior-itized list of things they want to address. The list of demands they face is impossibly long; legislators don't have enough time or enough money to do everything that they are asked to do, so they need to establish priorities, to decide which things really need to be addressed now.

Once again, we see the competitive nature of claimsmaking. Just as claimsmakers must compete for media coverage and public attention, they must also compete for places on legislators' agen-das. During this process, claimsmakers may wait years until they finally get legislators to address their concerns. Because laws touch on virtually all aspects of social life, there is terrific competition for legislators' attention among people calling for new laws or changes in existing laws. One result is the establishment of lob-byists, professionals responsible for knowing the ins and outs of the legislative process, who maintain networks of contacts with legislators and their staff members, and who understand how to effectively package claims so as to attract legislators' interest and support. Most industries, professions, and other well-established interest groups maintain permanent lobbying operations to try to influence lawmaking.

Recall the discussion of ownership in Chapter 3—how some claimsmakers become the established authorities on an issue, and how other people turn to those claimsmakers when questions arise regarding their issues. One way to maintain ownership of an issue is to establish a lobbying operation, so that someone is always ready to convey your views to those assembling legislation.

Attempting to influence policymaking can require patience. The political scientist John W. Kingdon (1984) offers one model for understanding how particular policies arrive at the top of the legislative agenda. He describes three streams: (1) the problem recognition stream, (2) the policy proposal stream, and (3) the political stream. Each stream is constantly flowing, but they often have minimal contact with one another. On occasion, however, the three streams seem to converge, and when they do, legislators are more likely to act.

The Problem Recognition Stream

What Kingdon calls the **problem recognition stream** is already familiar; it has been the focus of the preceding chapters. In the process of problem recognition, claimsmakers identify troubling conditions, name those conditions, devise compelling rhetoric to persuade others to become concerned about those conditions, and campaign to bring those conditions to the notice of the press, the public, and policymakers. These claimsmakers' efforts can receive a boost from current events—an attention-grabbing news story about a terrible crime or a natural disaster can catapult an issue into prominence. But most claimsmakers who hope to influence policy need to work to keep their constructions visible, interesting, fresh, and compelling so that they can maintain continual pressure for policymakers to act; thus the claimsmakers' particular views are readily accessible, should the policymakers' attention begin to turn toward their issues.

The Policy Proposal Stream

Kingdon's second stream—the **policy proposal stream**—consists of more specialized constructions, those that offer specific proposals for new legislation. Such proposals may be fairly general, in that they sketch broad ideological approaches toward a new policy; for example, at any given time, there are probably advocates calling for the government to create new programs to help the poor, as well as other advocates arguing that existing antipoverty programs are misguided and ought to be cut back. Other policy proposals may be quite elaborate and specific; advocates may design detailed plans for action or even draft suggested legislation for consideration.

All sorts of people work at devising policy proposals: in addition to the various experts, think tanks, and officials discussed in Chapter 4 who may develop proposals as part of their claimsmaking, there are lobbyists, as well as legislators and their staff members. Whereas outsider claimsmakers tend to concentrate their activities in the problem recognition stream, the policy proposal stream features far more insiders, those members of the polity who populate particular policy domains. Just as claims compete for public recognition, policy proposals compete for policymakers' attention. Again, patience is required: policy advocates must continually test the waters, constantly revise and repackage their proposals, and wait for a moment when those proposals can get a hearing (see Box 7.1).

The Political Stream

Finally, what Kingdon calls the **political stream** refers to what we might think of as the current political situation. Who has been elected, what ideologies do they hold, and what interests do they

Box 7.1 Waiting for the Next Policy Wave

The political scientist John W. Kingdon (1984) quotes an analyst for a Washington interest group:

> When you lobby for something, what you have to do is put together your coalition, you have to gear up, you have to get your political forces in line, and then you sit there and wait for the fortuitous event. For example, people who were trying to do something about regulation of railroads tried to ride the environment for a while, but that wave didn't wash them in to shore. So they grabbed their surfboards and they tried to ride something else, but that didn't do the job. The Penn Central collapse was the big wave that brought them in. As I see it, people who are trying to advocate change are like surfers waiting for the big wave. You get out there, you have to be ready to go, you have to be ready to paddle. If you're not ready to paddle when the big wave comes along, you're not going to ride it in. (p. 173)

The competition for space on policymakers' agendas is intense, and not all claims can succeed. This quote suggests that advocates need to be persistent, prepared, and flexible enough to take advantage of shifts in the policymaking environment. There may be various ways to frame an issue in order to advance the desired policies.

tend to represent? A new president or a new congress may favor particular approaches to government (such as being relatively sympathetic or unsympathetic toward government regulation). Any legislature's activities reflect its composition: Does one party have a dominant majority? Do the legislature and the chief executive come from the same party? What other issues are competing for the politicians' attention? Is the economy fairly robust, or are budgets tight? Such factors shape the degree to which legislators believe they have a free hand. Politicians also track public opinion, and they may respond to perceived shifts in what the public favors. The political situation is constantly evolving, affecting what legislation might receive consideration—let alone pass—at any given time.

The Policy Stream Model: Convergence of the Three Streams

Kingdon's policy stream model (Figure 7.1) illustrates how these three streams come together and assumes that, at any given moment, people are actively promoting the recognition of different problems, the adoption of different policies, and assorted political opportunities. All of these people are competing for attention and influence over the policymaking process. This intense competition ensures that most of these efforts will fail; it is just too hard to gain a place near the top of the agenda. However, sometimes the streams converge, with each reinforcing the other's influence. Sometimes a particular construction of a troubling condition complements a particular policy proposal that, in turn, coincides with the current political alignments. In those cases, proposals for new policies stand a much better chance of being enacted.

The competitive world of policymaking, with its cacophony of diverse claims demanding attention, helps explain why policy domains are so important. Policymakers cannot hope to master all of the issues, to stay on top of every topic. Instead, people specialize; they become familiar with one or two domains. Legislatures, for example, assign their members to committees (and often those committees are divided into more specialized subcommittees) charged with overseeing particular sorts of legislative proposals, and many committees can be seen as belonging to particular policy domains. These committees are much smaller than the larger legislative body, and they offer individual legislators opportunities to become relatively familiar with the issues within a specific policy domain. Policy domains bring knowledgeable people together: lob-

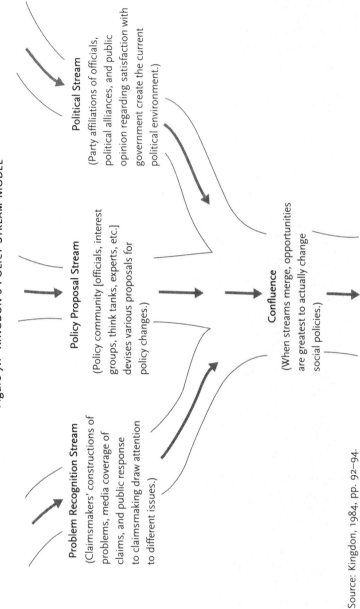

Figure 7.1 KINGDON'S POLICY STREAM MODEL

Problem Recognition Stream

(Claimsmakers' constructions of problems, media coverage of claims, and public response to claimsmaking draw attention to different issues.)

Policy Proposal Stream

(Policy community [officials, interest groups, think tanks, experts, etc.] devises various proposals for policy changes.)

Political Stream

(Party affiliations of officials, political alliances, and public opinion regarding satisfaction with government create the current political environment.)

Confluence

(When streams merge, opportunities are greatest to actually change social policies.)

Source: Kingdon, 1984, pp. 92–94.

byists, officials from related agencies, and legislative staff members often specialize in particular policy domains, and they focus their attention on the committees most concerned with that domain. This greater familiarity with a domain's issues translates into influence; committees' recommendations often influence the larger legislative body. After all, these committee members are the people most knowledgeable about the issue.

In advancing policies, legislators can draw upon a repertoire of tactics. Once they decide to emphasize particular issues (rather than any of the multitude of other possible issues they might promote) and choose to endorse specific policy proposals (among the broad array of available choices), legislators can adopt a public posture to promote their chosen policies: they can make speeches, publish their thoughts, appear on television programs, and generally seek to draw attention to their proposals. Others work backstage. Whether their efforts are public or relatively private, legislators must try to muster allies among their colleagues; they must find others who share their concerns and are willing to join the cause.

Legislators' committee positions serve as an important resource; legislators can use their committee positions to hold hearings to draw attention to the issue they're promoting. They can invite people to testify at these hearings, to present their views. Note that the power to control these invitations, to decide who will speak at these hearings, allows legislators to ensure that the hearings will highlight particular positions or proposals. Again, hearings vary in the degree to which they seek publicity. Sometimes witnesses are chosen for their ability to draw media coverage; hearings featuring show-business celebrities, sympathetic victims who can recount their sufferings, or figures who have been implicated in scandalous events are more likely to become subjects of media reporting. Well-orchestrated hearings—that is, those that attract heavy media coverage and involve dramatic presentations by witnesses—can help increase an issue's visibility and can give a cause the momentum needed to get legislation passed.

Sometimes this process results in what seems to be a significant, sudden policy change: the passage of a pathbreaking law. However, when we step back from the legislature's final vote and examine the streams leading up to the shift, we may recognize that the legislators' change of heart was preceded by social changes, particularly in problem recognition—in how claimsmakers, the media, and the public constructed the troubling conditions. There also may have been a long series of policy proposals appearing to be headed nowhere, before someone devised what proved to be a winning package. And often the political situation will have changed as well, making available the necessary votes. In other words, dramatic new legislation tends to emerge only when the three policy streams converge. For example, although earlier laws treated adolescent runaways as delinquents, subject to incarceration in juvenile facilities, by the 1970s Congress had shifted to a new policy affirming that running away was not a criminal matter and funding shelters to protect—but not detain or return—runaways (see Box 7.2).

More often, however, legislative reform is incremental, rather than sudden. A first bill may create a tentative, exploratory program, with advocates settling for a modest, compromise measure that can be implemented. They hope this new policy will be a foot in the door—that once they have gained this initial level of acceptance, it will be possible to press for further policy measures. Passage of a first, relatively minor law may be followed by a series of additional laws over the next few years that expand and further institutionalize the policy shift. For example, the initial federal hate crime law was the Hate Crimes Statistics Act (1990), which merely required that the FBI begin keeping records of reported hate crimes (Jenness & Grattet, 2001). The Hate Crimes Sentencing Enhancement Act, which followed in 1994, allowed federal judges to impose harsher sentences on those convicted of some hate crimes. In the meantime, most state legislatures passed their own hate crime statutes, and in many cases they passed additional laws that expanded the definition of hate crimes or increased the penalties

Box 7.2 Devising a New Runaway Policy

Before 1960, adolescents had limited rights, and running away from home was treated as a type of delinquency; runaways could be turned over to the juvenile justice system. During the 1960s, however, social constructions of running away began to shift. In part, there were legal challenges to the constitutionality of "status offenses" (behaviors such as running away that were illegal only because the individual was underage); state courts began to rule that incarcerating youths for these offenses violated their rights. As the emerging hippie counterculture celebrated being independent and being on the road, the number of runaways seemed to rise. However, some claimsmakers warned that many of these runaways had few resources, were vulnerable to exploitation, and survived by becoming prostitutes; runaways, they argued, needed protection and support (Staller, 2006).

Some within the hippie community, such as the Diggers (a group that sought to provide communal social services) tried to help newly arrived runaways find food, shelter, and other necessities. These early efforts led to the establishment of grassroots shelters for runaways, such as San Francisco's Huckleberry House. A runaway could come to a shelter and receive help; these shelters would not force their adolescent clients to contact their parents (although this stance was sometimes of questionable legality).

In 1974, Congress passed the Runaway and Homeless Youth Act, a law that provided federal funding for shelters, to help protect youths from exploitation, but did not require shelters to notify parents of their children's whereabouts. In other words, the new law redefined running away—which up to that point had been considered illegal—as a right that should be protected.

for those convicted. Over time, then, the domain of hate crime policy expanded.

Although policymaking is obviously a key stage in the social problems process, it has largely been taken for granted by sociologists (political scientists have tended to be the social scientists most interested in policy formation). The remainder of this chapter will try to suggest some sociological dimensions for analyzing the policymaking process; it will look at social organization and the pressures on policymakers before turning to policies as social constructions, to the rhetoric of policymaking.

PRESSURES ON POLICYMAKERS

We have already noted that policymakers operate under constraints. Lots of people are insisting that they take action, yet policymakers have limited resources at their disposal. Hence, they must set priorities and establish an agenda. But the effect of these constraints varies among policymakers—and among the issues that they are asked to resolve.

We tend to think first of the most visible, most contentious policy issues. For example, consider abortion: this issue can be easily understood by most people; it leads different people to have sharply opposing views about what policy ought to be, so policymakers cannot possibly satisfy everyone; and those conflicting opinions sometimes are expressed with great passion. Topics related to abortion policy—legislative action, court decisions, and so on—are the subject of considerable media coverage, and however policymakers act regarding abortion is likely to become widely known and is sure to anger at least some people.

However, hot-button issues like abortion are atypical. Much policymaking is almost invisible. We can presume that an agency in the federal government sets, say, standards for the composition of the concrete used in federal highways. This is a basically technical matter: most of us don't know anything about the chemical and physical properties of concrete. We probably prefer that the government build the best-quality highways (so that the roads won't deteriorate quickly) at the lowest possible cost, but we have no idea what sort of concrete composition is required, and we expect some-body else—presumably experts in that agency—to handle the matter. On the other hand, we might imagine that the people who manufacture concrete—who doubtless view the federal government as a major customer—will have strong opinions about concrete policy: they probably want to encourage concrete consumption, but they don't want those policies to cut into their profits. Probably the industry employs lobbyists to work with legislators and officials in the various agencies that determine concrete-related policies. This sort of insider claimsmaking leads to policies being made almost entirely out of the public view.

This is why policy domains (Burstein, 1991) are so important. Each domain contains the people who are most interested in—and most knowledgeable about—a particular set of issues. Although we might agree that, as taxpayers, we all have an interest in whether the government buys the best concrete at the lowest possible price, few taxpayers have the time or energy to pay attention to that policy domain, let alone to play an active part in that policymaking process. This means that, within some domains, policymakers have a relatively free hand: they aren't closely watched, and they aren't subjected to strong, competing pressures.

Policymakers respond to this freedom in different ways. At least sometimes, policymakers adopt relatively activist stances to take advantage of their powers. For example, when Congress passed the Rehabilitation Act of 1973, the law contained a section prohibiting discrimination against "handicapped" persons (Scotch, 2001). This was a minor provision in a much larger, apparently routine bill designed to renew a federal vocational rehabilitation program; the antidiscrimination section attracted little notice while the bill was being considered in Congress.

However, officials at the Department of Health, Education, and Welfare's Office of Civil Rights (OCR) took an active role in interpreting the new law's provisions very broadly. They argued that the law's antidiscrimination section required altering a wide range of social arrangements previously taken for granted, such as modifying curbs and other physical barriers to wheelchair access. The OCR found allies in the emerging disability rights movement, and the agency's broad interpretation led to far-reaching changes, such as requirements that public buildings be refurbished to be accessible to the disabled. It is quite possible that, without the OCR's decision to promote an expansive interpretation of the new law, disability policy would not have changed as dramatically or as quickly as it did. In contrast, we can imagine occasions when agencies might choose to turn away from potential policymaking opportunities and decide simply to continue administering ongoing policies.

Of course, there is always the possibility that officials will suddenly find that what in most years would be routine, virtually invisible decisions suddenly are subjected to the glare of publicity. How a state's wildlife agency manages, say, its river otter population, is not ordinarily a major public issue, but under the right circumstances, it can become a contentious topic (see Box 7.3). In such cases, policies that usually might be shaped by insider claimsmaking may be subjected to countervailing demands by all sorts of insiders and outsiders, the policymaking process now made visible through media coverage.

It is also not certain how policymakers will respond to such conflicting demands. Although at first glance it might seem obvious that officials are influenced by lobbying efforts, the evidence on this score is relatively weak (Burstein & Linton, 2002); and perhaps contrary to popular belief, a fair amount of evidence suggests that legislators are responsive to public opinion (Burstein, 1998). We might suspect that insider claimsmaking is most likely to be effective when policymaking is not especially visible. This does not mean that policies are necessarily made in secret or that the process is always corrupt, but simply that much policymaking occurs outside the spotlight of media coverage. When policymaking attracts more media attention, policymakers probably become more responsive to public opinion.

Box 7.3 Shaping Wildlife Policy

Policymakers sometimes have to socially construct nature. For instance, wildlife management agencies may confront competing definitions regarding the character of particular animal species. Should Missouri's river otters be viewed as delightful, playful creatures that should be allowed to roam freely, or should they be seen as destructive varmints that wastefully kill far more fish than they eat, and thereby ruin humans' fishing opportunities (Goedeke, 2005)? Or consider the case of the mourning dove in Wisconsin, which had been designated the state's official symbol of peace (Herda-Rapp & Marotz, 2005). Proposals to establish a dove hunting season led to a debate between opponents who objected to killing what they characterized as a friendly songbird, and proponents who argued that the dove should be recognized as a challenging form of edible game.

Wildlife agencies (Missouri's Department of Conservation dealt with the otter controversy; Wisconsin's Department of Natural Resources handled the dove debate) faced these competing constructions of wildlife and had to devise policies. In each of these cases, the agency's decision reflected its own organizational culture, which viewed wildlife as a resource to be managed. Because the larger predators that controlled the otter population were now gone, trapping otters was allowed; because hunting was unlikely to significantly reduce the large dove population, hunting was permitted. In making policy, emotional claims about playful otters or innocent doves received less weight than arguments about the need to oversee the balance of nature.

Note, too, that policymaking on an issue can occur in multiple arenas. More than one congressional committee may be involved with legislation related to a particular policy domain; proponents can launch proposals before each committee and then, depending on how the different committees respond, choose to concentrate their efforts in those arenas that seem to offer the best prospects.

In addition, policymaking arenas may be found at both the state and federal levels. Advocates can press for new policies at both levels: success at the federal level can provide momentum for further state-level campaigns; on the other hand, a successful state campaign or two may help persuade federal officials that they need to act. Similarly, those dissatisfied with the laws that are passed can press agency officials for interpretations that will shape policy implementation in particular directions; or if the agencies aren't responsive, it may be possible to appeal either the law's content or its implementation through various courts. Many doors offer openings to policymaking, so there are many opportunities for modest beginnings that get an issue's foot in the door and might lead to greater policy changes.

Although we tend to equate policymakers with government officials, remember that policymaking also can occur in the private sector. Corporations, churches, or other organizations can devise their own responses to claims about troubling conditions. Unlike government officials, who may be subject to countervailing pressures, private policymakers are less accountable to those outside their organizations. Foundations, for example, may donate money to implement social policies (see Box 7.4).

As private entities, foundations have considerable latitude in choosing which projects to support; and they are flexible, able to make decisions and even shift their priorities relatively quickly. In earlier decades, major foundations sometimes worked in partnership with the federal government: foundations funded experimental social programs, and then evidence that those programs had been effective was used to justify establishing federal social policies based on similar models, much as examples of successful state or local government programs can be used to promote federal legislation (Silver, 2006). In recent years, however, the federal government has tried to reduce its involvement in social programs by arguing that private, "faith-based" (that is, church-sponsored) programs can provide social services more efficiently or effectively than

---

Box 7.4 Foundations Fight Poverty

After Los Angeles experienced a major riot in the spring of 1992, Chicago foundations organized the Chicago Initiative, a collaboration between philanthropists and community-based organizations in their city (Silver, 2006). Their goal was to allocate money for youth programs that might help keep the inner city cool during what some feared might be a long, hot—that is, riot-prone—summer. Private funds were needed because the federal government's funding for antipoverty programs had declined markedly during the 1980s. Private foundations, however, had the flexibility to devise and implement a new policy within a few weeks.

The leaders of the community-based organizations that joined the Chicago Initiative did not necessarily share the foundations' concern that rioting was imminent in Chicago, but they hoped that the initial youth programs might evolve into larger-scale, broader-based antipoverty programs. Although the initiative's collaboration involved the organizers who served on panels that identified which groups ought to receive funding, the initiative's long-term survival depended on the foundations remaining interested in the project and continuing to give money to the cause.

However, the philanthropists proved unwilling to commit funds for the larger, long-term antipoverty programs that the organizers envisioned; they preferred to fund short-term projects. In fact, as concern about rioting receded, contributions to the Chicago Initiative fell, the collaboration disbanded after only three years, and the foundations' support shifted to other, fresher policies that attracted the funders' attention.

---

government agencies can. Thus, today's private efforts seem less likely to inspire larger public programs.

As we have seen, myriad organizational considerations can shape the direction of policymaking. Particular instances of policymaking will depend on the constellation of parties—claimsmakers, legislative committees, interest groups, official agencies, and so on—who are willing to weigh in on a particular issue. These actors become elements in Kingdon's (1984) policy proposal and political streams. But we should never forget that policy outcomes also depend on the problem recognition stream, on how social problems and their proposed policy solutions are constructed.

SYMBOLIC POLITICS AND THE RHETORIC OF POLICYMAKING

Policymakers must explain and justify their actions; that is, they must convince others that their policies are wise and appropriate. Such persuasion necessarily involves rhetoric—efforts to convince others that the new policies are the best courses of action. Why is this policy needed? What problem is it intended to solve? Why is this particular policy the most appropriate means for addressing the problem? To the degree that policymaking is a public act, policymakers need to anticipate and address such questions. This task requires yet another reconstruction, one that highlights certain aspects of the troubling condition and explains how and why a particular policy will solve the problem.

The political scientist Deborah A. Stone (1989) argues that policymaking involves the construction of **causal stories**. After all, a policy solution is most likely to be effective in solving a problem if it reflects an understanding of what causes that problem. Causal stories classify troubling conditions into familiar categories according to the nature of their causes. Different categories of causes invite different policy remedies. For example, a troubling condition might be depicted as having an accidental cause (which is to say that neither the events leading to the troubling condition nor their consequences were intentional). Put simply, accidents cannot be helped, so no one is blamed for them.

Other causal stories have other implications. Another popular explanation depicts social situations as caused by intentional action;

this is, for example, how we think of most crimes—that people know they are supposed to obey the law, but sometimes they deliberately break laws. A third causal story emphasizes inadvertent causes: people do things intentionally, but their actions have unintended consequences.

It is possible to devise competing constructions of the same troubling condition using all three types of causal stories. Consider Hurricane Katrina in 2005, which broke the levees in New Orleans and resulted in catastrophic flood damage. It is possible to construct the effects of the hurricane as an accident (the storm just happened to strike the city); or as a product of inadvertent causes (officials built the city's flood control system to withstand less severe storms because strong levees would have been much more costly, and it seemed unlikely that such a powerful storm would directly strike the city); or even as intentional (such stories might involve human intent [politicians willingly constructed levees that left the city's poorest districts at grave risk] or divine will [God was deliberately punishing New Orleans for its sinful ways]). Different causal stories carry different policy implications: Should the city be rebuilt? If so, who should pay for the rebuilding? Should anyone be blamed for the disaster?

Note that the choice of a causal story also affects the characterization of the people affected by the troubling condition—the policy's **target population**—in very different ways (Schneider & Ingram, 1993, 2005). Some causal stories depict troubling conditions as affecting vulnerable but morally worthy people—victims who deserve the policymakers' help and support. At the other extreme, stories can characterize target populations as villains—individuals who embody the troubling condition, and whose bad behavior needs to be controlled through the new policy's implementation. Note that different causal stories can construct the same target population in various ways, so, for example, drug addicts might be depicted either as villains (people who knowingly break the law) or as victims (whose hopeless lives lead to despair that causes them to turn to drugs).

Target populations can be relatively powerful (that is, politically influential), or relatively weak, and their status shapes policymakers' constructions. Contrast the differences in the ways politicians talk about Social Security (a program that benefits older citizens— one of the population segments most likely to vote) and welfare programs (which benefit poorer people who vote less often): whereas Social Security recipients are generally described as having a right to expect that their benefits will be protected, when it comes to welfare some politicians express skepticism that welfare recipients actually need—or deserve to receive—their benefits.

It is important to appreciate that there is nothing inevitable about these constructions; the same troubling condition could lead to policymakers devising very different causal stories and characterizing the target population in very different ways. A causal story that is widely accepted and is taken for granted at one time may fall out of favor, pushed aside by a rival construction that might have once been unthinkable but now has wide acceptance (see Box 7.5).

When new constructions take hold, people throughout the social problems process may begin to rework their positions to fit the new story. Prior to the environmental movement's rise, for instance, pesticide manufacturers marketed products under tough, militaristic brand names, such as Arsenal or Torpedo (Kiel & Nownes, 1994). However, once policymakers began to respond to claims about the dangers posed by pesticides and the need for tighter regulation of the industry, the companies began describing their products as "crop protection chemicals," and devised less threatening brand names, such as Accord or Green Mountain. The rise of a new causal story can force many parties to adapt.

Not all causal stories and their associated policies are equally attractive, equally compelling. Ideally a causal story needs to be easily understood. That is, a good causal story should be easy to tell, simple enough to be conveyed by the media (which—as described in Chapter 5—prefer stories that can be converted into relatively straightforward secondary claims), and easy for audiences

---

Box 7.5 New Causal Stories for Gender, Family, and Work Policies

In the half century after World War II, Congress addressed dozens of proposals that concerned work, family, and gender. Although in theory those issues might have been constructed in all sorts of ways, in practice just a few causal stories framed most of the discussions. Moreover, there were clear shifts, as a once dominant construction virtually disappeared and new ones replaced it.

In the postwar period, it was common to argue that men and women occupied *separate spheres*: men in the workplace, women at home. Women who worked were seen as exceptions, and not entitled to the same opportunities as males. However, this package of ideas lost favor, particularly after the 1970s, when the new women's movement insisted that males and females should have *equal opportunities* and receive equal protections under the law. Congressional sponsorships for legislation grounded in the separate-spheres model fell, while sponsorships for equal opportunity bills rose. Beginning in the 1980s, a third model also began to attract support. The *work–family accommodation* model argues that employers have obligations to acknowledge workers' family responsibilities by providing child care, paid leaves, and other forms of support (Burstein & Bricher, 1997; Burstein, Bricher, & Einwohner, 1995).

The assumptions shaping work and family policy changed markedly in a fairly short period. The once dominant separate-spheres model now seems antiquated, while proposals to ensure equal opportunity or require family accommodation measures would have seemed impossibly radical at the end of World War II.

---

to follow. It also helps if the problem can be presented as having a straightforward, easily understood solution, and if that solution can be promised to be economical. Policymakers would prefer to construct their policies as effective and inexpensive: "this should solve the problem once and for all." Of course, such policy claims create expectations among the policymakers' audiences.

Policymakers typically emphasize the *instrumental* purposes of their policies. That is, they claim that the policy is intended to make a difference, to correct or improve a particular troubling condition in society. Of course, such claims make sense. The content of policymakers' claims—the causal stories, the definitions of the target populations, and so on—depict the troubling condition as having particular sorts of features, and also present the policy as the appropriate measure needed to address the troubling condition's causes, the target population's needs, and other aspects of the policymakers' constructions.

However, analysts often argue that policies can serve *symbolic* purposes as well. That is, policies embody values, serving to promote particular constructions of the world. Consider drug laws. The historical record is filled with examples of efforts to ban the distribution and use of illegal drugs, and most of those efforts have failed. The classic example is the United States' experiment with Prohibition, the period when alcohol was treated as an illegal drug. During Prohibition, an illegal trade in alcohol flourished; it created new opportunities for organized crime and led to considerable corruption. After about a dozen years, policymakers reversed course, legalized alcohol, and sought to regulate drinking through various liquor control laws limiting the conditions under which alcohol could be sold and consumed. Of course, alcohol problems did not disappear; alcoholism remains a major health problem and drunk drivers continue to kill people, but most policymakers consider the problems associated with legalized alcohol to be less troubling than those that might emerge if alcohol again became a target of prohibition.

It is easy to make parallel arguments about the problems associated with laws against other illegal drugs (MacCoun & Reuter, 2001). However, many policymakers insist that legalizing drugs is unthinkable. Legalization might be interpreted as constituting approval of drug use; it would "send the wrong message"—that is, it would seem to endorse the wrong values. Maintaining a strong commitment to the prohibition of drugs may not have particularly positive instrumental effects: experts disagree, but it is at least possible to argue that the effects of legalizing drugs would be no worse than the consequences of our current prohibitionist policy. However, antidrug laws also serve important symbolic purposes: they affirm society's commitment to sobriety and other moral principles.

Symbolic considerations are important, particularly when policymakers are elected officials. Topics that become contentious public issues—alcohol in the decades leading to Prohibition, or such contemporary topics as abortion, drugs, and welfare—encourage policymakers to adopt positions that play well as symbolic politics. Such policies affirm that one is standing up for the right values, and policymakers can assert that, at least in principle, these policies should work (even when their track record suggests that, in practice, such policies do not work as anticipated).

The notion of symbolic politics reminds us that policymaking is also a form of rhetoric, that it can be intended to persuade audiences—a category that can include the media, the public, and even claimsmakers (whom the policymakers may hope to placate, so they will stop calling for further policy changes)—that the policymakers have done the right things for the right reasons. We need to be alert to the dramatic nature of policymaking, to watch for the ways that policymakers—particularly elected officials—put policymaking to symbolic uses.

The competition for policymakers' attention and the policymakers' own desire to get favorable publicity for their activities encourages dramatizing the creation of new policies. Thus, policymakers often announce new policies with considerable fanfare; for instance, the new policy may be given a distinctive name, in order to convey the sense that this policy represents a dramatic change from past practices. For example, American political leaders have a fondness for "declaring war" on social problems; there have been heavily publicized wars on poverty, cancer, drugs, and most recently, of course, terrorism (Best, 1999). War rhetoric conveys a sense of widespread commitment for eradicating a social problem;

calling a particular policy a "war" serves symbolic, not instrumental, ends.

The problem with this sort of war rhetoric is that it creates very high expectations. Americans tend to think of wars as relatively brief struggles that are supposed to end in total victory (for example, U.S. involvement in World War II lasted less than four years, and the Axis powers all surrendered). Our history is characterized by a series of short, generally successful wars; it is not marked by a Thirty Years' War or a Hundred Years' War. In fact, military conflicts that seem unlikely to be resolved quickly—Vietnam is the most obvious example—quickly become unpopular.

Of course, social problems are not clearly identifiable enemies that can be defeated and driven to public surrender. There isn't one form of cancer; there are dozens. Curing cancer would actually require many different cures. Similarly, people are poor for lots of different reasons, and no single policy is likely to address all of those causes; eliminating poverty is likely to require attacking many different causes over a long period. Solving social problems usually takes time and often occurs piecemeal (see Box 7.6).

Because successful policies often proceed gradually, their contributions may go almost unnoticed, although they can transform society's face over time. Consider the impact of childhood vaccination programs, stricter fire codes, or mandatory educational requirements—all policies that we take for granted. Such policies do not result in dramatic year-to-year changes, but over decades they can produce profound transformations. A look back in time can produce surprising revelations: in 1900, measles was one of the ten leading fatal diseases (U.S. Census Bureau, 1975, p. 58); today, of course, measles has virtually been eliminated. It is a shock to realize that this disease—now easily managed through childhood vaccinations—was once a serious threat to life. The policy's success is simply taken for granted.

Compare such quietly effective policies with the noisy announcements heralding many new policies. The announcement of a new

Box 7.6 The Undeclared War on Traffic Fatalities

In 1966, 50,894 Americans died in traffic accidents; in 2004, there were only 42,636 such deaths. In fact, the decline has been much more dramatic than those numbers suggest: deaths fell even as the population grew by 50 percent, the number of drivers doubled, and the miles driven tripled. The number of traffic fatalities per 100 million miles driven dropped from 5.5 in 1966 to 1.4 in 2004 (National Highway Traffic Safety Administration, 2005, p. 15).

Numerous apparently mundane policy changes account for this improvement, including the following:

- *Better cars*. Various safety features (such as seat belts, padded dashboards, electric turn signals, and air bags) became mandatory.

- *Better roads*. Various road improvements were made, including additional lanes, controlled-access highways, broader shoulders, and better signs.

- *Better drivers*. Tougher limits were imposed on alcohol consumption, and licensing was both delayed and made a graduated process for beginning drivers.

No one declared war on traffic fatalities, and no single policy change can account for the declining death toll. Rather, lots of minor policy changes nibbled away at the problem, but the cumulative effect is impressive.

This example serves as a reminder that often social policies are effective because of the combined effect of many small improvements, rather than dramatic policy pronouncements—such as heavily promoted wars on social problems—designed to get politicians favorable headlines.

war on a particular social problem raises expectations and thereby creates opportunities for prospective critics. After four or five years—roughly as long, remember, as Americans expect a war should last—it will be possible for critics to point to evidence that

Figure 7.2 POLICYMAKING IN THE SOCIAL PROBLEMS PROCESS

poverty or drug use or whatever the current pressing issue is continues to exist, and to argue that the new policy has failed. In other words, policies enacted with an eye toward symbolic politics are often vulnerable to critiques that are themselves grounded in symbolic arguments.

In summary, policymaking has important sociological dimensions (see Figure 7.2). Policies emerge only under favorable social conditions, and they involve yet another reconstruction of the troubling conditions—this time by policymakers who must devise a plausible causal story, depict a suitable target population, and so on. Nor is this the end of the matter. We have already noted that the tendency to herald new policies in dramatic terms, as the means by which a troubling condition can be defeated or eliminated, sets the stage for future critics. We will have more to say about the process of evaluating social policies in Chapter 9. Before examining the construction of those critiques, however, we need to explore how policies are implemented through social problems work—the topic of the next chapter.

MAKING CONNECTIONS

- *Activists compete for attention from policymakers. Chapter 3 describes how these outsider claimsmakers influence the policymaking process.*

- *Policy changes frequently result from a shift in how the public or the media construct a troubling condition. See Chapter 6 for more on the role of public reactions in the social problems process.*

- *After policymakers ratify a new policy, it still must be implemented. The next chapter explores how social problems workers put a policy into action.*

CASE STUDY
MAKING POLICY ABOUT GLOBAL WARMING IS A
TOUGH PROPOSITION

Evidence that overall planetary temperatures are rising has become widely accepted, and there is fairly broad agreement that human activity is contributing to this global warming. In particular, claims-makers argue that emissions of carbon dioxide and other "greenhouse gases" cause Earth's atmosphere to gradually retain heat (Cline, 2004). There is less agreement about what sorts of social policies are needed in response.

The principal international effort to address global warming has been the introduction of the Kyoto Protocol. Recommended following a 1997 conference in Kyoto, Japan, that drew representatives from many countries, the protocol set goals for reducing greenhouse gas emissions. In particular, it called on developed nations to reduce their emissions below 1990 levels by 2012, although it placed no restrictions on developing nations. Developing nations resisted being constrained under the treaty on the grounds that requiring their compliance would increase the costs of further development and slow their progress, placing an unfair burden on their already poor populations. However, the Kyoto Protocol's concession to these nations meant that such large, rapidly developing countries as China and India were not required to reduce emissions and, in fact, could be expected to significantly increase them.

A large share of the world's countries ratified the Kyoto Protocol (although a great many of these were not required to reduce emissions, so that ratification was a largely symbolic act). The United States did not ratify the agreement. President Bill Clinton signed the treaty in 1998, but he chose not to send it to the Senate for ratification (where he knew it would be voted down). After George W. Bush assumed office, he rejected the agreement and stated that the evidence for global warming was ambiguous and that the Kyoto Protocol could not control global warming.

Global warming presents policymakers with a complicated situation. Making claims about global warming involves developing complex models that can predict climate changes decades—even centuries—into the future. These models are constantly being modified, to take additional factors into account. For example, the Intergovernmental Panel on Climate Change issued a report in 1990 predicting that the average global temperature would increase 2°C to 5°C by the year 2100; subsequent reports in 1997 and 2001 revised those predictions to 1°C to 3.5°C and 1.4°C to 5.8°C, respectively. That is, the same group, working with the best available evidence, modified its predictions downward in 1997, then upward in 2001 (Barrett, 2003). (In 2007, they issued a new report predicting increases of 1.8°C to 4.0°C [Intergovernmental Panel on Climate Change, 2007].)

Just as scientists' models of climate science are not precise, the models developed by economists to estimate the costs and benefits of different policies for dealing with global warming also are of uncertain value. Even if everyone agrees that our planet is growing warmer, and even if there is fairly general consensus that human activity is contributing to the warmer temperatures, it is not clear which sorts of policies are needed, or which might be most effective.

In trying to confront climate change, policymakers face two key problems. The first is that this is a *global* problem. Those opposed to the Kyoto Protocol argued that, even if the developed countries met their goals for reduced emissions, global warming would continue because the developing nations could be expected to increase emissions, so that more—not fewer—greenhouse gas emissions would continue to enter the atmosphere. In fact, under the terms of the treaty, even many developed nations were allowed to meet their emission goals without actually reducing emissions. The treaty allowed nations to meet their goals through various forms of bookkeeping; for example, Canada would be credited with exporting "clean" energy to the United States and be able, in effect, to subtract those clean energy exports from its emissions total. There was general agreement among experts that, although the Kyoto Protocol might be a first step, even if fully implemented it would not significantly reduce global warming (Lutzenhiser, 2001).

The second problem is that global warming is a *long-term* process: its effects will emerge gradually, over years. None of the experts offering projections for 2100 could expect to be alive at the end of the twenty-first century. It may be a long time before the impacts of climate change are felt, and it may be decades before policies implemented today have any noticeable effects.

In contrast, policymakers tend to have a *short-term* focus. Although the Kyoto Protocol had support from U.S. environmentalists (who were able to mobilize expert endorsements from large numbers of scientists affirming the threat posed by global warming), the policy was strongly opposed by business interests. Business leaders argued that they would be required to spend significant sums to reduce emissions, that this would raise their costs, and that they would find themselves even less competitive in global markets (particularly if they were forced to compete with developing nations that would not be required to bear the costs of complying with the treaty). Although opponents of the Kyoto Protocol managed to mobilize their own experts—who (initially) questioned whether global warming was actually occurring, or who (later) suggested that the warming trend might be partially, perhaps even largely, part of the nature cycle of planetary warming and cooling—the core concerns of opponents were the economic costs of complying (McCright & Dunlap, 2003).

Global warming, then, poses significant challenges to policymakers. No single nation can unilaterally address a planetary problem, and different nations have their own goals and interests that need to be addressed in any effort to establish the sort of international cooperation that reducing global warming will require. Moreover, global warming is a long-range problem, and policymakers are rewarded for thinking in the short run. Clearly the Kyoto Protocol did not generate the confluence of Kingdon's problem recognition stream, policy proposal stream, and political stream. Dealing with global warming will continue to present a challenge for future policymakers.

QUESTIONS

1. What major policies are in place to regulate greenhouse gas emissions and global warming?

2. What problems confront policymakers as they try to address global warming?

3. Why do policymakers have few incentives to address environmental problems like global warming or greenhouse gas emissions?

8

Social Problems Work

The previous chapters explored the initial stages of the social problems process: claimsmaking, media coverage, public reaction, and policymaking. At each of these stages, people construct and reconstruct social problems: claimsmakers first draw attention to troubling conditions, the media then transform the claimsmakers' primary claims into secondary claims, next the public adds its own interpretations, and finally policymakers reframe issues in ways that can be addressed by new social policies.

This chapter concerns social problems work—the next stage in the social problems process. In this stage, too, people reconstruct the meaning of the troubling condition—but with a difference. The earlier constructions—during the stages from claimsmaking through policymaking—tended to characterize social problems in fairly abstract, general terms, as widespread, even society-wide problems. For instance, claimsmaking about the problem of poor people without medical insurance is likely to discuss the numbers of the uninsured poor, whether those numbers are rising or falling, how much caring for the uninsured costs, and so on. These claims may feature a typifying example or two, but the focus tends to be broad—on the implications of the troubling condition for the larger society. That is, claimsmaking, media coverage, and policy-making tend to take what sociologists call a **macrosociological** approach.

In social problems work, the focus narrows. *Social problems work* consists of applying constructions of social problems or social policies to their immediate, practical situations (Holstein & Miller, 2003b; Miller & Holstein, 1997). Instead of discussing, say, crime in the abstract, people doing social problems work construct specific events as instances of crime, or they conclude that some events should not be treated as crimes. Social problems work is how people apply constructions of social problems in their everyday lives.

Most obviously, people engage in social problems work when their jobs require that they implement social policies. For example, medical professionals such as doctors and nurses will encounter sick people who don't have medical insurance, and they must decide what to do in such cases—whether to provide care or turn the ill away. Such social problems work is where "the rubber meets the road"—occasions when general, theoretical constructions about social problems or social policies must be applied to real-world situations. Although some sociologists define social problems work more broadly, to encompass any occasion when people apply their constructions of social problems (for instance, in everyday conversations), this chapter will emphasize the social problems work done by "street-level bureaucrats" (Lipsky, 1980): people who work as police officers, teachers, social workers, doctors and nurses, counselors, and so on—those who have to implement whatever policies have been devised for dealing with troubling conditions.

Social problems work often occurs in face-to-face interactions—for example, when a doctor examines a patient, a teacher instructs a student, or a police officer questions a suspect. To describe the participants in these interacting pairs, we will refer to **social problems workers** (that is, the doctors, teachers, and others whose jobs involve carrying out social policies) and their **subjects** (the people—variously called addicts, clients, offenders, patients, suspects, victims, defendants, and so on—who in some way embody a socially constructed social problem). Therefore, parts of this chapter will adopt a more **microsociological** perspective, focusing on the dynamics of these interactions between individual social problems workers and particular subjects. In order to understand these face-to-face encounters, however, we must also consider the larger social context within which these interactions develop. This chapter will begin by considering this context and, in particular, the nature of the jobs that social problems workers do. Then, after exploring the nature of interactions between social problems workers and their subjects, we will expand our focus to consider the sorts of social problems work that occur in everyday life.

ON THE JOB

Social problems workers find themselves squeezed between great expectations and mundane reality. The expectations travel from the top down; they are imposed on social problems workers by the larger society, by policymakers, and particularly by those who directly supervise what social problems workers do. At the grandest level, these expectations come from the larger culture's understanding of social problems work. In general, we expect doctors to heal the sick, teachers to help their students learn, police to fight crime by enforcing the law, and so on. These expectations are reaffirmed by popular culture. Think of all those television series featuring dedicated doctors and nurses, cops and prosecutors, teachers, and so on. In general, these heroic figures confront and solve instances of social problems in each episode: patients are healed, criminals are brought to justice, or whatever. Because most of us have fairly limited real-world contacts with social problems workers, these idealized images may shape how we think of social problems work; we may imagine that social problems work is as straightforward and effective as these melodramas imply.

Further, social problems workers operate within broad-based institutions—such as medicine or the legal system—that state both general principles and specific rules that should govern the social problems workers' actions. Police, for example, enforce the criminal laws that define not just the nature of various crimes, but boundaries for legal police conduct. The activities of different social problems workers are governed by various institutional sets of rules—professional codes of conduct, standards for appropriate behavior, and so on. These rules provide another layer of expectations that constrain how social problems workers should act.

Finally, most social problems workers belong to particular organizations—a police force, hospital, or welfare agency—that have bureaucratic hierarchies, including supervisory personnel who have their own expectations for their subordinates. Organizations vary in the importance they place on implementing particular policies; for instance, some police departments assign a much higher priority to enforcing hate crime laws than other departments do (Jenness & Grattet, 2005). A police chief may decide that traffic offenses are becoming a problem in the community and order the department's officers to be especially vigilant about ticketing traffic offenses, or a hospital administrator may discourage medical personnel from ordering expensive tests. In these examples, officers who fail to issue tickets and doctors who continue to require lots of tests may become targets of their supervisors' disapproval. Obviously such organizational expectations act as further constraints on social problems workers.

The combination of cultural, institutional, and organizational expectations may be thought of as pressing social problems workers from above; these are all ways in which the larger society tries to shape how social problems work is conducted (see Figure 8.1). At the same time, social problems workers find themselves confronting the realities of the particular people and situations they encounter. Police officers observe minor traffic violations, or see a group of youths congregating on a street corner or an intoxicated

Figure 8.1   SOCIAL PROBLEMS WORKERS IN THE MIDDLE

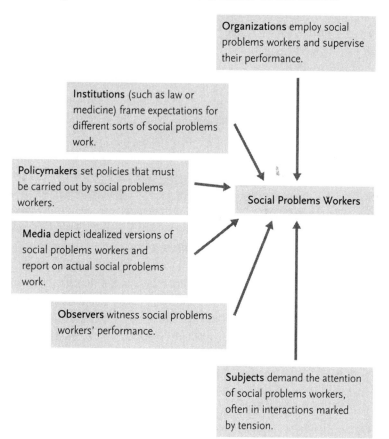

Organizations employ social problems workers and supervise their performance.

Institutions (such as law or medicine) frame expectations for different sorts of social problems work.

Policymakers set policies that must be carried out by social problems workers.

Social Problems Workers

Media depict idealized versions of social problems workers and report on actual social problems work.

Observers witness social problems workers' performance.

Subjects demand the attention of social problems workers, often in interactions marked by tension.

person shambling down the sidewalk, or answer a call about a domestic dispute. These are all occasions when the officers face choices: Should they ignore what they see? Should they investigate further, by speaking to the individuals involved? Or should they take official action, such as issuing a ticket or making an arrest? During any day on the job in social problems work, lots of decisions of this sort will need to be made.

All this means that most social problems workers have considerable discretion. Their supervisors cannot oversee all of their actions, and on many occasions a social problems worker may conclude that "going by the book"—following the institutional and organizational rules—isn't the wisest, or best, course. Society tends to idealize social problems work, but social problems workers recognize that what they do must be practical. They may have reservations about the wisdom of the policies that they are expected to execute—those policies may seem too idealistic to fit the gritty, practical world that the social problems workers confront—and they may choose when to invoke—and when to ignore—particular policies (Åkerström, 2006). In short, they must draw upon their own experiences, as well as their conversations with other social problems workers about how best to do their jobs, in order to decide what to do in any given instance.

Social problems workers vary in the amount of decision-making discretion they have; the lone police officer on patrol is harder to supervise than a social welfare case worker whose supervisor's desk is only a few feet away. In general, the historical trend has been for institutions and organizations to try to reduce the independence of individual social problems workers in the name of ensuring a higher standard of performance. For example, it used to be common for new police officers to learn on the job, by being partnered for a time with an experienced officer who could show the ropes to the newcomer; increasingly, this sort of informal apprenticeship has been replaced by academies where officers-in-training receive weeks of classroom training on criminal law and police procedure.

Similarly, medicine changed during the early twentieth century: medical schools began being accredited, states established procedures for licensing physicians, and there were other formal developments designed to ensure that all doctors would have at least a minimum set of qualifications and be able to provide at least a minimum standard of care (Starr, 1982). In much the same way, recent efforts by the federal government to use standardized testing to measure the performance of students in the nation's schools are an effort to improve the caliber of instruction in individual classrooms.

In other words, the discretion of social problems workers can itself be constructed as a social problem in that it can lead to inconsistent work that may be, among other things, corrupt or incompetent. Therefore, reformers devise policies to press social problems workers to be more consistent, and to meet higher standards of performance. Such reforms emphasize professionalism; they encourage social problems workers to think of themselves as having special training and qualifications, and to aspire to meet their professions' high standards (Freidson, 1986). These reforms often require paperwork: social problems workers are required to provide records of their actions, or even to apply for approval to proceed—measures intended to give supervisors more control over the individual social problems worker's performance. Still, there is an inherent problem: grand principles, whether they are laws or professional standards, must be translated into practical actions. The social problems worker remains the front-line figure, the person who has to have some discretion to assess particular situations involving particular subjects and decide what ought to be done.

The tendency toward the professionalization of social problems work has other consequences. Our discussion of claimsmakers (particularly in Chapter 3) noted that claimsmaking campaigns often originate with activists who may have personal experiences with a particular troubling condition, or who may hold ideologies that help them frame critiques of existing social arrangements. Such activists invest time and energy in claimsmaking because they feel strongly that this issue is important and must be addressed. In some cases, activists may even engage in private policymaking by establishing their own grassroots programs to address troubling conditions. For example, after some members of the hippie community became concerned about the vulnerability of adolescent runaways, they established shelters to provide runaways with food, shelter,

Box 8.1 Professionals Take Over Helping Battered Women

When the women's movement began to expand in the 1970s, its leaders initially concentrated their attention on particular issues, including domestic violence. Activists argued that the criminal justice system—as an arm of the larger patriarchal society—failed to protect battered women. These activists began to establish local shelters where women might find protection from their abusers, and they framed the problem of domestic violence and the role of the shelters in feminist terms.

At first, shelters received their funding from charitable contributions, but over time it became difficult to maintain the needed level of giving. Increasingly, shelters began seeking funding from local governments, and those local governments began hiring social welfare professionals to administer the shelters. But these new social problems workers constructed the troubling condition of domestic violence differently from the shelters' founders; their definition of the problem depended less on an ideology of sexual politics and more on psychological theories of family dynamics. Many of the activists found their influence over the shelters they had started diminishing (Tierney, 1982).

Rape crisis centers followed a parallel path from feminist activist origins to professional control (Matthews, 1994). Such transitions reveal societal assumptions about the need for social problems workers to have particular credentials; in general, formal credentials have become increasingly important in most forms of social problems work.

and other basic necessities (Staller, 2006); similarly, early feminists created centers for rape counseling and shelters for battered women (see Box 8.1).

Such grassroots operations tend to be staffed by volunteers and equipped through donations, but it is difficult to maintain them on that basis. The need for stable funding—to cover salaries and other costs—eventually leads these agencies to request government support. But this support usually comes at a cost; the agency may be expected to demonstrate that it is a professional operation, staffed by social problems workers who hold the appropriate credentials (rather than sharing the ideological positions of those who started the grassroots operation) and who can be counted on to abide by whatever legal constraints come with government funding.

There are exceptions to this pattern of professionalization. The obvious example is Alcoholics Anonymous (and the other twelve-step programs modeled on AA) that consist solely of people "in recovery." AA is an all-volunteer organization that refuses to acknowledge the relevance of professional credentials; its members turn to one another for support because AA's ideology insists that only those who have experienced alcoholism and recovery are qualified to guide those with drinking problems toward sobriety (Rudy, 1986). Even here, however, the emergence of health insurance provisions to cover alcohol and drug rehabilitation treatment have led to the creation of careers in alcohol and drug counseling, in which individuals who have themselves passed through the recovery process can become "professional ex-s" employed by rehabilitation centers to lead AA-like groups (J. D. Brown, 1991). Thus, the practical problems of maintaining the funding needed to support a stable program of social problems work tend to foster at least a sort of professionalism among social problems workers.

All this means that social problems workers have difficulty maintaining the ideological and emotional edge that helps motivate primary claimsmakers. At earlier stages in the social problems process, troubling conditions have been constructed and reconstructed, often in melodramatic terms, to make claims as persuasive as possible. In the construction of new crime problems, the crimes tend to be depicted as terribly harmful, and the criminals who commit those crimes tend to be characterized as callous, brutal, terrible people. Similarly, other troubling conditions, such as poverty, tend to be characterized as grave threats that inflict harm on innocent, good victims. Most claimsmaking portrays a melodramatic world, populated by evil villains and innocent victims.

In contrast, the people whom social problems workers actually meet on the job present more variety, complexity, and ambiguity than most social problems constructions promise. Police officers find themselves dealing with lawbreakers who may be hurt, frustrated, angry, sick, drunk, desperate, and so on—in other words, very different sorts of people from the melodramatic evildoers who must be brought to justice by, or the sympathetic victims who require the protection of, television's heroic cops. Similarly, other social problems workers meet people who are less admirable, less noble, and less innocent than the victims portrayed in many claims. Social problems work is not so clear-cut, so unambiguous, as claimsmakers and policymakers imply it will be.

CONSTRUCTING CASES

Typically, social problems work entails detailing with a series of individuals, subjects who require attention. On a given shift, a police officer encounters any number of people; the officer may stop some of them, others may hail the officer, or the dispatcher may send the officer to a place where someone thinks the police are needed. Similarly, a physician deals with a series of patients who feel sick, a social worker meets with various clients who may need assistance, and so on.

Each contact with a subject requires the social problems worker to assess the nature of the encounter: the police officer needs to decide whether a law has been broken and, if so, what the specific violation was (this was a robbery, that was an illegal turn); the doctor needs to decide whether the patient is actually ill, what the illness might be, and how best to treat it; and so on. Note that social problems workers may decide that there is really nothing wrong, or at least that there isn't anything wrong enough to require official action: the police officer may simply warn the person to stay out of trouble; the doctor may decide that further treatment is unnecessary.

A central theme in social problems work is the construction of **cases;** that is, social problems workers must decide whether particular subjects represent *instances* of a previously constructed troubling condition that requires attention through the application of an appropriate policy. Thanks to institutional and organizational expectations, social problems workers have an array of categories or labels that they might apply to the subjects who become their cases, as well as procedures for dealing with those cases (Chambliss, 1996). But first, subjects must be classified as cases; that is, individual people's practical problems must be translated into the categories (crimes, diseases, and so on) used by the social problems workers. Studies of social problems workers find that they consider a wide range of factors in making these assessments, asking questions such as:

* *What seems to be the problem?* Most obviously, social problems workers must label their subjects by categorizing their troubles. Such assessment involves yet another process of social construction. Consider a physician. Doctors are trained to recognize different diseases: a doctor who meets a new patient will ask questions designed to identify a familiar pattern of symptoms, such that the doctor can, with some confidence, declare that the patient suffers from a particular disease. Labeling the patient's disease will, in turn, allow the doctor to prescribe the appropriate treatment for that illness. Just as doctors construct individual patients as having particular maladies, other social problems workers classify their subjects into familiar categories: police officers must decide whether a crime has been committed (and if so, which crime) and whether there is sufficient evidence to make an arrest; educators must determine which students are having trouble learning, and then seek to identify

the source of the difficulty (perhaps by diagnosing a particular learning disability); and so on.

Often a social problems worker is able to conclude that a particular subject does not meet the standards to become a case, or that the subject represents a sort of case that a different kind of social problems worker handles. Such rejections or referrals may frustrate both subjects and social problems workers. If a physician proves unable to classify a patient's symptoms, the patient is likely to be dissatisfied with the doctor (and the doctor may conclude that there is nothing really wrong—that the patient is just a hypochondriac, someone who complains without a valid medical reason).

- *Which aspects of the case are relevant?* The need to classify each case into a familiar category leads social problems workers to focus on those features of the cases that are relevant for purposes of classification or treatment. For example, a doctor trying to diagnose an illness will be interested in particular symptoms that can help distinguish between different possible diagnoses, but may be uninterested in hearing about other symptoms that can't help with the diagnosis. These narrowly focused concerns may produce tension between the social problems worker and the subject: the social problems worker may dismiss some of the subject's concerns as irrelevant (which may frustrate the subject), and the social problems workers may in turn be frustrated by the subject's failure to grasp which information needs to be reported.

- *Does this seem to be a serious matter?* (For example, has someone been seriously injured?) Obviously, the more serious the problem, the more likely it is to be pursued—and to be assigned a higher priority—by the social problems worker. Differences regarding these judgments also can lead to tension between subjects and social problems workers. People may try to convince police officers, for example, that a fight was just a minor misunderstanding, that everyone has calmed down and that there's no need to make an arrest; on other hand, patients may insist that their symptoms are serious, and that the doctor needs to take action.

- *What is the nature of the subject?* Social problems workers may classify subjects by race, gender, social class, age, education, or any of the other status categories commonly used to locate individuals within their larger social context. Often cultural expectations dictate that different kinds of people should be treated differently—most people would doubtless agree that a police officer ought to treat a child of six differently from someone who is sixteen, or sixty-six for that matter. In other instances, subjects may suspect that the social problems worker is unjustly focusing on race or class; for example, an African American motorist who has been stopped may suspect that the police officer has engaged in racial profiling. Subjects and social problems workers may disagree about the relevance of the subject's characteristics for doing social problems work; for instance, subjects may complain that people of their status receive more—or less—attention from social problems workers than the circumstances of their cases warrant.

  Social problems workers often are more concerned with other, nondemographic aspects of their subjects. For instance, an individual's demeanor may affect the social problems worker's actions. Is the person calm or upset? Is the social problems worker being treated respectfully? Those who challenge the authority of police officers are more likely to wind up arrested than those who remain calm and respectful. Another consideration is the individual's career as a subject. Some subjects come to the attention of social problems workers again and again; they become the equivalents of students repeatedly sent to the vice principal's office. Social problems workers often become frustrated with such repeaters, particularly if those subjects seem to have ignored earlier advice or admonitions.

• *Are other people watching?* The knowledge that there is an audience observing the social problems worker's interactions with a subject can make things more complicated for both parties. During a conversation between a police officer and a teenager, the presence of other youths may make it harder for either party to back down. In particular, audiences may make social problems workers more careful, so as to avoid criticism for their conduct. Here, too, both parties may become frustrated because the other is, in a sense, playing to the gallery.

• *Are there work-related considerations?* Is the social problems worker's shift about to end? No one is eager to spend after-hours time filling out paperwork. Has the social problems worker's boss encouraged—or discouraged—particular practices? All manner of organizational and individual considerations can shape social problems work.

In particular, a social problems worker's job is often complicated by a heavy case load. For example, doctors may be expected to deal with many different patients, just as social workers or public defenders are assigned many clients. There may be a constant influx of new cases—new patients, new arrests, and so on—that need to be addressed by social problems workers. A social problems worker can ill afford to devote too much time to any one case, lest the flow of new cases create an unmanageable backlog, a queue of other people needing that worker's services. This pressure to deal with cases in an efficient, expeditious manner encourages social problems workers to focus on just the professionally relevant features of each case. But, of course, this narrowing of focus creates yet another source of tension: subjects may feel that their cases are not receiving the careful, individualized attention they deserve.

Box 8.2   Prosecutors Categorize Rape Victims

When reports of sexual assaults reach prosecutors, they must examine the records and interview the victims to decide how cases should
be handled. Using their knowledge of the law and the courts, prosecutors must identify the legally relevant features of each case—
elements that will make it easier or more difficult to gain convictions.

Victims vary, both in the circumstances surrounding their crimes
and in their determination to have officials pursue the case. On
some occasions, prosecutors may conclude that the evidence is
strong, even though the victim has reservations about pursuing the
case; in other instances, the victim may appear determined, even
though the evidence is weaker. Prosecutors must manage victims,
by guiding them to understand the legally relevant aspects of their
cases. In some instances, the attorney may encourage the victim to
pursue the case (by, for example, suggesting that officials will be
able to protect the victim from retaliation, or encouraging the victim to get counseling that might make it easier for her to testify);
in others, the prosecutor may subtly discourage a victim from pursuing a case (for instance, by emphasizing that this particular sort
of case is difficult to win) (Frohmann, 1998).

Most social problems workers face two challenges: (1) categorizing the particulars of the subject's circumstances into a type of
case and (2) guiding the subject in understanding the implications
of this construction for their lives. Both social problems workers and
their subjects need to reconstruct the particular events, to relocate
them within a more general framework.

In short, social problems work is complicated; many factors can
influence how social problems workers decide to deal with particular cases. At the same time, they usually find themselves under
pressure to be efficient, to deal with cases as quickly as possible,
so as not to get backlogged. Social problems workers typically
resolve this dilemma by devising *routines*, standard practices that

allow them to sort through cases, classify them, do what needs to be done, and then move on to the next case (see Box 8.2). For example, both prosecutors and defense attorneys learn to deal with their heavy criminal-court caseloads by negotiating guilty pleas (so that many cases can be handled in a relatively short amount of time). Lawyers on both sides must review the record to identify the key relevant features of each case; this evaluation allows them to classify these cases not just in terms of which law was violated, but also in terms of the seriousness of the defendant's particular offense, which in turn enables them to figure out reasonable terms for negotiating an appropriate guilty plea.

THE SUBJECT'S VIEW

As the preceding discussion has made clear, social problems workers are encouraged to view the people they deal with as cases, as instances of a particular disease, crime, or other troubling condition, rather than as unique individuals. But, of course, the people who constitute those cases—those who, depending on the particular kind of social problems work, are termed patients, complainants, defendants, students, clients, and so on—do not see things that way. These subjects tend to view their experiences as special, unique. They want to discuss their particular symptoms, the reasons they had for making particular choices or taking particular actions, the specific series of events that led them to the social problems worker.

A person who feels sick and goes to the doctor experiences illness as a personal, unique series of events and wants the doctor to return his or her body to good health. People's perspectives as subjects within the medical system—or with any other form of social problems work—are personal, individualistic. We would prefer not to be treated as "just another case." It can therefore be shocking to discover that, among themselves, social problems workers may refer to their subjects not as individuals, but as types of cases. For example, hospital personnel may speak of "that stomach ulcer in Room 313"; such depersonalization violates the subject's expectations for individualized social problems work (Chambliss, 1996).

We have already noted that tensions may arise because social problems workers and their subjects are likely to view their interaction in very different ways. The differences in the perspectives of the social problems worker who needs to classify subjects into cases of familiar categories, and the subjects who want to have social problems workers acknowledge them as individuals with unique problems creates another, familiar tension. Subjects often criticize social problems workers for being uncaring or insensitive, even as social problems workers complain that subjects expect individualized treatment for what, in the social problems workers' view, are common, routine problems.

Often, then, social problems work requires guiding subjects to redefine both their selves and their problems. An individual whose drinking has led to difficulties at work or at home is likely to explain those difficulties in idiosyncratic terms: if only my boss weren't so unreasonable, if only my spouse were more understanding, if only people could recognize that sometimes I need a drink; oh, maybe sometimes I drink a little too much, but it doesn't really hurt anyone else; and so on. The individual subject is likely to present a unique, autobiographical account of the circumstances that brought him or her to the social problems worker's attention: if only people would try to understand my point of view, they would recognize that what I did was reasonable.

The social problems worker's task is to help the subject rework that idiosyncratic account into a more general construction. The subject needs to reinterpret whatever unique combination of events led to the encounter with the social problems worker, to learn to construct those events as instances of a larger troubling condition— excessive drinking, family violence, criminal activity, or whatever.

Ideally, the subject will adopt the new identity offered by the social problems worker: "I am an alcoholic"; "I am a battered wife, and my husband is an abuser"; and so on.

Twelve-step programs, for example, demand that subjects undertake this sort of redefinition of self. Alcoholics Anonymous meetings begin with participants identifying themselves as alcoholics, and the program's first step is to admit to being powerless over alcohol. In other words, subjects are urged to identify themselves as instances of a general type of problem (so that they say, in effect, "I am an alcoholic, and my personal troubles are just one instance of the larger problem of alcoholism"). The subjects are helped to understand that what once seemed to them to be their personal, unique circumstances can be understood—are understood by the social problems workers and others—as just another case of a general problem (see Box 8.3).

Social problems workers not only find it necessary to convert individual subjects into cases in order to do their jobs effectively, but they also may believe that subjects need to identify themselves as cases if they are to benefit from the process. Some social problems work is based on force, or *coercion*: people who are arrested by police, brought to trial by prosecutors before judges, and sentenced to prison or probation are usually reluctant participants in the process; most would prefer to avoid the social problems workers' attentions. Even so, coercive social problems workers try to gain their subjects' cooperation using a combination of sticks ("You don't want to make this any harder on yourself") and carrots ("Be cooperative, and you may get a break"). Subjects who constantly offer maximum resistance make the social problems worker's job difficult; it is usually preferable to convince subjects to go along with the process, at least to the extent of accepting being defined and treated as a case.

Of course, not all social problems work is coercive; many social problems workers offer desired *services* to subjects who seek them out, providing different sorts of aid, assistance, or therapy. For

Box 8.3 Drug Treatment Helps Clients Define the
Dangers Out There

Contemporary culture medicalizes alcoholism and drug abuse; it
argues that addicts have a disease, but that treatment programs can
help their clients recover. For recovery to succeed, the clients must
acquire new ways to understand themselves and their worlds. Drug
treatment, then, is designed to teach clients to construct their worlds
differently. Ideally, clients learn to share the perspective of the drug
counselors and other social problems workers.

One aspect of this perspective is ecological. That is, clients learn
to divide the world into two places: inside the program, where they
can be safe and supported in their recovery efforts; and "out
there"—the dangerous world beyond the program (Weinberg,
2000). Social problems workers encourage clients to redefine the
outside world—which is, of course, where they have lived most of
their lives—as dirty and depraved, filled with temptations and bad
people. In this view, these dangers outside help explain why so many
former clients relapse after they leave the security of the residential
program. Drug treatment programs offer an alternative; clients must
adopt a different way of thinking about themselves, drugs, and the
larger world that they can retain and continue to use once they leave
the program. This explains why most drug treatment emphasizes
the importance of continuing to remain active in self-help groups
throughout recovery, in order to reinforce the program's perspective.

Drug treatment programs are an example of how social problems work often seeks to guide its subjects in reconstructing the
meanings of their lives. In the social problems workers' view, such
reconstructions are essential to resolving the subjects' problems.

example, physicians, social welfare workers, drug counselors, and
so on see themselves—and are probably seen by their subjects—
as helping the subjects deal with their difficulties. Yet again, a key
to these services is persuading the subject to accept the social problems worker's construction of the case, first to concede that the

social problems worker has correctly defined the problem and to adopt the suggested identity ("Okay, you're right, I'm an alcoholic"); and second, to follow the social problems worker's recommendations for addressing the problem. Following the prescribed program often involves adopting the social problems worker's construction of the situation, so subjects ideally acquire a new view that is supposed to help reduce or even solve their personal difficulties.

This process of subjects accepting the social problems workers' constructions is not always smooth. The social problems workers' redefinitions may be resisted by some subjects who insist on alternative interpretations (see Box 8.4). In general, subjects who have more resources (more money, more education, more social support, and so on) find it easier to resist whatever pressures the social problems workers apply, but even subjects with limited resources may be able to resist. A homeless person may insist on living on the street and refuse to enter a shelter, or someone arrested for violence against an abortion clinic may insist that this was a moral act in accordance with God's law (a view that even many abortion opponents would reject). Note that these subjects' acts of resistance may have different degrees of social support: on the one hand, for example, a homeless person may be unable to explain the decision to live on the streets in terms that make sense to anyone else; on the other, some abortion opponents may endorse the morality of antiabortion violence.

Much resistance, though, is less active, less visible. Doctors advise countless patients to eat less, stop smoking, drink in moderation, and get more exercise. To the doctors' frustration, many patients fail to follow this sensible advice and continue to suffer deteriorating health. Most forms of social problems work have these sorts of repeat subjects: most people who go through drug treatment programs return to drug use, most inmates released from prisons wind up back in prison, and so on. Often, of course, it is possible to construct these repeaters in sympathetic terms, as victims of larger social forces (for example, not only do ex-inmates

Box 8.4 Struggling over Defining the Problem with Unwanted Pets

People bring pets to animal shelters when the animals become inconvenient: perhaps a new landlord doesn't allow pets, or a cat has begun urinating outside the litter box. They want to turn the animals in to the shelter, perhaps hoping that someone else will adopt them.

Shelter workers tend to see giving the animal up as a last resort. In their view, humans should be committed to their pets and should make every effort to accommodate the animal. They might suggest other options to the client: find another landlord who permits pets; or try to resolve the urination problem by giving the pet different food, administering a prescription drug, or using behavioral conditioning. Among themselves, shelter workers tend to be critical of clients who surrender their animals (L. Irvine, 2003).

However, many clients do not consider themselves committed to their pets to the degree that shelter workers believe they should be. They don't feel guilty about abandoning their animals, and they often resist adopting alternative ways of resolving the problem, particularly if the suggestions are costly or may not work. In this case, the clients usually have the upper hand. Shelter workers are reluctant to refuse animals if clients insist on turning them in, because they fear that the animals may be abandoned or otherwise harmed. Although they may not approve, they admit the animals to the shelter.

Most social problems workers have the upper hand in interactions with their subjects, but in some circumstances, as in the case of workers at animal shelters, the subjects may be able to resist the social problems workers' constructions.

retain the disadvantages [such as limited education and job prospects] that initially encouraged their involvement in crime, but having been imprisoned usually further reduces their options, making recidivism more likely). Still, many social problems workers place much of the blame on the subjects, arguing that, if only the subjects had been sincere, determined, and otherwise virtuous, they might have avoided becoming repeaters.

In general, social problems workers prefer their subjects to be compliant, willing to adopt the workers' constructions, so that their interaction with the subjects can be cooperative, and the social problems work effective. However, at least some social problems workers anticipate resistance and noncooperation; the police, for example, have the power to arrest and restrain suspects, regardless of whether those subjects acknowledge the officers' authority. Other subjects may choose to go through the motions, viewing temporary submission to the social problems workers' authority as a necessary annoyance. Social problems workers, in turn, may watch for—and insist on—evidence of the subject's genuine cooperation. For instance, a drug court that offers clients the possibility of avoiding imprisonment by participating in therapeutic programs may expel clients who fail to participate fully in the program, sending them back into the penal system (Burns & Peyrot, 2003). Because so many tensions are built into the relationships between social problems workers and their subjects, the social problems workers' hopes often are disappointed and it is not surprising that they may develop a certain cynicism about their work.

LOOKING OVER THEIR SHOULDERS

Social problems workers face an additional consideration: they know that they may be held accountable for their performance. Figure 8.1 illustrated how social problems workers find themselves in the middle, experiencing pressures from many directions. In particular, individual workers have supervisors, bosses who oversee how social problems work is done. These supervisors have expectations: they probably expect social problems workers to be productive (that is, to deal with their cases quickly and efficiently, so that the agency's work doesn't back up); they may assign priorities, telling their workers to treat some cases as more important, deserving more careful attention than others; they want their workers to avoid mistakes or other actions that might result in critical attention being focused on the agency; and so on. Most social problems workers understand their supervisors' expectations, and they usually try to avoid displeasing their bosses.

Similarly, supervisors have others looking over their shoulders, and not just their own superiors within their organization's hierarchy (very large agencies may have several levels of authority between the agency head and the lowly, street-level social problems workers who actually deal directly with the agency's subjects). But agencies operate within a larger environment: most depend on a legislative body or other outsiders for their funding; there may be professional bodies that oversee professionals' conduct (such as state boards that license physicians); and an agency may become the subject of media coverage, or even a target of claimsmakers' criticisms. It is very easy for attention to turn to criticism, and for criticism to lead policymakers to begin interfering with an agency's operations.

Therefore, everyone involved at all levels of social problems work—for example, from the police chief to the cop on the beat—must consider not just how best to deal with the subjects of social problems work, but how those dealings might be regarded by others. The responses of social problems workers to these considerations revolve around two central principles.

First, social problems workers try to control the flow of information about their activities. They generally prefer that others learn about the work they do directly from them. Thus, agencies issue formal reports summarizing their activities, and they may employ public relations specialists to help guide media coverage of the agency's activities. Having control over information means that social problems workers may try to choose what they report; they may even try to cover up some information, to keep it secret. Not

Box 8.5 PLAYING THE NUMBERS GAME

Statistics have emerged as a vital way of tracking both the scope of social problems and the performance of social problems workers. When people report crimes to the police, for example, local law enforcement agencies tally those reports and submit their figures to the FBI, which uses them to compute the local crime rate (calculated as the number of crimes known to the police per hundred thousand people in the population). A lower crime rate is desirable: it suggests that the community is safer, and that the police are doing an effective job.

Periodically, particular police departments are revealed to have reported distorted—almost always lower—numbers of crimes. One way to do this is to record reports of serious crimes as instances of less serious crime categories. For instance, a report of rape (considered a serious crime that should be reported to the FBI) might be recorded as a complaint about a sexual misdemeanor (which would not be counted in calculating the crime rate). If done systematically, distorted reporting can result in a much lower crime rate (and praise for the city and its police) (Butterfield, 1998).

It is often possible for social problems workers to play these numbers games, to create statistical evidence that seems to document their effectiveness, thereby protecting themselves from the criticism of outsiders. However, revelations of dishonest reporting cause statistical scandals and lead to demands for more uniform, more carefully controlled recording practices. Of course, these reforms invite social problems workers to search for new ways to circumvent the new restrictions.

surprisingly, social problems workers may seek to release information that portrays their activities in the best possible light, even if doing so requires distorting what they report (see Box 8.5). This sets the stage for an ongoing struggle between various levels of supervisors who want to know what social problems workers do so that they can be held accountable, and the social problems workers who seek to manage what others learn about their work.

The second principle is that social problems workers try to limit outsiders' authority over their activities. Here, their argument is that only social problems workers can truly understand the nature of their work and the pressures under which they operate. To the degree possible, they want their performance judged by others who share their views of the job—that is, colleagues, fellow social problems workers who can be expected to sympathize with their position and endorse their actions. For example, teachers' unions often object to outsiders' proposals to award teachers merit pay on the basis of their students' test performance (the teachers argue that test results reflect too many things the teachers can't control), just as police often resist reforms that would create review boards with civilian (nonpolice) members overseeing complaints of police misconduct (on the grounds that outsiders cannot understand the real-world pressures that police face). Social problems workers object to such proposals because they give outsiders a measure of power over social problems work.

Social problems workers vary in their ability to control information and ward off outsider interference with their activities. In general, the more resources the subjects of social problems work command, the more likely it is that social problems workers will be scrutinized by outsiders and the more carefully they need to monitor any behavior that might be observed. For example, whereas police in an upper-middle-class suburb may view themselves as providing services to the community's residents and strive to maintain good relations with the local press and with the community generally, police in lower-class urban neighborhoods may have a freer hand because their work tends to be more hidden from public view.

When social problems work—such as health care, teaching, or policing—is directed toward subjects who are relatively poor and powerless, what happens is far less likely to attract public attention and concern than when comparable services for wealthier subjects are seen as failing. Moreover, poorer populations tend to have more problems that require more services, so social problems workers who deal with poorer subjects often find themselves swamped with work, compared to those working with better off, less needy subjects. At the same time, policymakers tend to be more responsive to middle-class demands for improved social problems work, so resources tend to flow to those social problems workers who need them relatively less. All this ensures that the quality of social problems work suffers—particularly work directed at less advantaged subjects—so social problems workers feel an even greater need to manage information. The result is a cycle of disappointment and fresh complaints about failing schools, unprofessional policing, and so on.

EVERYDAY SOCIAL PROBLEMS WORK

This chapter has focused on police, social workers, and other people who do social problems work for a living, carrying out the formal policies enacted to address claimsmaking about troubling conditions. However, we should recognize that we all sometimes become amateur social problems workers. Chapter 6 noted that the public reconstructs social problems claims in their everyday conversations. Similarly, ordinary individuals become aware of shifting constructions of troubling conditions, particularly via media coverage of claimsmaking and policymaking, and they find countless occasions to apply these constructions in their everyday lives.

Consider, for example, changing expectations regarding race and gender. The everyday world has become less segregated. Discrimination can take many forms; the southern states' legalized systems of racial segregation that were the targets of the civil rights movement (that is, laws that segregated everything from schools and hospitals to drinking fountains) are only the most obvious example; other forms are less blatant. For instance, prior to the emergence of the women's movement, women made up only a small minority of admissions to medical schools and law schools. Things have changed; most careers—like most neighborhoods, most schools, and most other settings—are more open to people of different races and both sexes. This is not to imply that there is absolute equality everywhere we turn. There is not. But expectations—and complaints—have shifted; for example, where activists once campaigned to open business schools to women students, they now complain that women in business confront a "glass ceiling" that makes it hard for women to move into the upper reaches of corporate leadership.

Everyday life is filled with occasions when people's behavior reflects changes in the larger culture, such as increasingly widespread assumptions about racial and sexual etiquette—the growing sense, for example, that blacks or women deserve to be treated with respect. Such changing manners, regarding how people respond to all sorts of differences—homosexuality, disabilities, unmarried couples cohabitating, and on and on—may be seen as one of the most common forms of social problems work, even if much of it has come to be taken for granted, as simply the way people think they ought to act. Of course, managing such reactions may be quite conscious, as when couples struggle to define what equality in marriage means in practice (see Box 8.6).

One form of everyday social problems work, then, is to smooth over what once might have been awkward occasions. Close personal relationships—ties between friends or family members—may offer the most extreme examples. Here, people know one another well; each person is understood to be a unique individual, with his or her own character and patterns of behavior. Such relationships can be seen as the opposite of the efforts of professional social prob-

Box 8.6 Everyday Social Problems Work about Marital Equality

Many Americans—including those who are married—would accept the principle that marriage should be an equal partnership. But what does equality mean? Some social scientists tend to assume that they can use a standard scale to measure the relative power of husbands and wives to determine which marriages are equal.

In practice, however, husbands and wives must construct the meaning of equality within their own marriages. When interviewed, individuals point to very different sorts of evidence to demonstrate which aspects of their marriages are or are not equal. These accounts can highlight familiar issues: some emphasize issues of power (that is, a spouse's refusal to give in on different issues reveals power); others focus on whether spouses perceive the household labor as being divided equitably; and still others find equality in intimacy and caring for one another. Other accounts are more idiosyncratic: a wife argues that her marriage cannot be equal, because she is more intelligent than her husband; or a husband refers to his religious beliefs as providing a foundation for ensuring true equality within his marriage (Harris, 2006).

Even when the larger culture supports the value of marital equality, individuals must negotiate the meaning of equality for their own relationships. Each husband and wife, then, is a potential social problems worker, who can construct particular incidents within his or her marriage as evidence of a larger troubling condition ("our marriage isn't equal") that ought to be addressed.

lems workers to classify their subjects into cases belonging to particular categories.

A consequence of such highly personalized understanding of one another is that families and friends are often slow to construct those they know well as instances of larger troubling conditions. Cousin Joe may get drunk a lot and even hit his wife, and Jane next door may often get moody, but it is possible for those who know Joe and Jane to tell themselves that these are just personal quirks: "Joe's under a lot of strain." "That's just how Jane is." It often takes time for friends and family to begin to use the larger culture's vocabulary of social problems—to speak of alcoholism, or domestic violence, or depression.

The media offer guidance for such everyday social problems work: many television talk show episodes are designed to help viewers reinterpret interpersonal problems as instances of larger social problems, and to offer advice—where to seek help, and so on. For example, friends, family members, and coworkers may be urged to stage an "intervention" to pressure an individual to acknowledge and do something about his or her drinking problem. In this way, ordinary people are encouraged to think that they, too, can assist professional social problems work, that they can recognize things that happen as instances of troubling conditions and respond appropriately, by guiding the subject toward professional social problems workers.

Social problems work, then, is a key stage in the social problems process because it connects general discussions of macrosociological social problems with the practical realities of individuals' lives. At one time or another, all of us experience troubling conditions, either personally or through our contacts with other people, and we all come into at least occasional contact with professional social problems workers. On these occasions, the currently available constructions of troubling conditions can affect us in many ways—through media messages, through the policies interpreted by social problems workers, and so on. What happens to us, what happens to those around us, and how we understand what's happening when we become involved with social problems work are all part of the social problems process. And, in turn, people's experiences with social problems work can lead to various reactions, which will be addressed in the next chapter.

MAKING CONNECTIONS

- *Through their jobs, social problems workers transform the meaning of a social problem from an abstract, general condition to a specific or immediate situation.*

- *The measurement of social problems workers' success will be discussed in the next chapter, on policy outcomes.*

- *Social problems workers frequently become targets themselves of claims by activists and experts and are subjected to new policies to address repackaged social problems. Chapters 3 and 4 explain how claimsmakers frame troubling conditions.*

CASE STUDY
TEACHERS AS SOCIAL PROBLEMS WORKERS IN A WORLD OF STANDARDIZED TESTING

Concerns that American schools are failing (that is, that American students are not being taught as well as students in other countries' schools) led to passage of the federal No Child Left Behind Act of 2001. The law requires that, in order to qualify for federal education funding, each state must establish a system of standardized testing that gives all public school students in grades three through eight annual tests in reading and mathematics, each school's test scores must be made public, and schools where students' scores do not meet "adequate yearly progress" goals must be penalized (Karen, 2005).

This policy holds schools responsible for their students' academic performance. That is, the failure of students to perform at an appropriate level is taken to mean that the school has fallen short. When this happens, the law requires that parents be provided with options to move their children to other schools that are more effective (that is, where students achieve higher scores); if schools continue to fail to meet their annual goals, stiffer penalties can be imposed. This policy puts considerable pressure on principals—who in turn pressure teachers—to focus on test scores as the central measure of educational effectiveness. A school or teacher with low-scoring students is not doing well enough.

Such high-stakes testing turns teachers into social problems workers who must implement a policy that makes improving students' performance on standardized tests a central goal. Of course, teachers have always been expected to help students learn, but policies that emphasize test results presume that such results are the best, the most important, measure of whether learning has taken place. In other words, such test-based policies lead the social problems workers—the teachers—to focus their work around achieving higher test scores. Critics (Bracey, 2006; S. L. Nichols & Berliner, 2005) argue that this policy negatively shapes teaching in various ways:

- *Most obviously, teachers may "teach to the test."* To the degree that teachers know what sorts of questions will be on the test, they may focus on making sure that their students can answer such questions. Those topics that are not expected to be on the test become considered less important and receive less coverage.

- *The schools' curricula change.* Americans expect schools to teach all manner of lessons, including good health practices, music appreciation, and on and on. However, given the testing policy's emphasis on reading and mathematics, it should be no surprise to find teachers spending more time on those test-related topics, while downplaying other subjects.

- *School officials may resort to cheating.* In numerous cases, teachers or administrators have reportedly cheated—in an effort either to make sure that students receive high test scores (for example, by telling students the answers to the test questions), or to exclude the test scores of students expected to receive low test scores (for example, by deliberately assigning such students incorrect ID numbers, so that their tests would be thrown out). There have been dozens of reports of schools and school districts using ways of reporting false data to improve their statistical showings.

- *Low achievers may be excluded.* In some cases, low-achieving students have been pushed out of schools ("administratively withdrawn") so that they would not be tested, or they have been excluded from testing so that their scores would not count against the school. For instance, some evidence suggests that, where students pursuing GEDs do not count against a school's test scores, more students are encouraged to leave school and pursue GEDs.

• *Standards may be lowered.* Under the No Child Left Behind Act, states can set proficiency standards; that is, they define the level of acceptable performance. Some state legislatures have realized that there are advantages to having lower—not higher—standards. Raising standards jeopardizes future federal funding, by making it more difficult for schools to demonstrate adequate progress. However, lowering standards makes it easier to attain the goal.

None of this should seem surprising. Whenever the performance of social problems workers is monitored by others—and we have noted that, because they are people in the middle, most social problems workers experience such monitoring in one form or another—we should expect them to try to put the best face on what they do. To the degree that police feel pressured to keep the crime rate low, they will be tempted to take various actions to try to minimize the crime rate—perhaps by not making formal records of some reported crimes, or by classifying certain serious crimes as minor offenses that aren't included in calculations of the crime rate.

Teachers are no different. If students' standardized test scores become the central criterion for assessing how well teachers are doing their jobs, then some teachers will certainly search for ways to ensure that their students score well. Nor is such behavior restricted to teachers. The preceding examples show that principals, district administrators, and even state legislators have become involved in efforts to manipulate the testing process so that schools can report desirable test scores.

The student-testing example illustrates the tensions among the principled goals of claimsmaking, the way those goals become operationalized in specific policies, and the street-level practices of social problems workers. Like many other social policies, the No Child Left Behind Act had a lofty rationale: society should ensure that schools do a good job of teaching students. The law operationalized that abstract goal into a specific policy, by requiring that states institute standardized testing programs, and by setting standards for adequate performance.

Although few might disagree with the general principle that schools ought to teach well, any policy to assess the quality of teaching inevitably affects what is understood to be good—or poor—teaching. Using standardized test scores as *the* measure creates a temptation to evaluate all aspects of teaching in terms of their impact on those scores, which leads teachers and other educators to concentrate on manipulating the outcome, rather than on the actual process of education. Inevitably, the particulars of any policy affect how the social problems workers—in this case the teachers—choose to perform.

QUESTIONS

1. Why should teachers be considered social problems workers?

2. What new policies are teachers implementing?

3. Why have these policies become the target of criticism from activists and experts?

9

Policy Outcomes

The social problems process can be lengthy. In its typical form, as described in earlier chapters, claims lead to media coverage, public reaction, and policymaking, and the resulting policies shape social problems work. At each stage in this process, actors reconstruct the troubling condition: just as media workers repackage the primary claims of activists and experts into secondary claims that fit the media's requirements for suitable news or entertainment, social problems workers must figure out how to bring the idealized generalities that inspired the social policies to bear on the gritty, practical situations they confront. At every stage in the social problems process, there are likely to be shifts in how the troubling condition is understood, as it is constructed and reconstructed by different people.

This chapter concerns what we can view as the final stage in the process: its *policy outcomes*, reactions to the way that social problems workers have implemented policies. There is a broad range of possible outcomes. At one extreme, we can imagine everyone agreeing that a particular policy solves the problem; perhaps all interested parties smile, dust off their hands, and turn their attention to something else. The Nineteenth Amendment to the Constitution, which granted women the vote throughout the United States, might be an example; women's right to vote became a part of the political landscape that is now simply taken for granted. However, this sort of complete satisfaction with social policy is probably rare. At the other extreme, a policy may be completely rejected, perhaps because it is seen as having failed to work, or even as having made things worse. For instance, the Eighteenth Amendment, which established Prohibition of alcohol as the law of the land, was quickly found unsatisfactory and repealed (via the Twenty-first Amendment). Most policies fall between these extremes and are seen as flawed—satisfactory in some respects, but unsatisfactory in others.

In most cases, policies fail to make the troubling conditions that they are intended to address vanish. This should not come as a surprise. Crime, racism, poverty, and most other troubling conditions are unlikely to disappear simply because a particular policy has been implemented. These conditions tend to have multiple causes—consider all of the various things that might lead someone to commit a crime—and it is unlikely that any one policy can address them all. It is almost certain that more will remain to be done. This helps explain why so few social policies are regarded as completely successful.

It is significant that our culture speaks of social *problems*. The very term implies that there must be a solution; after all, school-children learn to *solve* arithmetic *problems*. We might use other terms to characterize society's troubling conditions. We might call them **social conditions**, an expression that does not seem to imply the same confidence that there must be a solution; or **social issues**, a term that draws attention to disagreements or debates without necessarily raising expectations that they can be resolved. But because we think in terms of social *problems*, people often judge social policies as falling short if they don't solve everything; they tend to criticize policies that don't work, construct interpretations for those policies' shortcomings, and make recommendations regarding what ought to be done differently.

This chapter will focus on such critiques—what we will call *policy outcomes*. As we will see, the range of such outcomes is very broad. Even when people agree that a policy is flawed, they may have very different interpretations about what the flaws are, what causes those flaws, and how the flaws might be repaired. This chapter cannot possibly explore all of the many ways that people respond to social policies; it can only sketch some key features about policy outcomes. The discussion will begin by considering how policy outcomes can evolve into new claims, then turn to the types of people who participate in constructing policy outcomes, as well as the rhetoric they tend to favor.

NEW CLAIMS BASED ON POLICY EVALUATION

As suggested already, general acceptance of a social policy's success may be relatively rare. Certainly our attention is drawn to cases of vocal critical reactions, in which people charge that the policy is somehow imperfect. These reactions can be viewed as new claims, claims that the flawed social policy itself now constitutes a troubling condition that needs to be addressed. Although such claims about policies' flaws can take many forms, we can identify three general types of critiques about social policies.

Critique #1: The Policy Is Insufficient

The first critique is that the policy is *insufficient*. Here, critics argue that the policy was a step in the right direction, but that it doesn't do enough and, as a result, has fallen short of what is needed to eliminate the troubling condition that it was intended to address. For example, critics might argue that an antipoverty program, although it may help some poor people, is insufficient to end poverty; or that a civil rights law does not do enough to eradicate the legacy of racism. An insufficient policy, according to its critics, does too little.

The critique of insufficiency is often promoted by those who supported the original claims that led to implementation of the social policy. Having identified a particular troubling condition and having successfully urged policymakers to act, they now claim that the policy just wasn't enough, that the policy needs to be extended or expanded to deal better with the troubling condition. Often these new claims are part of a broader strategy. After all, when claimsmakers first draw attention to a troubling condition, they may anticipate considerable resistance from the press, public, and policymakers who find the claims too unfamiliar or the claims-makers' proposals too radical. Although they may privately think that eliminating the troubling condition will require extensive—and expensive—policy changes, claimsmakers may fear that it will be impossible—at least at first—to convince the public and poli-cymakers to buy into such far-reaching changes. It's better to call for specific, narrower—and cheaper—policies; that is, it's better to ask for something that others might be willing to give. And, as dis-cussed in Chapter 7, policymakers may adopt a similar approach, settling for a modest initial program in hopes that it will be a foot in the door. Once many people accept the need to do something about the troubling condition, it may be possible to mount a new campaign, arguing that the original policy is insufficient, and that more needs to be done.

Critique #2: The Policy Is Excessive

The second critique is the opposite of the first, stating that the pol-icy is *excessive*. The argument is that the policy goes too far, that it does too much and needs to be rolled back. For example, some critics argue that laws protecting endangered species are too broad (in that they block economic progress in order to protect minor, unimportant species), too cumbersome (in that there are too many bureaucratic steps required to demonstrate compliance with the laws), and not in society's best interest (in that the requirement to protect endangered species impedes society from achieving other important goals). These, too, are claims—claims that policies have an inappropriate, damaging impact.

Those who present claims about excessive policies are likely to have resisted those policies in the first place. They may have seen the proposed policy as threatening their interests or their values, yet failed to block the policymaking process. Now they have returned to argue that the policy has, in fact, proven to be excessive, and they may seek to cut it back. In particular, they may try to convince media workers, members of the public, and policymakers who supported the initial policy that they made a mistake, that it is time to backtrack and undo the damage.

Critique #3: The Policy Is Misguided

Finally, policies may be critiqued as *misguided*. Once again, these evaluations are claims that the policy has led to a troubling condition, but in this case the claim is not so much that the policy goes too far or not far enough, but that it heads in the wrong direction. There are various bases for making such claims. For example, the critics can argue that the *construction of the troubling condition* that led to the original policy was mistaken, that the problem needs to be understood in completely different terms.

Such claims often offer alternative definitions of the troubling condition that are grounded in a different underlying ideology. For example, concerns about the spread of sexually transmitted diseases among adolescents and about teenage pregnancy have led liberals to advocate policies for sex education and for providing youths better access to contraception and abortion (J. M. Irvine, 2002). In effect, such programs of reproductive health services define the troubling condition as caused by society's failure to deal effectively with the reality of widespread adolescent sexual behavior. These programs had long met resistance from—and were sometimes blocked by—conservatives who worried that sex education and reproductive health services might promote adolescent sexual activity.

However, the emergence of HIV/AIDS as a major health risk led many schools and communities to adopt expanded new programs. After the programs were in place, some conservatives presented an alternative construction of the troubling condition by arguing that it was the liberals' policies that were promoting sexual activity among the young; their counterclaims argued instead for abstinence-based programs designed to discourage premarital sexual behavior. There are many similar examples, cases in which critics argue that the assumptions behind social policies—such as those dealing with poverty or homelessness—are mistaken, and that only by reinterpreting the nature and causes of the troubling condition can effective policies be designed and implemented.

Other critiques may generally accept the initial construction of the troubling condition, yet argue that the *policies* that emerged were in some way misguided. For example, Lipsky and Smith (1989) argue that constructing social problems as emergencies often wastes resources (see Box 9.1). Emergencies are defined as short-term challenges for which policymakers tend to adopt short-term solutions, but it often might make more sense to establish long-term arrangements to deal with such conditions. For instance, instead of viewing homelessness as an emergency that requires short-term shelter and other assistance, it might be less costly and more helpful in the long run to establish programs to make stable, low-cost housing available for longer periods. Just because people agree about the nature of a social problem doesn't mean they won't disagree about how best to deal with it.

One important theme in critiques about misguided policies is that the policies actually make things worse, that they exacerbate the troubling conditions they are designed to eliminate. That is, these claims often describe policies as having *ironic* consequences. For instance, critics argue that antidrug policies actually encourage

Box 9.1 The Problems with Emergency Policies

Some troubling conditions are constructed as emergencies—sudden, unexpected crises that demand a short-term response. (Think of disaster relief efforts after a hurricane or a flood.) Often, emergency responses are administered by private organizations (such as the Red Cross), rather than by government agencies. In fact, policymakers may favor treating social problems as emergencies because then they are not bound to a long-term commitment to provide services.

However, critics charge that emergency response programs raise some important concerns (Lipsky & Smith, 1989). These programs can be very expensive. They tend to concentrate on immediate, short-term issues (such as providing food or shelter today), while doing less about long-range problems (such as helping the people being served to become less dependent on this aid). They do not necessarily administer their services evenhandedly; some people may qualify for help, while others are turned away. And if the demand for the program continues—and as complaints about how the program is administered increase—policymakers may be pressured to redefine the troubling condition not as an emergency, but as an enduring issue that requires a more institutionalized response.

In other words, emergency responses can avoid criticism—but only as long as people continue to view the troubling condition as an emergency. This illustrates how constructions of troubling conditions need to match constructions of social policies. Once the two no longer coincide, criticism is likely to emerge.

the spread of illicit drugs (for example, they might argue that arresting drug dealers increases the risks of dealing and reduces the supply of drugs, leading to higher drug prices, which in turn attract more people to the now even more lucrative business of drug dealing), or that programs designed to lift people out of poverty actually increase the numbers of poor (here the argument might be that, the more generous social welfare programs become, the more likely it is that people will choose to remain dependent on welfare rather than working) (MacCoun & Reuter, 2001; Murray, 1994). Note that the former critique tends to be favored by liberals, while the latter usually is presented by conservatives; claims that policies have ironic consequences are not limited to particular ideologies. Such claims often describe a vicious cycle: a troubling condition leads to a policy that makes the condition worse; in response, the policy is expanded (because that's how people have agreed to address this issue), which in turn causes the condition to get even worse, and so on. Critics insist that the only way to break this cycle is to devise completely different policies that approach the problem from a fresh direction.

A somewhat different critique of misguided policies is to argue that the implementation of the policy—the *social problems work*— violates the policy's true intent or purpose. Here, critics claim that the initial construction of the problem and policy—perhaps what was intended by its advocates to be a supportive, generous plan to help the afflicted—is being subverted by social problems workers. Such critiques may contrast the public face of a policy with its hidden workings, arguing that, for example, job training programs usually do not help their clients to find good jobs so much as steer them into low-paying, dead-end jobs (Lafer, 2002). Alternatively, the critics may argue that the social problems workers are abusing their positions, wasting resources, or paying too little attention to the needs of those the policy is meant to help. Claims about police brutality or police corruption, for instance, are less about flawed laws than about problems with the ways the laws are enforced.

In short, there are various ways to construct the workings of social policies as imperfect—as troubling conditions in their own right. The social problems process does not usually come to an end after a particular social policy has been implemented. Rather, new social policies often provide the raw material for launching yet another social problems process, one in which critics construct

Figure 9.1 ONE SOCIAL PROBLEMS PROCESS CAN INSPIRE OTHERS

Claims-making → Media Coverage → Public Reaction → Policy-making → Social Problems Work → Policy Outcomes

A Social Problems Process

Policy goes too far

Policy doesn't go far enough

Policy based on wrong view of condition

Policy based on wrong principles

Policy improperly implemented by social problems workers

Possible Claims for Launching a New Social Problems Process

claims that the policy is doing too little, too much, or the wrong thing; that this in itself is a troubling condition; and that something ought to be done about it. In fact, dissatisfaction with the operation of current social policy is an element in most claimsmakers' rhetoric. A glance back at the examples in earlier chapters will reveal that many of the claimsmaking campaigns we have discussed throughout this book have focused, at least to some degree, on the deficiencies of existing social policies. This means that social problems processes can be linked through time: when one runs its course, it often inspires one or more new claimsmaking campaigns, as illustrated in Figure 9.1.

ACTORS, EVIDENCE, AND EVALUATION

The previous section described several ways to criticize the workings of social policies. But who presents these critiques? And what sorts of rhetoric do they use to make their claims convincing? This section considers some of the actors who play prominent roles in constructing outcomes to the social problems process, as well as the sorts of evidence that they are likely to feature in their claims.

Most obviously, social problems workers can become critics. As noted in Chapter 8, it is not unusual for social problems workers to be ambivalent about the policies that they must implement. Moreover, they have a good sense of what is—and isn't—working. Social problems workers often have to report to their supervisors about what they have been doing. Because most social problems workers keep records, they have two important advantages in debates over social policy outcomes: they understand how social problems work is actually practiced, and they have access to those records. Again, Chapter 8 noted that social problems workers seek to control information about their work, and this desire shapes their claims. They have an interest in convincing other people that they're doing a good job and, perhaps, that they would be able to do an even better job if only they had more resources—more personnel, a bigger budget, and so on. Thus, social problems workers may be reluctant to challenge either the basic policies that they are supposed to implement, or the manner in which they actually implement those policies, unless they can, in the process, advocate receiving additional resources for their agencies.

Because they control their agencies' records, social problems workers are particularly likely to support their claims with evidence of organizational activity—that is, measures of how much work they do. It is relatively easy for them to compile this information: police departments can tally the number of arrests made during the previous year, hospitals can count the number of patients, and so on. Social problems workers can use these data to demonstrate that they have been busy doing what they are supposed to do, and they often argue that the fact that they are busy is evidence that they need bigger budgets and additional personnel to handle the demand for their services. In other words, social problems workers are particularly likely to use measures of organizational activity to support claims that existing policies are insufficient, and that they need to be expanded to give social problems workers more resources (see Box 9.2).

Sometimes the social problems workers' *subjects*—the people whose lives constitute the troubling condition that the policy is supposed to address—offer their own evaluations. For example, poor people may criticize antipoverty programs for not doing enough to help poor people, just as both people who have been arrested and crime victims may complain about mistreatment at the hands of the criminal justice system. Again, as noted in Chapter 8, subjects often are frustrated in their dealings with social problems workers, and they may be dissatisfied with the actual implementation of social policies.

Like social problems workers, subjects have the advantage of firsthand experience with how policies work, and they are most likely to draw upon these experiences for evidence to support their

Box 9.2 JUSTIFYING MORE RESOURCES FOR
SOCIAL PROBLEMS WORKERS

Because social problems workers usually collect statistics about their activities, they are often able to offer their own interpretations of what those numbers mean. Imagine that an agency reports that it dealt with more cases this year than last year. For example, a hospital might report that it served an increased number of patients during the current year, or a police force might note that number of reported crimes rose over last year's total. In response to this news, the agency might call for more resources—a bigger budget, increasing the number of social problems workers, and so on—in order to cope with the demand for its services.

Now imagine that this year's numbers are *lower* than last year's, that the number of patients or reported crimes fell. The agency may argue that this evidence means it has been effective, and it may further suggest that additional resources would allow it to be even more effective.

In other words, evidence that cases have increased and evidence that cases have decreased can both be used by social problems workers to justify calls for additional resources. Social problems workers and the agencies for which they work are interested parties in discussions of policy outcomes, and they often find occasion to promote their interests.

claims. Thus, they tend to favor anecdotal accounts—this is how the policy failed to work in our particular cases, or in the cases of people we know—which then serve as typifying examples for what are constructed as larger policy failings. (Recall a lesson from Chapter 2: typifying examples are rarely typical; they are chosen because they offer compelling illustrations of claims.)

Whereas social problems workers usually argue that policies are insufficient, subjects' critiques can be more varied. Subjects, too, may claim that the policy is insufficient; for example, they might argue that there are long waiting lines and other delays because there aren't enough social problems workers to aid the subjects who need services. Or they may warn that policies are excessive; for instance, they may charge that people who commit minor criminal offenses may suffer unreasonably harsh, life-damaging penalties. Or subjects may insist that the policies are misguided; for example, they may claim that social problems workers ought to help their subjects, rather than coerce them. Properly chosen typifying examples can support any of these critiques.

Compared to social problems workers, subjects tend to have significant disadvantages when critiquing policies. To the degree that subjects draw upon their own personal experiences to document the policy's shortcomings, audiences may dismiss the subjects' claims as self-interested. Moreover, the subjects of many kinds of social problems work have relatively few resources (that is, they have limited money, education, and social status), and the very fact that they are subjects can be stigmatizing (in that they may have been labeled as criminals, mentally ill, and so on). Although it is not impossible for low-status or stigmatized subjects to devise claims criticizing how a particular social policy operates, these disadvantages can make it much harder to get the media, policymakers, and other audiences to attend to the subjects' claims.

The prospects are better for a third set of critics, those whose claims launched the initial social problems process—the *original activists and experts* who first drew attention to the troubling condition and the need to do something about it. These people may already have the advantage of ownership; that is, the media and policymakers may be used to listening to what these claimsmakers have to say about this troubling condition. In particular, experts' critiques may seem more credible because they have professional credentials, and these experts may be seen as offering authoritative assessments. Claimsmakers' criticisms that the policy they promoted has somehow failed to deal effectively with the problem, then, stand a somewhat better chance of being heard than do critiques from other people.

In fact, such dissatisfaction from claimsmakers may be expected. As noted in Chapter 7, policymakers may have altered the claimsmakers' original proposals; social policies often are products of compromise, as policymakers try to placate both claimsmakers who are calling for action and opponents who want to do nothing, or as little as possible, or perhaps something very different. To the degree that a policy was a compromise measure, everyone may anticipate that the initial claimsmakers will still be dissatisfied and want more, that they are likely to argue that the policy was insufficient and call for further reforms.

Activist and expert claimsmakers alike may draw upon both anecdotal responses and measures of social problems workers' activity to document their claims that policies are insufficient. Like subjects, they can use typifying examples to show that the policy doesn't do enough to help those affected by the troubling condition. Expanding the policy may require nothing more than increasing resources (bigger budget allocations and so on), but it may also involve domain expansion (see Chapter 2). Here the claimsmakers argue that the policy defines the troubling condition too narrowly, that a broader definition is needed so that a larger share of those affected can be helped.

Alternatively, like social problems workers, claimsmakers can point to statistical evidence (perhaps collected by social problems workers) to demonstrate that there is a growing problem requiring further action. After social policies are established to deal with previously neglected troubling conditions, social problems workers' statistics often display a marked jump. For example, the campaign to draw attention to child abuse led to laws requiring that doctors, teachers, and others report instances of suspected abuse; not surprisingly, the number of reported cases increased dramatically. But child abuse claimsmakers could then use these statistics to argue that the increased numbers of reports proved that child abuse was a growing problem, that current policy responses were insufficient, and that additional resources were needed to fight child abuse.

Policies may be critiqued not only by the claimsmakers whose efforts led to policymaking, but also by *rival activists and experts*. These are people who opposed the original claims and the resulting policy, whose counterclaims proved unsuccessful during the social problems process. They are, of course, predisposed to be critical; and they are particularly likely to argue either that the policy is excessive, or that it is misguided. In their view, the policy was a failed experiment: it didn't work, and it may even have made things worse. These rival claimsmakers call upon policymakers to undo the damage, and they warn that expanding the policy will only exacerbate matters (see Box 9.3).

These rival claimsmakers also can draw upon both anecdotal and statistical evidence. Their typifying examples point to subjects whose lives have been harmed by their contacts with social problems workers implementing the policy (for instance, a nice middle-class college student who suddenly faces felony charges for possessing a small amount of drugs, or a welfare recipient who is discouraged from finding work by a system of benefits that encourages dependency). Similarly, they can interpret the available statistical evidence as showing that the policy is having negative effects (that, say, the war on drugs has imprisoned large numbers of people, and a disproportionate share of these are African Americans; or that people are remaining welfare recipients for longer periods of time than under the preceding policy). Note that, just as initial claimsmaking campaigns can be mounted by either liberals or conservatives, these critiques by rival claimsmakers who opposed those campaigns are not restricted to one ideology: both liberal and conservative claimsmakers can frame parallel critiques of policies that each opposed.

Thus far, we have examined policy critiques by four different groups: (1) social problems workers, (2) subjects, (3) the initial

Box 9.3 Drug War Critics Call for Peace

For decades, drug policies have been debated by those who argue that tough antidrug laws are needed to control drug distribution and use, and those who insist that antidrug policies only make things worse. During the past twenty years the federal government has pursued a vigorous war on drugs. What do the rival claimsmakers opposed to drug policy say?

Some critics develop principled arguments. For example, libertarians reason that laws should not interfere with an individual's choices, even choices to use drugs. Others make the argument that marijuana, at least, is no more harmful than alcohol, so if one is legal, what basis can there be for forbidding the other? More often, however, the critics identify practical problems by pointing to harms caused by antidrug policies: drug enforcement is costly (the tab runs to billions of dollars each year); a large share of prison inmates were convicted on drug charges (not only is it expensive to incarcerate these people, but after they are released, they will have the burden of a felony record); the immense profits from drug dealing encourage organized crime and official corruption; the fact that drugs are popular means that a large share of the population has broken the law—and perhaps learned to hold laws in contempt; and so on. These are well-established critiques, readily available whenever a new antidrug policy is introduced (Bertram, Blachman, Sharpe, & Andreas, 1996).

In response, drug war advocates have their own set of claims to use in rebutting proposals to reduce antidrug efforts. They argue that society must not give in to criminality, that drug use would increase without tough drug enforcement, and so on. This debate has continued for decades. Positions in such long-standing debates become familiar and well articulated.

claimsmakers whose activities led to the policies, and (4) opposition claimsmakers who stood opposed to the original claims. Each group tends to favor particular arguments, and to rely on particular sorts of evidence. Although some successful policies can lead to social problems work that attracts minimal criticism, other, more contentious issues inspire prolonged, visible debates. Topics such as abortion, gun control, drug law enforcement, environmental regulation, health care, and welfare policy are widely known to be issues about which people have disagreed in the past, disagree at the present, and in all probability will continue to disagree in the future. Such contentious policies attract many critics—sometimes from all four groups—but often their critiques tend to be discounted because each group is widely understood to have a vested interest in a by now predictable position in the debate, and therefore cannot be counted on to be an impartial judge of a policy's effectiveness. Is there no way to develop accurate, objective assessments of how social policies work?

THE SEARCH FOR IMPARTIAL EVALUATIONS

Doubts about whether interested parties can be trusted sometimes lead to efforts to solicit impartial evaluations of how well policies work. The most obvious of such efforts take the form of **evaluation research** (Rossi, Lipsey, & Freeman, 2004). Evaluation research usually involves some sort of social scientific assessment of a policy's effectiveness; the hallmarks of such research are efforts to create objective measures of a policy's costs, benefits, and outcomes. Often the evaluators are outsiders, chosen because they do not come from within the ranks of social problems workers, although such evaluations also can be done by insiders. The real issue is not who does the evaluation, but whether the methods used to produce the evaluation can lead to information that others will find convincing.

In theory, the most compelling evidence would come from careful experiments to assess the policy's effectiveness. At a minimum, two matched groups of subjects would be compared: social problems workers would apply the policy to the experimental, or treatment, group; and the control group would experience something else (usually whatever social problems workers did before the policy was implemented). In practice, experimental designs are often more elaborate: there may be several treatment and control groups that undergo slightly different conditions. Well-designed experiments can provide fairly convincing evidence regarding whether a policy works better than whatever preceded it.

There are, however, significant problems with experiments. One problem is that experimental research tends to be time-consuming, in part because designing the research, carrying it out, and then analyzing the results can take a long time. But experiments also take time because the evaluators may want to wait to follow up the subjects who experience the policy. It may take time for the policy's effects to be felt, or a policy's early effects on the subjects' lives may wear off over time; since it takes a while for either of those consequences to become apparent, researchers may prefer to make their final measurements years after the subjects' contacts with social problems workers end. In addition, experimental designs, because they can be elaborate and take years to complete, are often costly. As a practical matter, people engaged in policy debates are often too impatient to wait for experimental results that may not be available for years, as well as unwilling to pay for such expensive research.

Therefore, evaluation research usually winds up using less compelling, nonexperimental methods to study policy effectiveness. Often such studies consist of two sorts of comparisons. The first is across time: the evaluators compare a particular measure of the old and new policies' effectiveness (for instance, under our old policing policy the crime rate was X, whereas under our new policy it is Y). Second, evaluators may compare different places (other cities, states, or countries) to see whether our policy seems to be more effective than those used elsewhere.

The evidence produced through such comparisons is weaker than the findings of experiments because the differences between the old and new policies may actually have been caused by another factor (such as the economy booming or declining), or perhaps the other places used for comparison aren't really comparable (for instance, City A's agencies are known to be corrupt, City B has a very different ethnic composition, and so on). Such comparisons pose complicated problems for researchers: both the troubling conditions that the policies are designed to address and the policies themselves are likely to vary from time to time and place to place; in addition, policymakers, social problems workers, and others may insist that they already know whether and why a policy works, so the evaluators' findings may not be welcome (see Box 9.4).

There is another problem: to hold down costs, nonexperimental research often winds up measuring policy effectiveness using whatever data have already been collected. In practice, this usually means using the records kept by the social problems workers—the measures of organizational activity discussed earlier, such as the number of arrests or the average amount of time that clients continue to receive welfare benefits. This information may be suggestive, but it often doesn't answer the key questions: Do lots of arrests mean that crime is under—or out of—control? Do clients stop receiving welfare benefits because they have been helped out of poverty, or because they have become frustrated with the policy and have given up?

Since it is difficult to produce high-quality, inexpensive data quickly, evaluation research rarely provides the last word in assessing policies' effectiveness. Too many questions remain. Typically, such research depends on the records compiled by social problems workers, and those records have limitations. Imagine an effort to evaluate a new antidrug policy. Evaluation researchers might try to compare available measures of organizational activity, such as the number of drug arrests or the value of the drugs seized before and after the policy's introduction. But note that this approach raises various questions: Are those records accurate? (How, for example, is the value of the drugs seized calculated?) Were the records kept in the same way before and after the policy was introduced (or was

Box 9.4 Why Did Homicide Rates Fall?

Homicide rates—and crime rates generally—fell during the 1990s after reaching fairly high levels at the beginning of the decade. The drop took many commentators by surprise; some commentators had even predicted that homicide rates would soar to new heights during the 1990s. What accounted for this unexpected decline?

In New York City, officials insisted that the city's homicide rates fell because of tough new policing policies. In particular, police had been ordered to crack down on panhandling and other minor forms of public disorder as a way of signaling that lawbreaking would not be tolerated. Insisting that the decline in homicides was proof that those policies had worked, officials took credit for the drop. In other cities, where police had introduced other sorts of initiatives, such as focusing on gun violations, officials argued that it was *those* policies that had cut crime (Rosenfeld, Fornango, & Baumer, 2005).

The problem, of course, is that homicides declined during that period in most major cities—some of which had no new policies, while others had adopted a range of different policies. Perhaps New York's police practices had affected crime rates, but then again, perhaps the drop in crime reflected factors that had nothing to do with the department's policies (remember that the 1990s were a period of considerable economic prosperity, which may better explain why the crime rate fell in many cities). When social scientists used sophisticated statistics to try to figure out which factors were at work, New York's policies did not seem to have been particularly effective, although the city's officials insisted that those analyses were mistaken—that of course their policies had worked and could be credited with the decrease in homicides.

there perhaps a more systematic effort to count every case once the policy went into effect)? And, after all, what do such measures mean? Do more drug arrests and more drugs seized mean that the policy is working (because, presumably, drug dealers and drugs are being taken out of circulation), or do they suggest that the policy is failing (because there seem to be more dealers to arrest and drugs to capture)?

In short, evaluation research tends to rely on imperfect, ambiguous data, and the correct interpretation of its results is often unclear. Depending on the assumptions that evaluators bring to their work and the choices that they make in deciding how to measure the policy outcomes, it is often possible for evaluators to come to very different conclusions. And although evaluation research is theoretically impartial, evaluators can be "hired guns," brought in to buttress a particular tale. A policy's advocates may commission research that allows them to point with pride at evidence of their policy's success, while the policy's opponents may present their own research suggesting the policy's shortcomings. Not surprisingly, then, evaluation research often fails to gain acceptance as the authoritative, impartial, last word on a policy's impact.

The knowledge that evaluators may design research that seems to affirm their prejudices sometimes leads to efforts to devise special high-status, impartial bodies to evaluate policies and issue recommendations. At the highest level, the president and/or Congress often appoint national **commissions**; and state or local authorities may appoint similar bodies (Zegart, 2004). The commission members tend to be visible figures known for their integrity and chosen to represent a range of interest groups (for instance, leaders from business, labor, law, the media, and religion; members from both political parties; males as well as females; individuals from different regions and ethnic groups; and so on). In other words, the commissioners are meant to represent a broad range of those concerned with the policy. Such "blue ribbon" commissions may be appointed with great fanfare with the expectation that the commission's findings will also be well publicized, accepted as authoritative, and used to guide future policy.

Of course, selecting commissioners who already hold important positions and lead busy lives means that they will have difficulty devoting much time to the commission's work. The actual work

Box 9.5 A Tale of Two Pornography Commissions

During the 1960s, appellate courts began striking down laws against pornography on First Amendment grounds. In 1968, President Lyndon Johnson (a Democrat) appointed a national Commission on Obscenity and Pornography to recommend changes in pornography policy that would pass constitutional challenges. The commission's members included lawyers, social scientists, members of the media, and representatives of organized religion; in addition, three commission members had been active in antipornography campaigns.

The commission sponsored a great deal of research that generally failed to demonstrate that pornography caused significant harms. In 1970 it released its report, which concluded that most restrictions on pornography were unnecessary. The three antiporn members of the commission openly criticized the report, and both Richard Nixon (a Republican who had since become president) and Congress repudiated the report's recommendations.

In 1985, during Republican Ronald Reagan's second term, his attorney general established a new Commission on Pornography to recommend effective ways of constraining the spread of pornography. Critics charged that this commission was stacked with conservatives who would advocate tighter restrictions, and its report (released in 1986) met those expectations. By this time, however, most adult movie theaters had been replaced by pornographic videos, so pornography was less publicly visible, and this commission also failed to have much impact on social policy. Like its predecessor, the second commission attracted public attention but failed to redirect policy (Hawkins & Zimring, 1988).

tends to fall upon the less well-known staff members, who assemble evidence about the policy's workings and guide the commissioners in making their recommendations. Moreover, a commission's recommendations may prove unpopular (see Box 9.5). Commissions tend to be appointed precisely because an issue is seen as divisive, so it is almost inevitable that whatever is recommended will prove controversial. Although commission recommendations sometimes receive considerable media coverage, they often fail to lead to the significant policy changes that the commission hoped to achieve.

One other category of actors who play an important role in evaluating policy outcomes deserves attention: the *appellate courts* (see also Chapter 7). Policymaking often involves creating new laws, and social problems work often leads to legal actions. In turn, the people who find themselves targeted by new social policies can appeal their cases to higher courts. These appellate courts may rule on the constitutionality of the policies, affirming some, striking down others, and clarifying still others. In the United States, a bill passed by legislators and signed into law by a president (in the case of federal legislation) or a governor (in the case of state legislation) may be modified—even ruled illegal—by appellate courts. Such court rulings may reject the policy itself, or the ways in which social problems workers implement that policy. This power makes courts important players in shaping policy outcomes.

Legislators are supposed to represent the popular will (recall Chapter 7's discussion of the various pressures they face), while courts are intended to provide a check on legislative enthusiasm. This means that even the most successful claimsmaking campaigns—those that elicit media coverage, mobilize public concern, and see their claims translated into new policies—may be constrained or rejected by the courts. For example, legislators often promote laws against burning the American flag, laws that have considerable vote-getting appeal (Welch, 2000). However, the courts have tended to recognize flag burning as protest, a form of political speech, protected under the First Amendment. Similarly, courts often constrain overly broad interpretations of new policies, restricting the grounds for defining, say, hate crimes (Jenness & Grattet, 2001) or sexual harassment (Saguy, 2003). The courts' rulings, in turn, may be denounced, constructed as new troubling conditions by assorted claimsmakers, media workers, policymakers, or social problems workers.

In sum, courts, like evaluation researchers and commissions, are often seen as failing to resolve debates over policy outcomes. However much we might like to imagine that an impartial interpretation will resolve people's differences in policy debates, such solutions prove elusive. People continue to disagree about which policies can best address troubling conditions.

IDEOLOGICAL PREDISPOSITIONS

As we have seen in this chapter, there are many possible bases for criticizing how social policies are being implemented, as well as many types of people who might be moved to offer such critiques. From this we might conclude that all sorts of debates over policies are theoretically possible, but in fact, many policy discussions take fairly predictable forms.

Key to many policy debates is **ideology**. Within contemporary America, many people—including activists, experts, media workers, members of the general public, policymakers, and social problems workers—can locate themselves on a political spectrum that is understood to run from left to right—that is, from those who have relatively liberal views to those who hold relatively conservative views. Precisely how individuals construct this ideological spectrum varies: just as conservatives may lump together people who variously think of themselves as liberals, progressives, or radicals, and who recognize these as important distinctions; liberals may not appreciate the range of positions among those on the right.

In general, however, when discussing social problems, those on the left tend to emphasize the importance of equality and worry that society discriminates too much on the basis of race, class, and gender; they favor social policies that promote equality and dis-

courage discrimination. And in general, those on the right emphasize the importance of liberty and social order; they worry that
excessive social policies may constrain liberty and, in the process,
damage overall societal well-being. Of course, these are questions
of emphasis: few Americans would denounce either equality or liberty, yet they may disagree about their relative importance, or the
best ways to achieve these values in particular situations.

This means that debates over social policies often break down
into those favoring a more liberal position opposed to those favoring a more conservative stance. Each ideological side has its own
activists in social movement organizations, think tanks filled with
experts, media commentators, and policymaking politicians; the
same people tend to find themselves allied over a range of policy
debates. In fact, when individuals thought to be associated with a
particular side break ranks on an issue and agree with those they
usually oppose, the split is considered remarkable, something worth
mentioning. Thus, when discussions about a particular policy outcome begin, it is often possible to predict who will line up on which
side of the issue.

Not all ideologies fit neatly on the familiar liberal–conservative
continuum. Think of libertarianism (usually viewed as a form of
conservatism, but one that leads to what are typically thought of
as liberal positions on issues related to drug use or sexual behavior), various religious doctrines (which can vary a great deal,
depending on the theological interpretations being advanced), or
feminism (which is centrally concerned with improving women's
place in society). In addition, there are professional ideologies; professions have distinctive views of troubling conditions and how they
ought to be addressed. For example, recall Chapter 4's discussion
of medicalization: medical authorities tend to favor constructing
troubling conditions as medical problems that ought to be solved
through medical solutions.

Ideologies are not unrelated to *interests*. Ideologies allow individuals to appeal to principles, such as equality, liberty, or women's

rights, to argue that these values *should* guide how society responds to troubling conditions (for example, a liberal might criticize a particular social policy because it fails to alleviate the inequalities at the root of the troubling condition, and a conservative policy critique might focus on how the policy unreasonably constrains people's liberty). In other words, ideologies allow their adherents to construct principled arguments, to claim that this is the right thing to do because it is consistent with a particular value. At the same time, people frequently adopt ideologies that support their interests (for example, a large share of feminists are women whose interests the ideology advances, just as medical authorities often stand to benefit from medicalizing troubling conditions). The link between ideology and interest creates rhetorical opportunities for those who oppose a particular ideology: they can charge that proponents of a particular claim may be motivated less by a principled sense of what is right than by their self-interest, by the advantages they stand to gain if their claims succeed.

The tendency for ideological critiques to invoke values creates a range of questions that might be addressed in policy debates. On the one hand, critics can focus on practical questions: Is the policy effective? Does it do what we want it to do? Does it work better or cost less than alternative policies? On the other hand, critics can emphasize principles: Is this policy consistent with important values? Is it morally sound? Is it the sort of thing we ought to be doing? Policy debates often conflate these two approaches, so that opponents denounce one another's practical claims for being unprincipled, while rejecting the opposition's principled claims as impractical. Of course, an inability to agree on the questions that ought to be asked virtually guarantees that people will be unable to agree on the answers.

Ideologies, then, can be seen as predisposing how people may respond to policy outcomes. When people are allied with particular ideological stances—whether of a political, professional, or other nature—it is often possible to predict how they will respond to a particular social policy. Those whose ideology led them to favor the policy in the first place are likely to claim that any shortcomings are due to the policy's being insufficient, and to argue for expanding or extending the policy to make up this shortfall. In contrast, those who stood ideologically opposed to the initial policy are more likely to claim that the policy is excessive or misguided, that it needs to be cut back or redirected. Although ideologies do not control how everyone approaches policy outcomes, they often shape the responses of at least some participants in the discussions.

Once again we see the subjective nature of the social problems process. Just as claimsmakers must construct troubling conditions so that people become concerned enough to do something, and just as policymakers and social problems workers must construct practical responses to that concern, so, too, must critics devise interpretations of the workings of policies. They may decide that a policy is a great success (remember granting women the vote; no one now advocates disenfranchising women), or they may decide that it works pretty well and just needs a bit of fine-tuning (maybe we ought to install another traffic light at that dangerous intersection). Or, of course, some people may argue that the policy isn't working all that well and that we ought to do significantly more, or maybe a lot less, or perhaps something completely different. At the stage of policy outcomes, the social problems process comes to an end—unless it inspires an entirely new round of claimsmaking.

MAKING CONNECTIONS

• *Policy outcomes are reactions to policies after they have been implemented by social problems workers. However, as this chapter and the following chapter explain, the social problems process is cyclical, so policy outcomes become the basis for new claims.*

- *Social problems workers can become compelling critics of policies. As Chapter 8 explained, they understand how social problems work is actually practiced and see policy flaws firsthand.*

- *Both activists and experts frequently use typifying examples (discussed in Chapter 2) to make new claims that criticize policies.*

CASE STUDY
Evaluating the Impact of Welfare Reform

In 1996, the federal government enacted the Personal Responsibility and Work Opportunity Reconciliation Act (PRWORA), a law that promised to "end welfare as we know it." Welfare programs that provided support to those in need had long been controversial. Critics argued that welfare had created a culture of long-term dependency, in which individuals found they could make more money remaining on welfare than they might earn from available jobs (Murray, 1994). Certainly this was not true for the many welfare recipients who had begun receiving benefits following a personal crisis such as a debilitating illness or divorce, but who soon left the welfare rolls. However, some individuals remained on welfare for years, and their children also became welfare recipients when they reached adulthood or began having children of their own. It was the prospect of long-term, intergenerational dependency that made welfare especially controversial.

PRWORA promised to end this cycle of long-term dependency. In particular, the law stipulated a lifetime limit for most recipients of no more than sixty months of cash assistance from federal funds, and it required recipients to work after receiving two years of cash assistance. Critics of welfare predicted that the reforms would not only get people off welfare, but also help them find dignity in work and encourage them to aspire to better lives. The critics of welfare reform offered a less rosy picture: welfare, they argued, was necessary because society simply didn't offer enough opportunities for decent employment; they foresaw an increase in poverty and homelessness once people lost the welfare benefits upon which they depended.

The debate over welfare policy was heated, and both PRWORA's supporters and its opponents made straightforward predictions—the former that the policy would succeed, the latter that it would fail. This debate ensured that the policy's outcomes would receive close attention. Not surprisingly, when they evaluated PRWORA's workings, both groups claimed to find evidence to support their views.

Before considering the rival constructions of PRWORA's outcomes, it is important to understand the economic and political context within which the policy took effect. The late 1990s were years of economic prosperity; the economy was booming and unemployment was low. So, during the period the program took effect, it was relatively easier for people moving off welfare rolls to find jobs. This economic context was significant because, on average, welfare recipients have less education and less work experience than other job applicants have, and when employment opportunities are scarce, they have more difficulty finding jobs. In addition, following the 1994 election, Republicans controlled Congress; and beginning in 2001, of course, the president was also a Republican. Because Republicans had long been critical of welfare dependency, leaders in both Congress and the White House hoped to find evidence that PRWORA worked.

In fact, after the new policy had been in effect for five years, its supporters could point to evidence suggesting that PRWORA had succeeded (Hymowitz, 2006). The number of households receiving assistance fell dramatically—from about 5.1 million in 1994 receiving AFDC (Aid to Families with Dependent Children—the welfare program that had drawn the most criticism), to about 2 million in 2001 (sixty months after PRWORA took effect). (Under welfare reform, AFDC had been renamed by this point; it was now TANF—Temporary Assistance for Needy Families.) The proportion of single mothers who were working rose, and the proportion of births to single mothers grew much less rapidly under the new policy (suggesting that, without the prospect of welfare support, young, single women were more reluctant to bear children). All of this suggested that welfare reform had discouraged people from becoming and remaining dependent on welfare, and had encouraged them to join the workforce. Republicans pronounced the policy a success, and some called for further reforms to make welfare even more difficult to obtain.

However, 2001 also marked an economic turning point; the long boom of the 1990s was followed by a recession, when jobs were tougher to obtain. Unemployment began to rise, and PRWORA's critics could point to their own troubling statistical evidence. For instance, although the percentage of children living in poverty had fallen from 20.5 percent in 1996 to 16.2 percent in 2000, it was beginning to creep back up, and it reached 17.8 percent in 2004 (DeNavas-Walt, Proctor, & Lee, 2005, p. 52). Similarly, the number of Americans who lacked health insurance coverage, which had been below 40 million in 2000, climbed to nearly 46 million by 2004 (p. 60). Welfare reform, the critics charged, had created holes in society's safety net; former welfare recipients may have been working, but many of them remained poor and vulnerable (Eckholm, 2006).

In a sense, when PRWORA's advocates looked at the program's outcomes they saw a half-full glass, but when welfare reform's critics assessed those same outcomes they viewed the glass as half-empty. In part, these different assessments reflected different constructions of the problem that welfare ought to address. The proponents of welfare reform focused on what they saw as a self-perpetuating culture of dependency: welfare, they argued, encouraged people to settle for marginal existence; being required to work would lead former recipients to a better life marked by higher incomes, better self-esteem, more stable families, and more children in the next generation pursuing the American dream. From this perspective, just getting people off welfare was an important accomplishment.

In contrast, the critics of welfare reform tended to define the problem as one of poverty and inequality. Limited opportunities and racism made it too difficult for some Americans to attain a decent standard of living, and welfare provided essential support for those who needed help. PRWORA might push former welfare recipients into the workforce, but given their limited educations and work histories, many would find themselves taking jobs that paid poorly and didn't provide health insurance, so they would remain trapped in poverty. In this view, welfare reform had ignored the real problems that needed attention.

The continuing debate over welfare reform illustrates how policy outcomes are themselves social constructions. Even when everyone can agree on what the evidence says—and both welfare reform's proponents and its critics generally accepted the government's statistics about poverty, employment, and so on—they may not agree on what that evidence means. Whether one views a policy's workings as a success or a failure depends on how the problems to be solved are understood.

QUESTIONS

1. What were the goals of welfare reform?

2. How did opponents' and supporters' evaluations of the new welfare policy differ after five years?

3. Why were the two groups able to construct different conclusions from the same evidence?

10

Claims across Space and Time

The previous chapters have traced a six-stage social problems process from (1) the initial claimsmaking, through (2) media coverage, (3) public reaction, and (4) policymaking, and on to (5) the social problems work that implements the policy, followed by (6) policy outcomes. This sequence of stages should be seen as the natural history that a typical social problem might follow. To be sure, not every social problem fits the pattern exactly. Most important, many claims fail: they don't attract media attention, or they don't lead to public concern, or they don't lead to policy changes, or the policies are never implemented. The model sequence that has guided this book depicts a successful campaign to draw attention to a particular troubling condition and to get the larger society to try to do something about it. Many claims may follow different trajectories, but the model remains a useful framework for understanding the course taken by those claims that have the greatest impact.

There are, however, additional complexities that require some attention. Thus far, we have been thinking about social problems one at a time: here is how the U.S. Bureau of Narcotics constructed marijuana as a social problem in the 1930s, here is how today's authorities are constructing the crystal meth problem, and so on. Such **case studies** are useful, but it seems obvious that the marijuana and crystal meth cases might have some important features in common, even though they occurred decades apart. After all, both cases involve claims that a particular drug is harmful and ought to be prohibited. This similarity raises important questions: Are such drug problems constructed completely independently; that is, does each set of claimsmakers start from scratch in assembling its claims, and do policymakers adopt a fresh approach each time they encounter claims about a new drug problem? Or are there underlying similarities in the way drug problems and drug policies are constructed, and if so, what are they, and why do they occur? Does the history of previous claims about drugs affect current claimsmaking? Do claims about similar troubling conditions always take the same form, or are they affected by the social circumstances in which they emerge?

This chapter explores some of these issues; in particular, it considers how claims vary from place to place, and from time to time. It begins with comparative research, in which analysts compare what happens when claimsmakers raise claims about the same troubling condition in different places—in different cities, or in different countries. Then it examines diffusion, the way claims spread from one place to another. The third section of the chapter asks how claims evolve over time; it explores apparently cyclical claims—issues that attract considerable attention for a time, then fade from notice, only to be revived in a new wave of claimsmaking. The chapter concludes with a discussion of progress: claimsmakers tend to emphasize that things are getting worse, but is envisioning societal decay the best framework for thinking about social problems?

COMPARISON

Usually sociologists who study the construction of social problems conduct case studies. That is, they examine one instance, one case of the social problems process—how and why a particular problem was constructed in a given place at a given time. In fact, many studies focus on specific aspects of a particular case, so different analyses of the same case might consider, for example, just how the claims' rhetoric was assembled to make a persuasive argument, who made those claims, or how the media covered the topic.

The main advantage of the case study is that it permits a careful, detailed analysis of how one particular instance of the social problems process developed. Most of the points raised in the earlier chapters of this book are the product of sociologists' case studies, and a large share of the sources cited in this volume's references present such case studies. But case studies have a major disadvantage: there is no way of knowing whether the case being studied is fairly typical or quite unusual. Throughout this book we have been discussing things that can happen during the construction of social problems. When we first diagrammed the social problems process in Figure 1.1, the picture seemed simple and straightforward. But later chapters featured more detailed, more complicated diagrams of the various stages in the social problems process. These complications reveal that not all social problems follow exactly the same trajectory; there are important differences in how social problems can develop, so the particular case being studied may not always be all that typical.

The simplest way to study such differences is to compare two cases that we might expect to be fairly similar. For example, Cynthia Bogard (2003) examined how the problem of homelessness was constructed in two major American cities—New York City and Washington, D.C.—during the early 1980s. She found important differences. In Washington, activists—a self-styled group of "Christian anarchists"—promoted homelessness as a moral issue; they devised clever protests designed to attract media attention (in a city filled with media workers), and they sought to involve nationally prominent politicians in the issue. While acknowledging that many homeless individuals were troubled by mental illness or substance abuse, the Washington activists constructed the homeless as rational figures, who would stop living on the streets if only they had access to safe, nonintrusive shelters. In contrast, in New York City the issue of homelessness centered around a struggle between city and state officials over who ought to be held responsible for the condition—and pay the costs of fixing it. The state blamed the city for encouraging gentrification that had eliminated low-cost housing units and thereby had made their former residents homeless; the city, on the other hand, insisted that many of the homeless were seriously mentally ill individuals who now found themselves on the streets after the state had closed many of its mental hospitals. In New York, the homeless were typified as incapable of caring for themselves, and as a threat to public order. In short, the two cities featured different claimsmakers, with different interests, who constructed the homelessness problem in different ways.

Bogard's study shows that, even in dealing with the same problem during the same years, the social problems process can develop in different ways—with different claims made by different claimsmakers leading to different policies. There are all sorts of possible bases for making such comparisons:

- *Geography*. Bogard compared the social problems process in two cities, but it is possible to compare other geographic entities. Most obviously, analysts can compare how the same troubling condition is addressed in two or more countries (Best, 2001b).

- *Time*. Many social conditions have been around for a long time, so it is possible to compare two or more efforts to construct the same social problem in the same place during different times. For example, Philip Jenkins (2000) has compared different anti-cult campaigns in American history (his analysis is discussed later in this chapter).

- *Similar conditions*. Some troubling conditions are understood to belong to the same category of social problems, so the basis for comparison seems obvious. For example, Reinarman (1994) describes similarities among the ways that different drugs are constructed as social problems.

- *Similar constructions.* Sometimes analysts compare problems that seem to be constructed with similar claimsmaking rhetoric. For instance, Best (1999) compared freeway shootings, stalking, and other crimes characterized as "random violence," as well as how claimsmakers constructed different problems that involved "victimization."

- *Other bases for comparison.* Analysts might compare different campaigns by the same claimsmakers (for instance, examining how feminists—or medical authorities—construct various social problems), how different media construct the same problem, and so on. The bases for comparison are limited only by the analysts' imagination.

Figure 10.1 illustrates some of these forms of comparison among social problems processes. The top of the figure displays one six-stage social problems process (for a particular problem—call it Problem X). The same process is shown in reduced size at the center of the figure, where it is surrounded by other social problems processes that suggest various bases for comparison between the construction of Problem X and the construction of other social problems. Note that it is not necessary to compare the entire sequences of stages in two social problems processes; a sociologist might focus on comparing particular, even very narrowly defined topics (such as the use of statistics in two claimsmaking campaigns).

Comparison is a powerful method of analysis because it can help us discover both underlying similarities and unexpected differences. People involved in the social problems process sometimes assume that things have to be the way they are; they take it for granted that the problem pretty much has to be constructed in the terms with which they're familiar. One of the most important lessons from

Figure 10.1 BASES FOR COMPARISON AMONG SOCIAL PROBLEMS PROCESSES

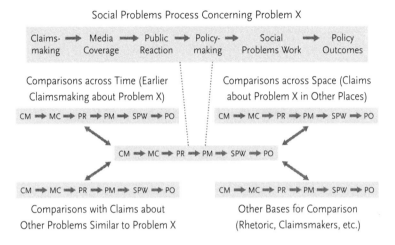

Social Problems Process Concerning Problem X

comparing social problems processes is that whatever we understand about social problems is a product of people's choices, that people—claimsmakers, media workers, policymakers, social problems workers, and so on—have chosen to highlight some aspects of a troubling condition while downplaying others. It can be hard to notice what those people have ignored, but comparisons often can help us recognize that choices were made, and to ask how and why those proved to be the favored choices.

Consider the issue of sexual harassment. Americans take it for granted that sexual harassment is a type of gender discrimination, and that it should be defined broadly to encompass not only demands for sexual favors but also inappropriate joking and other behaviors that create a "hostile environment" (Saguy, 2003). In France, however, sexual harassment has been defined not only more narrowly (encompassing only demands for sex), but also very differently (as sexual violence involving the abuse of hierarchical authority). These different definitions evolved through different processes: in the United States, court rulings gradually established the domain of sexual harassment; in France, courts cannot establish the law, so an act of Parliament was required—which was important because policymakers had to find a legislative consensus, and there was not enough support for a broader definition of what constituted sexual harassment. Press coverage also differed in the two countries. The American press devoted a large share of its coverage to scandals—claims implicating prominent politicians in sexual harassment. In contrast, considerable French media coverage focused on the "excesses" of *Americans'* treatment of sexual harassment; commentators argued that France should avoid copying the Americans' example. In other words, there were numerous differences in how sexual harassment was constructed in the two nations.

Comparative studies often reveal such differences in how social problems are constructed, even when we might imagine that the issue would have to be constructed in the same way. If cell phones pose a threat of exposure to radioactivity, as some claimsmakers suggest, presumably the physical processes that produce those risks ought to be the same everywhere, exposing cell phone users throughout the world to the same dangers. Yet different countries construct health risks from cell phones in very different ways (see Box 10.1). Comparative analyses, then, can expose the social processes that underpin the construction of even physical threats. Risks of radioactivity—usually thought of as understandable in terms of physics and biology—are socially constructed, as are all other social problems. Comparative research can help make such social processes visible.

DIFFUSION

Comparative studies reveal that the social problems process can lead to different outcomes in different places: two countries may

Box 10.1 New Technologies in Europe and the United States

New technologies sometimes become targets of claimsmaking consisting of warnings that the new change poses a threat of some sort and ought to be controlled through social policies. Such claims can show surprising variation from country to country.

For example, as cellular phones have spread rapidly in recent years, there have been warnings that they may pose a health risk. Americans are most familiar with claims that cell phones may cause brain tumors (the theory being that holding the phone next to the head exposes the brain to radiation that, in turn, leads to cancer). Europeans discount this concern, yet they worry about the risks of microwaves broadcast from cell phone towers. Some European countries regulate how far towers must be located away from schools; in the United States, however, these towers are rarely seen as a health risk. Presumably, if radiation or microwave exposure endangers health, Europeans and Americans would be exposed to the same dangers, yet claimsmakers on the two continents construct the problem differently (Burgess, 2004).

Food safety policies show a similar difference. Europeans irradiate food—which they view as a safe means of reducing food-borne disease, yet the United States has long resisted food irradiation (which some Americans mistakenly assume makes food radioactive). On the other hand, Americans have adopted genetically engineered food with relatively little fuss, while Europeans worried about "frankenfoods" have sought to block genetically engineered foods (Schurman, 2004).

In short, suspicions of the same technologies can and do take different forms in different places.

construct a given problem in much the same way; or they may construct that problem in rather—sometimes dramatically—different terms; or one country may define the troubling condition as a big deal, while the other may dismiss it as unworthy of concern. However, it is especially interesting when a problem attracts attention in different places at about the same time. Although it is possible that the social problems processes in different countries are completely independent, unrelated to one another, another possibility is that claims have spread from one country to another, and we can study this process (Best, 2001b).

Diffusion is the term used by social scientists to describe the spread of innovations. New things—new ideas, new inventions, and so on—emerge in particular places, but then they spread from one group to another. If one group figures out a better way to, say, make arrowheads, that group's neighbors may copy or adopt the method for their own benefit. The process of diffusion involves sources, or **transmitters**, passing the innovation along to **adopters**. Successful innovations can spread across many societies and over thousands of miles.

Diffusion can occur in the case of social problems claims. A claim may originate in a particular town, region, or country but then spread to other places. Not all claims experience diffusion, and of those that do spread, some travel farther and more widely than others. What accounts for these differences?

All social problems claims argue that a particular condition exists and that it is troubling. Successful diffusion of a claim requires that adopters accept that these basic ideas apply to the adopters' setting—their community or nation. Certainly diffusion requires accepting the notion that the condition exists; a society whose members doubt the existence of a condition is unlikely to be receptive to claims about that problem. For instance, being worried about witches requires that people believe in witches; regardless of how worried about witches a society of believers may become, they will find it hard to spread their concern to a society of nonbelievers. Similarly, the condition must be seen as troubling: a society with a traditional aristocracy might view a decline in deference as quite troubling, but their claims probably would have little appeal for members of democratic societies, who might agree that the condition exists but view this as a cause for celebration rather than concern.

For a claim to spread from one society to another, then, potential adopters of the claim must come from cultures and social structures that allow them to recognize both that their society has the condition about which claims are being made, and that that condition is troubling. This means that claims are less likely to spread to societies very different from those in which the claims originated. In particular, adopters need to view their society as similar to the society where the claims originated (Strang & Meyer, 1993). When similarities are harder to recognize, diffusion becomes less likely.

For example, it is easier for social problems claims to spread among countries with a common language and interwoven histories. In recent decades, many successful claimsmaking campaigns have originated in the United States and then spread to England, Australia, and Canada (for instance, concerns about satanic ritual abuse traveled from the United States to all three other English-speaking countries). In addition, claims that originated in those countries have traveled to the United States (concern about both bullying and road rage, for example, spread from Britain to the United States) (Best, 2001b). On the other hand, American constructions of social problems often meet resistance in France; French media tend to criticize American policies and present alternative constructions for social issues such as sexual harassment or immigration (Benson & Saguy, 2005).

Diffusion must occur through channels; that is, there need to be links, connections between potential transmitters and prospective adopters. Theorists of diffusion make an analytic distinction between **relational channels** involving interpersonal contact between transmitters and adopters, and **nonrelational channels**, such as mass media, that do not involve personal ties (McAdam & Rucht, 1993). In practice, the diffusion of claims usually combines both relational and nonrelational channels. Through informal ties (such as acquaintanceship) and more formal ties (such as memberships in the same professional organizations), people in different countries get to know one another well enough to establish relational channels: this person got to know foreigners while attending school abroad; these folks met at international conferences for police officers, or social workers, or whatever.

At the same time, information about social problems flows through nonrelational channels—through the press and entertainment media, through books and news broadcasts and the Internet. Relational and nonrelational channels are mutually reinforcing. Once again, it should be clear that a common language makes it easier for diffusion to occur through both sorts of channels. Translating claims into another tongue takes time; claims can travel faster when transmitters and adopters share a language.

All diffusion ultimately depends on the actors in the process— the transmitters and, especially, the adopters. Transmitters may make deliberate efforts to disseminate social problems claims to other countries. Drawing attention to troubling conditions is, of course, central to social problems claimsmaking, and some claimsmakers explicitly seek to spread their message to other nations. This is particularly true when claims depict large-scale, even global problems, such as population growth, ecological degradation, or economic globalization. Such claimsmakers become missionaries, seeking to spread their message abroad, through both relational and nonrelational channels. International social movements, for example, offer a way of spreading claims about troubling conditions to countries that might be expected to resist those claims (see Box 10.2).

In other cases, transmitters are more passive; their concern may be limited to their own country, even to a particular locality; they make no effort to promote the diffusion of their claims. Still, their claims may reach other countries, particularly via such nonrelational channels as media coverage, professional publications, and the like. Nonetheless, the key actors in diffusion are adopters.

Box 10.2 NATIONAL DIFFERENCES IN THE DIFFUSION OF LAWS AGAINST FEMALE GENITAL CUTTING

Female genital cutting (FGC)—removal of part or all of the clitoris—is widely practiced in several African countries. Feminists and international organizations began speaking out against the practice in the late 1970s, and international pressure has led most countries to adopt policies intended to end the practice (Boyle, Songora, & Foss, 2001).

The United States passed a law against FGC in 1996, but the issue attracted only minimal attention because the practice was unfamiliar to most Americans. The situation was very different in Egypt, however, where an estimated 97 percent of women have been circumcised, and where polls show that a substantial majority of women support the practice. On the one hand, the Egyptian government, which was concerned about the nation's international standing, found itself under pressure to adopt anti-FGC policies (the United States, for example, threatened to limit foreign aid to countries without laws against FGC); on the other hand, there was considerable popular support for maintaining the practice. The Egyptian government struggled to devise policies that give the appearance of compliance with international expectations, yet minimize popular opposition. In practice, this meant that FGC continued, although an Egyptian anti-FGC movement has emerged that presses for further change.

In contrast, the government of Tanzania—an ethnically diverse country that included groups that both did and did not practice FGC—used the international consensus that FGC was wrong to justify making the practice illegal. There is evidence that the practice began losing support under the new policy.

The impact of international efforts to spread claims and policies will depend on national differences. Changes that are uncontroversial in some nations may be bitterly resisted in others.

Prospective adopters must define conditions in their society as sufficiently like those depicted in the transmitters' claims before they will join in spreading those claims.

Of course, societies have differences as well as similarities. There are likely to be both cultural differences (that is, people in the transmitting society and those in the prospective adopting society are likely to construct the world in at least somewhat different terms), as well as differences in social arrangements (such as different legal or educational systems). Such differences are potential obstacles to diffusion; they make it easier for prospective adopters to conclude that a particular claim is not really applicable to their society. For example, tobacco smoking is much more common among males in Japan than in the United States or western Europe (Ayukawa, 2001). Whereas other countries' governments have launched vigorous public health campaigns to reduce smoking, Japan has been slower to take such actions. Why? In Japan, the government controls tobacco distribution and derives considerable revenue from smokers. Also it is hard to mobilize social movements in Japan to campaign against government interests. What is—and what is not—considered a social problem depends on a society's culture and social structure.

Therefore, diffusion is easier when claims are phrased in relatively abstract or theoretical language. **Theorization** is the presentation of claims that emphasize general, abstract principles and arguments: for instance, claimsmakers might describe sexism generally in terms of male, or patriarchal, domination rather than in terms of specific discriminatory practices; the former construction offers a general principle that might be detected at work in many different social settings, whereas the latter may seem applicable only in countries where those particular practices are common—and seen as troubling (Strang & Meyer, 1993). Theorization abstracts and simplifies. In the case of social problems claims, theorization smooths out the argument. It reduces specifics of limited, local relevance and rephrases the claim in broader, more general terms that make it more widely acceptable. The theoretical becomes significant; the practical, less important. Thus, a theorized claim is more easily spread to new societies, where it can be reformulated to take local culture and social structure into account.

As a result, claims about the same social problem often take somewhat different forms, depending on the social arrangements in different societies. In some cases, differences in social arrangements may make it hard for claims to travel successfully. In recent years, for example, British claimsmakers have focused on various types of bullying—not just bullying in schools, but also bullying in other settings, including the workplace (Furedi, 2001). The British campaign against workplace bullying received considerable support from that country's powerful trade unions. In contrast, efforts to construct workplace bullying as a problem in the United States (where unions are less influential) have been markedly less successful. The abstract—and already familiar—problem of bullying (particularly among children) spread easily, but the more specific construction of workplace bullying did not. Similarly, the abortion issue evolved differently in the United States and Britain (Lee, 2003). British law has long regarded abortion as a medical matter, subject to physicians' authority, but Americans have come to view it as a question of rights (see Box 10.3).

Contemporary commentators argue that globalization has become a central concept for understanding the world. Countries are increasingly linked through trade, rapid transportation, and essentially instantaneous communications. Money and jobs—but also ideas—flow more freely across international borders. This means that the future is likely to feature even more diffusion of social problems claims. In part, this is because some claimsmakers seek to construct global issues such as global warming or terrorism. In part, it is because some troubling conditions, such as epidemic disease, may start in one corner of the world, yet spread

Box 10.3 Postabortion Syndrome Travels to Britain

Arguments in favor of abortion rights tend to focus on the woman's rights or well-being. During the 1980s, abortion opponents advanced claims that abortion harmed women, that many women experienced mental health problems following abortion; these claimsmakers labeled these effects as *postabortion syndrome* (PAS) (Lee, 2003).

Within the United States there was a brief but intense controversy. The U.S. surgeon general held a formal inquiry into the health effects of abortion, but failed to issue a report. In addition, various professional bodies, including the American Psychological Association and the American Psychiatric Association made public statements arguing that PAS was not a significant problem.

In the early 1990s, somewhat after the American controversy faded, PAS claims emerged in Britain. Prominent American PAS activists traveled to Britain and met with antiabortion advocates, who in turn established their own investigative commission that warned against PAS. However, British law gives physicians control of abortion; abortion is not viewed as a right, but as a medical matter. The British medical establishment largely ignored the commission's report, and the concern with PAS never found its way into policymaking.

The diffusion of PAS illustrates that, although it is possible to spread claims, the reaction—or lack of reaction—will depend on the prospective adopters' culture and social structure. Changing abortion policy in Britain requires changing medical professionals' views, not simply making claims in public arenas.

great distances. In addition to these considerations, however, improved communications (such as the World Wide Web) give people around the world access to claims made in distant places, and at least some of those claims will be theorized in terms that make it easier for them to spread.

CYCLES IN CLAIMSMAKING

Early in the social problems process, it is very common for claims-making rhetoric to describe a troubling condition as new, or at least as deserving new concern because the condition is growing much worse. After the issue begins to attract more attention and people want to know more about it, there may be an effort to trace the troubling condition's history. For instance, claims about child abuse might include brief historical accounts stating that although adults have abused children for centuries, we now know better; or a history of poverty might argue that previous efforts to eliminate poverty have been misguided, and that a totally new approach is needed. Still, claimsmakers tend to focus most intensely on the troubling condition's current manifestations rather than its distant past. Most claims concentrate on the present situation and pay relatively little attention to the past.

This narrow focus is unfortunate because careful study of the history of a social issue can often place today's claims within an illuminating context. In particular, many troubling conditions are the focus of *cycles* of concern. That is, a troubling condition may become the focus of intense claimsmaking, then slip out of the spotlight for a while before returning as the focus of renewed attention.

A cycle of concern begins when a troubling condition that has been receiving little attention becomes the subject of claimsmaking (Downs, 1972). As a result, concern increases until it reaches a peak, then interest falls off once more, until the topic is again attracting little notice. This cycle is another way of thinking about the social problems process: attention increases as claimsmakers, media, the public, policymakers, and social problems workers become involved. But why does interest decline? Why doesn't it remain high? Why are there cycles of concern?

Part of the answer is that the social problems process values novelty. Claims that seem new or fresh compete more easily in the social problems marketplace to attract attention from the media, the public, and policymakers. This is why claimsmakers who come to own particular issues find it necessary to constantly update and repackage their claims (as discussed in Chapter 3). But even when claimsmakers work to keep an issue visible, they find themselves at an increasing disadvantage because other, competing claims that seek to draw attention to topics that have been neglected are likely to seem more novel. The fact that a particular claim has been occupying center stage for a while begins to make other claims seem fresher, more interesting, particularly to the media, which depend so heavily on presenting novel material. In addition, as noted in Chapters 8 and 9, once the social problems process reaches the stage of social problems work, there is likely to be some disillusionment. Very often the policies touted as the solution to the problem haven't really solved things; instead, the troubling condition endures, and people begin losing their enthusiasm for those policies.

All of this means that, however successful claimsmakers have been in managing to raise concern about a particular troubling condition, that concern eventually is likely to decline, so the issue moves out of the limelight. However, that need not be the end of the matter; once enough time has passed, the previous wave of concern is likely to be forgotten, thanks to all of the competing claimsmaking campaigns that have captured the attention of the social problems marketplace in the meantime. Conditions may once more become ripe for drawing attention to what now again seems to be a neglected topic. Therefore, we should not be surprised to discover that the histories of many social problems display sequential waves of concern interspersed with periods when the topic receives relatively little attention.

For example, consider three waves of intense concern about delinquent gangs—youth gangs—in twentieth-century America. The first began in the 1920s, the second in the 1950s, and the third in the 1980s. Each period was marked by warnings that today's gangs were much worse—larger, better organized, more dangerous—than gangs in previous eras. Each wave featured claimsmaking by experts, such as sociologists, psychiatrists, and criminologists; each became the subject of both sensational news coverage and popular cultural depictions of gangs. Nor did these waves begin in the twentieth century; waves of concern about gangs date back to the 1840s in U.S. cities, and to the eighteenth century in London (Pearson, 1983).

We can spot similar sequential waves of concern regarding many other issues. The historian Philip Jenkins has described the oscillating attention given to the sexual exploitation of children (Jenkins, 1998) and to cults (Jenkins, 2000) (see Box 10.4). The pattern turns up in surprising places; for example, Christian theologians periodically turn their attention to claims that there are "hidden gospels"—ancient manuscripts that were suppressed by religious authorities because they reveal that Christ's true message was antithetical to what the established church now endorses (Jenkins, 2001).

In each of these cases, a new set of claims attracts a great deal of attention for a time, but then concern begins to dissipate. When claimsmaking on the topic revives, usually people pay little attention to the previous wave of concern. The older set of claims—and the intense concern it generated—is often forgotten, as a new generation of claimsmakers reinvents the wheel. Even if the earlier claims are recalled, they tend to be dismissed: those people in the "good old days" may have thought they had a gang problem, but their gangs were nothing compared to ours.

What accounts for these waves of concern? One possibility, of course, is that the troubling conditions criticized by claimsmakers become more or less common over time, and claimsmaking merely tracks these shifts. Perhaps gang membership actually rises and falls in different historical periods. However, it is impossible to document such changes. There are probably always some gangs operating, but there is no long-term measure of such activity; in particular, in periods when gangs aren't a focus of attention, it is unlikely that anyone is charting gang involvement. When gangs

---

Box 10.4 Cyclical Concerns about Cults

The emergence of new religious movements has been a common thread in American history. In particular, the continuing arrival of immigrants introduces elements from different spiritual traditions that can be incorporated into new faiths. In spite of pronouncements that Americans support religious tolerance and freedom, these new religions are often constructed as social problems—as "cults."

The historian Philip Jenkins (2000) notes that these claims are cyclical—that anticult arguments flourished in the 1880s, the 1930s, and the 1970s and '80s. New religions tend to spread during the late stages of baby booms, when there are large numbers of adolescents and young adults (because younger people are more willing to experiment with different religious beliefs). Then, as the new religions grow to the point that they become visible, and as society enters a period of lower birthrates, it becomes easier to define the new religions as a danger to the society's precious young. Often race figures into these claims: in particular, there tend to be warnings that white youths are endangered by foreign, nonwhite religions.

In a few cases, new religions catch on; they continue to grow, their adherents age (and become wealthier), and the former "cult" becomes an established denomination. The Latter-Day Saints (or Mormons) offer the clearest example: persecuted for their unorthodox beliefs in the early nineteenth century, they evolved into an institutionalized religious faith. However, most new religions vanish and are forgotten, so when a new generation begins to experiment with unorthodox beliefs, the threat seems not just new, but unprecedented.

---

attract concern, we have no way of being sure that the reason for the concern is that they have become more active.

Another possibility is that dramatic events attract media and public attention to particular social issues. For example, Jenkins (1998) notes waves of great concern over sexual crimes against children (as well as periods of much lower concern about these crimes). To be sure, during the waves of concern, heavily publicized news reports described terrible sex crimes against children; however, there were similar reports during the periods of low concern. During the waves of high concern, such crimes were depicted as *instances* of the larger problem of sexual violence against children—proof that something needed to be done. In contrast, during the periods of low concern, press coverage of such terrible crimes treated them as aberrant, exceptional behavior—not as representative of a larger phenomenon. It is difficult to make a strong case that claimsmaking activity simply rises and falls along with the increases and declines of a potentially troubling condition.

How, then, should we understand these waves of concern? One clue is that some of the same issues—gangs, cults, sexual crimes against children, even hidden gospels—appear again and again. Such recurrence might seem only sensible; it doesn't seem surprising that people would worry about these topics. But such wave-like patterns seem more striking when we realize that they occur in other societies and involve constructions that strike us as peculiar, such as waves of concern about vampires in East Africa (White, 2000). The variation in the types of concerns that are prevalent in different societies suggests that certain problems may be particularly easy to construct in particular societies—that some combination of cultural and social structural arrangements may foster such recurring claims.

It may help to think of societies as having the equivalent of fault lines—or "axes of variation" (Erikson, 1976). That is, social arrangements can create tensions between groups—between youths and older adults, between immigrants and the native-born, and on and on. Such tensions can flare into claimsmaking whenever self-identified groups find themselves competing for scarce resources, or whenever one group controls another's access to such resources. Claimsmaking is particularly likely to increase during periods of relative scarcity, when the competition between groups is more intense (see Box 10.5).

Such tensions can be expressed in lots of different ways. Probably most often, people complain about specific individuals or particular actions: "He shouldn't have done that!" But sometimes tensions can be linked to larger claims, so that particular actions are understood as instances of a more general, troubling condition. At any given moment we can imagine that tensions inspire countless grievances—what we might think of as potential claims. Whether any particular grievance starts a full-scale social problems process will depend on contingencies: whether the grievance can be packaged as a rhetorically powerful claim, whether claimsmakers can mobilize sufficient resources, the nature of the other claims currently competing in the social problems marketplace, and so on.

The level of tension along societal fault lines can be understood as another contingency. Periods of higher tension probably increase the receptivity of the press, the public, and policymakers to claims. In some cases, these claims may even—at first glance—seem oblique. Late-nineteenth-century America, for instance, witnessed an active claimsmaking campaign against the English sparrow, a bird that had been imported to the United States in hopes that it would eat insects that infested urban areas (Fine & Christoforides, 1991). The sparrow was widely denounced in moralistic terms: it was lazy and dirty. The intensity of the antisparrow campaign seems surprising, until it is understood as part of the period's larger anti-immigrant claimsmaking. In the late nineteenth and early twentieth centuries, the United States was experiencing one of its periodic waves of opposition to immigration, and claims about the influx of a foreign bird paralleled worries about the country's ability to accommodate human immigrants. Although complaints about bird species aren't all that common, the larger tensions of the time gave the antisparrow claims visibility.

In addition to cycles of concern regarding particular issues, we can note periods when American society seems particularly open

Box 10.5 Chains of Social Problems

Cycles of concern over time are just one way that claimsmaking campaigns can be linked. Gary Alan Fine (2006) identifies four forms of social problems succession—processes that produce chains of linked claims:

1. *Incrementalism.* Claimsmakers and policymakers often campaign in stages, first seeking to gain acceptance for a modest policy that can serve as a foot in the door, a wedge for further domain expansion and additional policies. For example, a law requiring the collection of hate crime statistics can serve as a foundation for additional laws against hate crimes.

2. *Slotting.* Because arenas have limited carrying capacities, and because the media and the public eventually become bored with any claimsmaking campaign, issues tend to fade from view, creating a vacancy in the arena, a slot that can be filled by a new set of claims.

3. *Countering.* Contentious issues have well-established opponents who reliably offer counterclaims. Think of the long-standing abortion debate between pro-life and pro-choice advocates: any advance by one side—a favorable court ruling, new legislation, or whatever—is almost certain to inspire a new claimsmaking campaign by the opposition.

4. *Unintended consequences.* Policies don't always work as expected, and sometimes they create new troubling conditions that inspire their own rounds of claimsmaking. Not only did Prohibition fail to halt drinking, for example, but it led to claims denouncing organized criminal violence and corruption.

to claimsmaking. Three major periods of intense reform activity appear in U.S. history. First, in the decades preceding the Civil War (roughly 1830–1860), there was considerable social movement activity: the abolitionist campaign to abolish slavery, of course, but also intense interest in women's rights, new religions, the temperance movement against strong drink, opposition to immigration (particularly focused on anti-Irish sentiments), and so on. Second, the late-nineteenth/early-twentieth-century period featured a revived women's movement, further opposition to immigration (particularly from southern and eastern Europe), prohibitionist campaigns against alcohol and other drugs, and all of the other causes associated with the Progressive Era. And more recently, beginning in the 1960s and continuing to the present, there has been intense claimsmaking regarding civil rights, women's rights, a war on drugs, renewed concern about immigration (now from Latin America and Asia), and many other issues.

A comparison of these three periods shows that concerns with such fault-line topics as race, women's issues, immigration, and drug use do not just recur, but tend to emerge at roughly the same times. This concurrence suggests that conditions in some historical periods seem to foster claimsmaking. We might speculate that the impending Civil War left people unsettled and more open to the social problems claims of the first period. In the more recent period—as noted in earlier chapters—a new media environment and increasingly sophisticated claimsmaking methods have helped foster contemporary claimsmaking. Again, examining the social problems process across time reveals surprising similarities and differences that can help us better understand our contemporary arrangements for constructing social problems.

THE PROBLEM OF PROGRESS

Comparisons of claims across time raise another comparative question: Do things ever get better? That is, can we speak of social progress, or are things actually getting worse? It seems possible to make a strong case that there has been progress on many fronts: During the twentieth century, life expectancy rose markedly (a newborn male's life expectancy—46 years in 1900—rose to 73 in 2000, the improvement for females was even greater, and life expectancies for nonwhites grew more than those of whites). The percentage of young people graduating from high school climbed (from about 6 percent in 1900 to, according to some calculations, over 80 percent in 2000). The right to vote became more widely available (in 1900, few women, few African Americans in the South, and no one aged 18–20 could vote). And the standard of living improved (so that, for instance, access to indoor plumbing, electricity, and phone service—all relatively rare in 1900—became nearly universally available) (Best, 2001c). Isn't all this progress?

Most people would say yes, but claims about troubling conditions tend to accentuate the negative. Claimsmakers' rhetoric often insists that things are worse than they seem and that they are deteriorating, that real catastrophe lies ahead, that progress is only an illusion. Claimsmakers rarely speak of progress; they seem to fear that acknowledging societal improvements may encourage complacency and discourage taking the actions needed to address troubling conditions. This worry is understandable: it is probably harder to arouse concern about a troubling condition if people are focused on how much things have improved. In addition, however, four aspects of the culture and organization of claimsmaking make it easier to downplay progress:

1. *Perfectibility.* Claimsmakers often invoke **perfectibility** as a standard. That is, they declare that they won't settle for improving a particular troubling condition—that they are determined to eradicate the problem. As noted in Chapter 7, policymakers often "declare war" on social problems: heavily publicized wars have focused on such problems as poverty, cancer, drugs, and most recently, terrorism (Best, 1999). Similarly, our current education policy promises to "leave no child behind." But perfection is a very high standard; as long as one child is doing poorly in school, or one person is poor, there will be room for improvement—and therefore continued opportunities for claimsmaking.

2. *Proportion.* As big problems disappear, relatively smaller problems seem proportionally bigger than before. In 1900, many of the most common causes of death were infectious diseases. Vaccinations and antibiotics caused many of these threats to virtually vanish. Still, everyone is going to die from some cause, so attention can now focus on potentially fatal diseases—such as breast cancer—that received relatively little attention when influenza, pneumonia, and diphtheria were killing far more people. Similarly, ending the worst forms of racial inequality (such as lynching and institutionalized segregation in the South) allows attention to focus on those less violent, less systematic forms of racism that remain. This means that claimsmakers need never run out of conditions that might be constructed as social problems.

3. *Proliferation.* Contemporary society encourages the proliferation of social problems claims. Chapter 5 discussed the growing number of arenas where claims can be mounted, including the increasing number of television channels and the Internet's endless reach, which have made it far easier to promote social problems claims. At the same time, most of these emerging arenas address segmented audiences, giving claimsmakers the advantage of being able to direct their rhetoric toward the homogeneous audience most likely to be receptive. Claimsmakers can therefore avoid confronting criticism and counterclaims, particularly during the early stages of a campaign, when they are seeking to mobilize support. The disadvantage, of course, is that in a world with more arenas, it is harder to gain general public attention for one's claims. For example, it has become easier to promote environmental causes by communicating in arenas filled with environmentalists, but harder to get the attention of the whole society and keep everyone focused on environmentalist concerns.

4. *Paranoia.* Finally, social progress fosters paranoia—fears of societal collapse. How can claimsmaking rhetoric be made compelling in a

world characterized by social progress? One method is to warn that we are in terrible danger, that a collective catastrophe is on the horizon. Apocalyptic scenarios abound; claimsmakers warn about the threats of nuclear war, nuclear winter, global warming, over-population, pollution, resource depletion, epidemic disease, ethnic conflict, globalization, economic collapse, famine, genetic engineering, nanotechnology (tiny technological devices that might outcompete the natural biological system), or robotics (machines that might develop superior intelligence and eliminate people). Moreover, all of these fears focus on troubling conditions that have *social* causes and are therefore suitable subjects for claimsmakers. They can argue that progress is a temporary illusion and warn that what seems to be progress will, in fact, lead to disaster.

In short, the experience of progress has, in some ways, made it easier to construct social problems: claimsmakers can insist that social arrangements remain imperfect; they find it easier to draw attention to previous neglected problems now that some of the big problems of the past have been resolved; they can target and reach audiences likely to be sympathetic to their claims; and they can warn that progress is illusionary, just a predecessor of far worse problems.

Given these patterns, it should not be surprising that social problems claims feature the most urgent rhetoric. Not only can claims-makers draw attention to existing troubling conditions, but they can also predict alarming future problems. These are the secular equivalents of religious prophecies that the world will end on a particular date. It is worth noting that, in retrospect, these warn-ings often seem misguided. Consider alarmist warnings about AIDS in the late 1980s (in 1987, a leading television talk show host declared, "Research studies now project that . . . one in five het-erosexuals could be dead from AIDS at the end of the next three years" [Fumento, 1990, p. 3]); and the furor about the Y2K problem (the concerns that the world's computers would be unable to cope when the calendar changed from 1999 to 2000, and that the resulting crisis might threaten civilization itself).

Apocalyptic rhetoric helps make claims stand out in the social problems marketplace. Every year brings a flu season, and it is always possible to speculate that this year's flu may turn into a devastating pandemic (see Box 10.6). Accentuating a positive record of progress rarely makes claims more competitive, whereas offering a dire forecast can help grab the attention of media workers, the general public, and policymakers. Terrible fears make for good headlines, create good conversation topics, and offer policymakers opportunities to take a stand defending society from a threatening menace.

In short, the question is not whether there is or is not evidence of social progress. The point is that the social problems process pits claims against one another, and that claimsmakers can justify pessimistic rhetoric as a competitive strategy—the most effective way of arousing concern for their issues. This is one more way that the larger societal context shapes claimsmaking.

EXTENDING OUR FOCUS
ACROSS SPACE AND TIME

Although the case study is the typical method for studying the social problems process, this chapter has suggested that there is much to be gained from studying more than one case at a time. Comparisons allow us to compare and contrast social issues across space and time—to recognize that there are various ways to construct the same troubling condition, and that claims morph as they diffuse from one country to another, or as a new wave of concern breathes fresh life into a once visible issue that has since fallen out of favor.

Typically, claims emphasize troubling conditions in the here and now—and in the future. Claimsmakers warn that this is why things are bad now, and that there are reasons to worry that things might

Box 10.6 Avian Flu: Was the Sky Falling?

In late 2005, media commentators warned that avian flu—particularly the virus classified as H5N1—might become a pandemic (a global epidemic). Avian flu affects birds, but people who have considerable contact with poultry can sometimes become infected. Between 2003 and 2005, more than a hundred cases of avian flu in humans (mostly in Southeast Asia) were reported; about half of these people died. Although the H5N1 virus had been around for decades, there were warnings that the virus might mutate, so that rather than spreading from birds to humans, people could spread the infection to one another (Fumento, 2005).

Pandemics can be serious. The Spanish flu of 1918–19 killed 500,000 in the United States and 25 to 50 million worldwide. How serious could an avian flu epidemic become? The media carried stories speculating that it might kill 1 or even 2 million Americans, and 180 to 360 million—or even a billion—people around the world. Suddenly bird flu loomed as a big threat. There had been similar warnings in the past: the fears about SARS (severe acute respiratory syndrome) in 2003, an earlier H5N1 scare in 1997, and so on.

These worst-case scenarios ignored H5N1's failure over nearly half a century to mutate into a form that might be transmitted among people, the likelihood that only the most serious H5N1 cases were being reported (meaning that a large share of infections might not be serious enough to come to the attention of medical authorities— so the actual proportion of cases leading to death might have been far less than one-half), and the post-1918 improvements in medical treatment that could help control the disease's spread. Of course, such considerations would have made avian flu claims seem less compelling.

get much worse. Expanding our focus—thinking about claims more broadly, by considering how social problems were constructed in other places or during other time periods—can help us place those claims in context, to locate the social problems process within a larger framework, so that we can better understand how that process operates. Without such bases for comparisons, it is difficult to assess any particular set of claims.

MAKING CONNECTIONS

● *Although many troubling conditions follow the six stages of the social problems process, often claims fail to attract media attention (discussed in Chapter 5) or public concern (covered in Chapter 6).*

● *Comparisons across time or between places are a useful way of evaluating social problems and the choices made by social problems workers and policymakers. See Chapters 7 and 8 for more about social policy and its implementation.*

● *Looking at cycles of concern across time or between different countries reveals how conditions in some historical periods foster claimsmaking. Chapter 3 explains how activists exploit cultural opportunities when conditions are optimal for drawing attention to their claims.*

CASE STUDY
COMPARING CLAIMS ABOUT IMMIGRATION ACROSS SPACE AND TIME

The U.S. population consists of immigrants and people descended from immigrants; even those called Native Americans are descended from ancestors who crossed the land bridge from Asia to North America long ago. Once people settle in, however, they tend to forget their immigrant roots, even as they complain about the problems posed by new immigrants.

American history has been marked by three great waves of concern about immigration. The first of these occurred in the decades leading up to the Civil War, when millions of Irish immigrants fled poverty and famine to come to the United States. Most Irish were, of course, Catholics, and they were coming to a predominantly Protestant country, where they faced suspicion and hostility (Bilderback, 1989).

The second wave of opposition spanned the late nineteenth and early twentieth centuries. A growing share of these immigrants came from southern and eastern Europe; most of them did not speak English, and many came from Catholic, Jewish, or Eastern Orthodox cultures. Another, visibly different group of immigrants came from Asia, particularly China. This new wave of immigration inspired a great deal of opposition, including new laws making it much tougher to immigrate: the first laws sought to block immigration from China, Japan, and much of the rest of Asia, but this anti-immigrant campaign culminated in the 1924 National Origins Act, which sought to impose significant restrictions on further immigration from outside western Europe.

The third wave of concern began following World War II and has continued into the twenty-first century. This time, the largest share of immigrants comes from Mexico and other Latin American countries, although there are substantial numbers from Asia as well.

Immigrants coming from Europe and Canada—traditionally the major sources of immigration to the United States—are now a small minority. In addition, contemporary claimsmakers charge that most recent immigrants are undocumented—that is, that they entered the United States illegally. This claim has led to several laws intended to control illegal immigration, notably the Immigration Reform and Control Act of 1986, and the Illegal Immigration Reform and Immigrant Responsibility Act of 1996. In 2006, the public debate over immigration policy was revived, with those who advocated much tougher measures against illegal immigrants arguing against the proposals of those who favored opening pathways for current immigrants to move toward citizenship.

The history of opposition to immigration reveals some clear patterns. First, although there is not a perfect correlation, concern about immigration tends to rise and fall with the actual numbers of immigrants; all three waves of opposition occurred during periods when large numbers of immigrants were arriving.

Second, opposition tends to focus on immigrants who seem different—whose race, religion, or national origins are unlike those of most native-born Americans. Over time, of course, what seem to be insurmountable differences come to be accepted; the intense hostility that greeted Irish immigrants in the first wave, or Italian immigrants in the second, now seems misplaced.

Third, anti-immigration claims tend to call upon some of the same values, to use similar warrants. There is the fear that the immigrants' differences threaten the homogeneity of American culture, that the newcomers will fail to assimilate. There are concerns that, by increasing the supply of labor, immigration depresses wages, in that native-born workers find themselves competing against immigrants who are willing to work for wages that may seem quite low to Americans, yet are far higher than the immigrants could have earned in their countries of origin; in this way, claimsmakers argue, immigration harms American workers. The current wave of claimsmaking also argues that immigrants are a significant drain on medical care, school systems, and other social services, so that taxpayers wind up supporting individuals who, in many cases, have no legal right to be in the country (Newton, 2005).

Of course, immigration to the United States represents only a fraction of worldwide migration. Other countries also have significant levels of immigration, which often inspire their own claimsmaking. In Germany, claimsmakers worry about the impact of Turkish immigrants; in France, concern tends to focus on North Africans. Some of the same themes—such as the difficulties posed by the immigrants' cultural differences, or the economic impact of immigration—may be found in claimsmaking in different countries, although different specific issues tend to be emphasized in different places.

For example, Benson and Saguy (2005) studied how French and U.S. media covered immigration issues during the last few decades of the twentieth century. They argue that, whereas policy debates in the United States tend to emphasize "market-based" claims about individuals' contributions to the labor market, the French highlight egalitarian, nonmaterialistic "civic solidarity" claims. When they compared media coverage of immigration issues in leading newspapers and newsmagazines, they found that the French media tended to devote more attention to the problems faced by immigrants (such as poverty, discrimination, and the like); these could be seen as failures of the civic-solidarity ideal. Similarly, French media were much more likely to focus on cultural problems created by immigrants (such as Muslim schoolgirls insisting on wearing scarves in violation of rules against religious insignia); again, such a focus was consistent with the civic-solidarity theme, in that the media worried that immigrants threatened the solidarity of French culture.

In contrast, American media were consistently more likely to emphasize the fiscal problems created by immigrants (such as the costs of providing them with social services)—a concern consistent with Americans' market-based culture. Another interesting finding was that the French media's coverage of immigration issues in France often made comparisons with the situation in the United States, but American coverage of U.S. immigration issues only rarely mentioned the situation in France. This lack of attention to the French situation suggests that Americans are less likely to think comparatively about immigration.

Discussions of immigration—and most other social issues— tend to focus on the here and now. There is a tendency to forget or ignore what happened in the past or in other places. This lack of recall is unfortunate because studying claimsmaking across space and time often reveals important parallels and interesting differences.

QUESTIONS

1. In what different ways have Americans responded to immigration since the nineteenth century?

2. What do the three waves of concern about immigration have in common?

3. Compare the claims about immigration in the United States with claimsmaking in France and Germany. How are the issues different? How are they the same?

11

The Uses of the Constructionist Stance

Most of us find ourselves discussing social problems with friends or family members from time to time. In general, these everyday conversations focus on what we've called troubling conditions. People argue about the scope of conditions, or about what causes them (for instance, some may insist that poverty is caused by discrimination or a lack of good jobs, while others counter that poor people are at least partly to blame for their own problems). Reports from the media may be used to buttress one position or another (perhaps someone will refer to a radio talk show or a program on television about poverty). There may be disagreements about what should be done (should the government distribute more—or less—money to the poor?). In short, these conversations tend to treat social problems as though they are conditions that have an objective existence in our society.

Of course, this book has adopted a very different stance. It has been relatively uninterested in such social conditions, and has focused instead on what people think and say about social problems. Instead of treating social problems as social conditions, it has described a *process* in which people's ideas about social problems emerge and evolve.

Figure 11.1   Basic Model of the Social Problems Process

Claims- ⟶ Media ⟶ Public ⟶ Policy- ⟶ Social ⟶ Policy
making   Coverage   Reaction   making   Problems   Outcomes
                                          Work

Chapter 1 introduced a model of a social problems process with six basic stages: claimsmaking, media coverage, public reaction, policymaking, social problems work, and policy outcomes. That model (reproduced as Figure 11.1) provided the organizational framework for the chapters that followed, which, in general, dealt with successive stages in the social problems process.

While exploring the six stages in the social problems process, this book has remained focused on the subjective nature of social problems. Remember that what all phenomena that are considered social problems have in common is not a particular objective quality, some sort of harm or damage that they inflict on society. Rather, the one characteristic that all social problems share is subjective: people define them as troubling. Social problems are not conditions; they are *concerns*.

This subjective work—people's efforts to understand and draw attention to what they define as troubling conditions—occurs at every stage in the social problems process. It begins with claimsmakers' efforts to construct claims that will convince others to share their concern about a troubling condition. And at each successive stage in the process, people—media workers, members of the public, policymakers, social problems workers, and those who evaluate and criticize policies—rework the claims that come to their attention, and reconstruct the problem again and again so that their new understanding will be appropriate for their purposes. News workers repackage primary claims into secondary claims to fit the demands and conventions of news coverage, members of the public respond by interpreting these secondary claims to correspond with their own understanding of how the larger world works, policymakers make further alterations so that the troubling condition can be addressed through a formal policy, social problems workers try to apply abstract policies to practical situations, and various evaluators redefine what is needed according to their assessments of how well policies work.

In other words, social problems construction is not something that happens all at once, through the actions of a single set of actors at one stage in the social problems process. Instead, it is an ongoing process, in which different people work out different ways of making sense of the situations they confront. Any phenomenon can be understood in lots of different ways, and social construction is a process of making choices—of people in a particular situation choosing one perspective among all the possibilities. Each effort to construct or understand a social problem needs to meet two criteria: first, it needs to make sense to—and be useful for—whoever is producing the construction; second, it needs to be able to convince others—whoever the audience for that construction may be.

Social construction is thus an *interactive* process. People present their constructions to an audience of others (as when an activist holds a press conference, a legislator tries to convince colleagues to vote for a bill, or a case worker tries to persuade clients that taking a particular action will be in their best interest). Those others, however, may react in different ways (perhaps no reporters bother to attend the press conference, perhaps the legislature votes unanimously in favor of the bill, perhaps some clients reject the case worker's advice while others follow it). These reactions become feedback, and on the basis of the audience's response, the people offering the construction may continue pressing their claims, modify those claims to see whether a repackaged version might elicit a better response, or even decide to abandon the claims entirely. Although we may think of a claimsmaker addressing an audience, we should not imagine that that audience is passive. Rather, audiences react to claims, and claimsmakers are likely to revise their constructions in response to those reactions.

All of this means that our initial model of the social problems process, as illustrated in Figure 11.1, oversimplifies the process in some important ways. First, the arrows between stages imply that influence is unidirectional; they ignore the role of feedback and the interactive nature of the process. Second, the actors at the different stages in the social problems process do not necessarily limit their interactions to contacts with those in the next stage. Third, and very important, interactions also occur *within* each stage. That is, activists interact with others in their social movement organization, as well as with activists in rival SMOs, and with other sorts of claimsmakers, such as experts. Similarly, media workers interact with their colleagues and follow one another's coverage, and so on.

Moreover, when we look at interactions between actors in different stages, we realize again that the basic model's depiction of actors addressing only those at the next stage in the process is too simple. For example, the model suggests that claimsmakers will focus their attention on influencing media coverage, but claimsmakers may do far more. Sometimes claimsmakers bypass the media and directly address members of the public, policymakers, social problems workers, or even those who evaluate policy outcomes. There are many possible pathways through the social problems process. Figure 11.1 can be thought of as offering a simplified, fairly typical natural history—a framework for developing this book's argument. In contrast, Figure 11.2 gives a better sense of the complicated ways in which actors in different stages of the process can interact; it suggests the range of possible connections that might shape how social problems evolve.

Examine Figure 11.2 carefully, and note the following five features:

1. The five one-way stage-to-stage arrows found in the simplified model reappear in Figure 11.2 as thicker arrows—a reminder that these are particularly important links in the social problems process.

Figure 11.2 INTERACTIONS IN THE SOCIAL PROBLEMS PROCESS

2. Each stage in the social problems process is now represented by a box, and small circles within each box denote the various actors in that stage (that is, different claimsmakers in the claimsmaking stage, and so on). In turn, those circles are linked by two-way arrows suggesting interactions among the people at each stage.

3. Arrows connect each stage with every other stage, illustrating possible connections, in that it may be possible for actors at any stage to communicate with people anywhere else in the social problems process.

4. The arrows linking all the different stages go in both directions, to illustrate that there is always the possibility of feedback and social interaction.

5. The figure is laid out as a circle, rather than along a straight line, and there is a thick arrow between "Policy Outcomes" (which the basic model presented as the final stage in the social problems process) and "Claimsmaking" (which was, of course, the first stage). This arrow denotes how reactions to social policies often lead to new claimsmaking campaigns (as discussed in Chapter 9). The figure's roughly circular shape reminds us that the social problems process need not end—that critiques of social policies often inspire new cycles of claimsmaking.

Figure 11.2 is complex, but it reflects genuine complexities—the many possible pathways through the social problems process. Spend some time examining Figure 11.2. Pick one particular arrow and consider the sorts of activities it might involve. Then pick another. Do this until you are comfortable, until you understand how this complex figure depicts the overall social problems process.

These complexities become especially apparent when we compare social problems processes across space and time (the subject of Chapter 10). For example, many campaigns raise concern about dangerous drugs. Some of these efforts are remarkably successful at attracting intense media coverage, arousing great public concern, and inspiring new policies; the 1986 campaign to warn Americans about the dangers of crack cocaine is an obvious example (Reinarman & Levine, 1995). On the other hand, some campaigns flop, such as the 1989 effort to draw attention to "ice" (smokable crystal methamphetamine), although later campaigns to raise alarm about this drug had more success; or the 1993 warnings about "Cat" (methcathinone, a drug that—so far—has not aroused great concern) (Jenkins, 1999).

We can imagine a continuum of outcomes for antidrug campaigns that ranges from widespread, intense concern to indifference. Only by comparing antidrug claimsmaking campaigns—targeting different drugs, at different times, or in different places—can we begin to appreciate the many possible ways that the social problems process can unfold. And, of course, various claims about other troubling conditions—racial discrimination, ecological problems, and so on—will display similar variability in their outcomes.

In other words, our constructionist model—both the simpler version depicted in Figure 11.1 and the more complex version presented in Figure 11.2—should be understood as a tool, a framework that can be used to help us think critically about the social construction of social problems. Most days, newspapers present various stories that report on claimsmaking, policymaking, or social problems work; very often they also run stories about public reactions and evaluations of different policies. (And, of course, all of those stories are themselves examples of media coverage.) The constructionist model can be used to place all those stories in their broader context, to view them as parts of the larger social problems process. And that's worth doing, because we are constantly surrounded by examples of the social problems process.

IS THIS STUFF USEFUL?

As noted way back in Chapter 1, the constructionist stance for thinking about the social problems process is not the traditional approach to studying social problems. Most books about social problems have been—and continue to be—organized around a series of chapters that deal with different conditions considered to be social problems—crime, racism, and the like. Each chapter summarizes information about its problem: statistics about crime rates, theories of crime causation, and so on. This book has presented very little information of that sort.

The justification for this book's constructionist approach is that it is intellectually coherent. Rather than letting our attention drift as we examine, one at a time, crime and other specific phenomena that people consider social problems, this book has focused on the general topic of the social problems process—on the insight that the only thing the various conditions called social problems have in common is that they are socially constructed—and it has explored the ins and outs of that process.

This approach is intended to give you some tools for recognizing, thinking about, and responding to social problems claims. Ten years from now—or maybe twenty or thirty—you will encounter warnings about a terrible new social problem of some sort. There is no way of predicting exactly what the topic of those warnings will be—perhaps a new crime, or a new disease, or a new form of drug abuse. But we can be reasonably confident that you will run into such claims, because such claims have been an important part of the social landscape for a very long time, and there is no reason to expect that they will vanish—particularly not in a world where twenty-four-hour television news broadcasts, the Internet, and other forms of electronic communication make it incredibly easy to promote new claims. If anything, claims are likely to spread via ever more channels as new media evolve (consider, for example, the recent emergence of news bulletins transmitted to cell phones and other portable electronic devices). People who pay even min-imal attention to the media can expect to spend their lives bom-barded by such claims.

Moreover, the historical record is full of warnings about terrible problems that—in retrospect—seem mistaken. In the 1970s, some environmentalists warned that civilization was jeopardized by global climate change—that humans faced an impending ice age brought on by global cooling. Fifteen years later, fears about the threat of global cooling would be replaced by what seem to be their exact opposite—concerns over the danger of global warming. In another example, in the early 1990s some commentators warned that violent crime was about to spiral out of control—that a gen-eration of "superpredators" would be coming of age. Instead, crime rates fell fairly steadily during the years that followed. These claims received plenty of respectful attention when they first appeared, even though their forecasts proved to be quite wrong.

There are many other examples of urgent claims that hindsight lets us see as exaggerated, if not silly. There is a long history of crit-ics warning that the amusements of the young—games, toys, dances, movies, television, music, and on and on—endangered the next generation. Each successive style of rock music, for example, has been denounced as threatening the moral fabric of young peo-ple. There is an equally long history of commentators charging that the current wave of immigrants threatens the fabric of American society, that some new recreational drug is spreading out of con-trol, and so on. Such claims often acknowledge that earlier claims about similar problems exaggerated the threat, yet the claimsmak-ers insist that this new problem is different—the real deal—that it presents a genuine danger that must be addressed.

At one extreme, it is possible to treat all social problems claims as correct, true, accurate. When claimsmakers warn that a partic-ular troubling condition is this serious, affects that many people, and so on, we might simply accept those claims, even though we may realize that, in the past, many such claims have proven to be exaggerated or even false. In other words, every time we encounter a news story that warns we should be worried about a new problem, we could decide to worry. An alternative, but equally extreme stance might be to approach all claims cynically, to presume that they are wrong, false, bogus. We could suspect that claimsmakers are interested parties who are quite willing to say anything, that media workers are just trying to attract an audience, that politicians are cynically pandering to voters' concerns, and so on. That is, knowing that some social problems claims have been exaggerated in the past, we might simply discount and ignore any claims we encounter in the future. The first possibility encourages excessive credulity; the second fosters cynicism, apathy, and ignorance.

Obviously it would be desirable to find a middle ground between those extremes—a stance somewhere between credulousness and cynicism. That is, it would be better to approach claims thoughtfully—critically—so that we could weigh what we're told about social problems and make our own evaluations about the nature of those problems and the best ways of addressing them.

The constructionist model of the social problems process can help in this regard. Understanding that claims need to be made persuasive—that claimsmakers are competing to be heard in the social problems marketplace so that they can bring their claims to the attention of press, public, and policymakers—offers a useful foundation for thinking about social problems as a process. In particular, it can help us to think carefully about how the problem is being constructed, about the rhetoric of claimsmaking, who is making which claims, and so on.

By adopting a constructionist stance, we can identify interesting questions that we might ask about a set of claims. Is the problem clearly defined, or are we encouraged to understand it primarily through typifying examples? Is there any reason to suspect that those typifying examples may not be all that typical? If the claims feature statistics, where do those numbers come from, and how likely is it that they are accurate? What sorts of warrants are being used to make the claims compelling? How are the media covering the issue: What sources are they drawing upon, and how does what the media report differ from what the claimsmakers are saying? Are the media presenting different constructions of the problem, and what do those differences reveal?

Further questions arise at successive stages in the social problems process. Is the problem addressed in our everyday conversations? Is it a theme in stories or jokes that we hear from people we know, and if so, does the public seem to be constructing the problem in different terms from those that claimsmakers and the media are using? Which aspects of the problem do policymakers emphasize? Do their policy recommendations match their claims? Do they seem workable? How do social problems workers describe their activities and the clients with whom they work? Who criticizes social policies and why, and how do they frame their critiques?

Such questions give us tools that we can use to think critically about social problems. Note, however, that being critical does mean rejecting claims. The answers to the questions you ask may strike you as completely convincing; you may decide that some claims are quite correct, and you may even be moved to join some claimsmakers' causes. In some instances, though, questioning the claims might lead you to suspect that those claims are exaggerated or misguided. Thus, one goal is to become a thoughtful consumer of social problems claims.

There is also another way to use the constructionist approach. Studying how social problems are constructed—how some claims prove effective while others fall by the wayside—offers useful information for would-be claimsmakers. That is, constructionist research can be studied for its practical advice on how to arouse concern and mobilize action regarding whatever you might consider as troubling conditions (just as it can suggest how opposition to claims might be made more effective). Studying the social problems process offers lessons on how to assemble persuasive claimsmaking rhetoric, how to mobilize effective adherents, how to incorporate expert knowledge in campaigns, how to elicit media coverage and attract public attention, how to understand the concerns of policymakers and social problems workers, and so on. If you are inclined to take an active part in the social problems process, the constructionist stance can help you ask—and answer—very practical questions. It is a perspective that can benefit participants, as well as observers.

What constructionism cannot do is tell you which conditions ought to concern you. You have your own values, your own sense of what is or is not troubling, what needs to be changed, and what sorts of changes are needed. You may be attracted by the ideologies of liberals or conservatives, of feminists or fundamentalists. Those are choices you need to make, and the constructionist stance does not provide the grounds for preferring one choice over another. The goal of this book has not been to tell you *what* to think about various social conditions, but rather to offer guidelines for *how* to think about the social problems process. If this book advocates a moral position, it is that it is desirable for people to think critically about that process, to engage the claims they encounter.

I hope you will find these ideas useful in the years ahead. Good luck.

Glossary

abeyance A period when a social movement is relatively inactive.

activists Members of a social movement organization who make claims about social problems. Compare *experts*.

adopters The people who accept new innovations as part of the process of diffusion. Compare *transmitters*.

agenda setting Choosing which claims will receive the attention of media or policymakers.

arena A public venue where social problems claims can be presented.

audience The people whom claimsmakers seek to persuade with their claims.

audience segmentation Targeting media presentations for particular audiences.

beneficiaries People who stand to benefit from a social movement's success. Compare *constituents*.

bias A tendency for media workers' personal beliefs and views on an issue to interfere with balanced and impartial coverage.

biomedicalization The process of arguing that biological processes are the root cause of many troubling conditions.

carrying capacity The number of issues that can receive attention in an arena.

case An instance of a previously constructed troubling condition that requires attention through the application of appropriate policy.

case study An examination of a particular problem.

causal story A story that classifies a troubling condition in a familiar category according to the nature of its cause.

claim An argument that a particular troubling condition needs to be addressed.

claimsmakers People who seek to convince others that there is a troubling condition about which something ought to be done.

claimsmaking The process of making claims, of bringing a troubling condition to the attention of others.

commission A special, high-status group—often created at the national level—that evaluates policies and issues recommendations.

conclusion The part of a claim that specifies what should be done, what action should be taken to address a troubling condition.

condensing symbol A shorthand element—such as a landmark narrative, typifying example, slogan, or visual image—that evokes a package.

conscience constituents People who contribute money or even join demonstrations because they believe in a particular cause, although they do not expect to be direct beneficiaries of that cause.

constituents People who support a social movement. Compare *beneficiaries* and *conscience constituents*.

constructionism A sociological approach that focuses on the process of social construction.

contemporary legend A story, also called an *urban legend*, spread from one person to another and believed to be true by teller and listener.

counterclaim An argument that directly opposes a particular claim.

countermovement A movement that opposes a social movement by promoting counterclaims that challenge the opponent's claims.

cultural opportunity A situation when a shift in popular ideas makes it possible to change how a particular troubling condition is addressed. Compare *political opportunity*.

cultural resources Cultural knowledge that can be incorporated in claims.

diagnostic frame A social movement's depiction of the nature of a problem. Compare *prognostic frame*.

dialog An exchange of ideas between two or more persons.

diffusion The process by which innovations spread.

domain expansion Redefining a troubling condition to encompass a broader array of cases.

evaluation research A social scientific assessment of the effectiveness of a specific policy.

experts People—such as physicians, scientists, lawyers, and officials—who have special knowledge and claim to speak with special authority. Compare *activists*.

feedback The phenomenon in which a particular cause produces an effect that in turn affects the cause.

focus group A set of people that researchers select to discuss certain topics in order to learn what the public is thinking.

frame alignment Ways in which activists try to promote a social movement's frame to prospective members.

frame amplification Ways in which activists appeal to prospective members by arguing that a social movement's frame is consistent with popular beliefs.

frame bridging Ways in which activists appeal to prospective members thought to be already sympathetic to a social movement's frame.

frame dispute A disagreement between groups of activists about how to frame a particular troubling condition.

frame extension Ways in which activists appeal to prospective members by extending a social movement's frame to encompass the concerns of those prospective supporters.

frame transformation Ways in which activists appeal to prospective members by inviting them to reject familiar views of the world and adopt the activists' very different perspective.

framing The way in which claimsmakers construct claims about a troubling condition.

ground The portion of a claim that argues that a troubling condition exists.

ideology A system of beliefs regarding how society does and should operate.

inertia A reluctance to alter existing social arrangements.

insider claimsmakers Claimsmakers who have easy access to publicity and people in positions of power. Compare *outsider claimsmakers*.

joke cycle A set of jokes that share a form or topic and are popular for a period of time.

landmark narrative A typifying example that dominates news coverage of a troubling condition, shaping the terms in which the problem is covered and how the news audience understands the problem.

macrosociology Sociological studies concerned with whole societies. Compare *microsociology*.

master frame A broad construction that can be easily modified and applied to many troubling conditions.

media coverage Attention from mass media outlets, such as newspapers and television, that can bring claims to the attention of a wide audience.

medical model A general framework for thinking about medical matters as diseases that require treatment.

medicalization The process of defining a troubling condition as a medical matter.

microsociology Sociological studies concerned with interactions between individuals. Compare *macrosociology*.

motif A recurring thematic element in legends and jokes.

motivational frame A social movement's justification for taking action.

naming Coining a term to identify a troubling condition.

natural history A sequence of steps or stages often found in a particular process.

news work The job of locating and presenting news to the larger public.

nonrelational channel A link in diffusion that does not involve a personal connection between a transmitter and an adopter. Compare *relational channel*.

objectivism A school of thought that defines social problems in terms of objectively measurable characteristics of conditions. Compare *subjectivism*.

outsider claimsmakers People who lack easy access to publicity and to people in positions of power. Compare *insider claimsmakers*.

ownership Having one's construction of a troubling condition become widely accepted.

package A familiar construction of a particular troubling condition, including specifications of its causes and solutions.

perfectibility Using the eradication of a troubling condition—instead of its improvement—as the standard for evaluating a social policy.

piggyback To link a new troubling condition to an already established social problem.

policy domain The part of the political system that focuses on a particular troubling condition.

policy outcome The result of how a particular social policy is implemented.

policy proposal stream A set of policy proposals that policymakers hear for addressing a troubling condition.

policymakers People who are able to establish a social policy of some kind.

policymaking The process of devising policy to address a particular troubling condition.

political opportunity A situation when a shift in power makes it possible to change how a particular troubling condition is addressed. Compare *cultural opportunity*.

political stream The current political situation recognized by policymakers in which a troubling condition might be addressed.

polity Groups and individuals who have easy access to policymakers.

popular culture Commercial entertainment.

population All those described by a statistic. Compare *representative sample*.

position issue A troubling condition about which people disagree. Compare *valence issue*.

primary claim One of the initial claims, usually presented by activists or experts, that begin the social problems process. Compare *secondary claim*.

problem recognition stream The set of claims that policymakers hear about a troubling condition.

prognostic frame A social movement's description of what needs to be done about a particular troubling condition. Compare *diagnostic frame*.

relational channel A link in diffusion that involves interpersonal contact between a transmitter and an adopter. Compare *nonrelational channel*.

representative sample A sample that accurately reflects the diversity of the population.

resource Anything that can be drawn upon to construct a claim.

resource mobilization Collecting and assembling money, members, and other resources needed by a social movement.

rhetoric The study of persuasion.

sample A subgroup used as a basis for statistical generalizations about a population.

sample survey A poll administered to a sample in order to generalize about opinions or other characteristics of a population.

secondary claim The media's transformation of a primary claim. Secondary claims are usually shorter and more dramatic than primary claims.

segmentation See *audience segmentation.*

SMO See *social movement organization.*

social condition A social circumstance or arrangement.

social construction The process by which people continually create—or construct—meaning.

social issue A topic of social concern that is characterized by disagreement or debate.

social movement A general cause that motivates activists and social movement organizations to address a particular troubling condition.

social movement organization (SMO) A particular organization that belongs to a social movement.

social problems marketplace The public forum where claims are presented and discussed.

social problems process The process through which particular troubling conditions come to be constructed as social problems.

social problems work The application of constructions of a troubling condition or a social policy to practical situations.

social problems workers People who do social problems work.

sociological imagination The ability to see private troubles in terms of larger public issues.

statistic A number that measures or characterizes a particular situation.

subjectivism A school of thought that defines social problems in terms of people's subjective sense that something is or isn't troubling. Compare *objectivism.*

subjects The people (variously called addicts, clients, offenders, patients, suspects, victims, defendants, and so on) who in some way embody a socially constructed social problem.

target population The group of people intended to be affected by a social policy.

theorization The presentation of claims using abstract principles and arguments.

topical joke cycle A joke cycle about a particular event.

transmitters The people who promote new innovations as part of the process of diffusion. Compare *adopters.*

troubling condition A condition that becomes a subject of claims.

typifying example A particular instance chosen to illustrate a troubling condition—often a dramatic, disturbing, or memorable case.

urban legend See *contemporary legend*.

valence issue A troubling condition about which there is general agreement. Compare *position issue*.

variant A version of a contemporary legend or joke.

warrant The portion of a claim that justifies doing something about a troubling condition.

References

Åkerström, M. (2006). Doing ambivalence: Embracing policy innovation—At arm's length. *Social Problems* 53: 57–74.

Alterman, E. (2003). *What liberal media? The truth about bias and the news.* New York: Basic Books.

Appleton, L. M. (1995). Rethinking medicalization: Alcoholism and anomalies. In J. Best (Ed.), *Images of issues: Typifying contemporary social problems* (2nd ed., pp. 59–80). Hawthorne, NY: Aldine de Gruyter.

Armstrong, E. M. (2003). *Conceiving risk, bearing responsibility: Fetal alcohol syndrome and the diagnosis of moral disorder.* Baltimore: Johns Hopkins University Press.

Ayukawa, J. (2001). The United States and smoking problems in Japan. In J. Best (Ed.), *How claims spread: Cross-national diffusion of social problems* (pp. 215–242). Hawthorne, NY: Aldine de Gruyter.

Barker, K. (2002). Self-help literature and the making of illness identity: The case of fibromyalgia syndrome (FMS). *Social Problems* 49: 279–300.

Barnes, F. (2004, May 28). Liberal media evidence. *The Daily Standard.* Retrieved from www.weeklystandard.com.

Barrett, S. (2003). *Environment and statecraft: The strategy of environmental treaty-making.* New York: Oxford University Press.

Becker, H. S. (1995). The power of inertia. *Qualitative Sociology* 18: 301–309.

Beckett, K. (1994). Setting the public agenda: "Street crime" and drug use in American politics. *Social Problems* 41: 425–447.

Beckett, K. (1996). Culture and the politics of signification: The case of child sexual abuse. *Social Problems* 43: 57–76.

Benford, R. D. (1993). Frame disputes within the nuclear disarmament movement. *Social Forces* 71: 677–701.

Benford, R. D., & Hunt, S. A. (2003). Interactional dynamics in public problems marketplaces: Movements and the counterframing and reframing of public problems. In J. A. Holstein & G. Miller (Eds.), *Challenges and choices: Constructionist perspectives on social problems* (pp. 153–186). Hawthorne, NY: Aldine de Gruyter.

Benson, R., & Saguy, A. C. (2005). Constructing social problems in an age of globalization: A French-American comparison. *American Sociological Review* 70: 233–259.

Berger, P. L., & Luckmann, T. (1966). *The social construction of reality: A treatise in the sociology of knowledge.* Garden City, NY: Doubleday.

Berns, N. (2004). *Framing the victim: Domestic violence, media, and social problems.* Hawthorne, NY: Aldine de Gruyter.

Bertram, E., Blachman, M., Sharpe, K., & Andreas, P. (1996). *Drug war politics: The price of denial.* Berkeley: University of California Press.

Best, J. (1990). *Threatened children: Rhetoric and concern about child-victims.* Chicago: University of Chicago Press.

Best, J. (1991). "Road warriors" on "hair-trigger highways": Cultural resources and the media's construction of the 1987 freeway shootings problem. *Sociological Inquiry* 61: 327–345.

Best, J. (1999). *Random violence: How we talk about new crimes and new victims.* Berkeley: University of California Press.

Best, J. (2001a). *Damned lies and statistics: Untangling numbers from the media, politicians, and activists.* Berkeley: University of California Press.

Best, J. (Ed.). (2001b). *How claims spread: Cross-national diffusion of social problems.* Hawthorne, NY: Aldine de Gruyter.

Best, J. (2001c). Social progress and social problems: Toward a sociology of gloom. *Sociological Quarterly* 42: 1–12.

Best, J., & Furedi, F. (2001). The evolution of road rage in Britain and the United States. In J. Best (Ed.), *How claims spread: Cross-national diffusion of social problems* (pp. 107–127). Hawthorne, NY: Aldine de Gruyter.

Bianco, A. (2006). *The bully of Bentonville: How the high cost of Wal-Mart's everyday low prices is hurting America.* New York: Doubleday.

Bilderback, L. (1989). "A greater threat than the Soviet Union": Mexican immigration as a social problem. In J. Best (Ed.), *Images of issues: Typifying contemporary social problems* (pp. 223–241). Hawthorne, NY: Aldine de Gruyter.

Bishop, G. F. (2005). *The illusion of public opinion: Fact and artifact in American public opinion polls.* Lanham, MD: Rowman & Littlefield.

Blumer, H. (1971). Social problems as collective behavior. *Social Problems* 18: 298–306.

Bogard, C. J. (2003). *Seasons such as these: How homelessness took shape in America.* Hawthorne, NY: Aldine de Gruyter.

Boyle, E. H., Songora, F., & Foss, G. (2001). International discourse and local politics: Anti-female-genital-cutting laws in Egypt, Tanzania, and the United States. *Social Problems* 48: 524–544.

Bracey, G. W. (2006). *Reading educational research: How to avoid getting statistically snookered.* Portsmouth, NH: Heinemann.

Brewer, P. R., & Wilcox, C. (2005). The polls-trends: Same-sex marriage and civil unions. *Public Opinion Quarterly* 69: 599–616.

Bronner, S. J. (1988). Political suicide: The Bud Dwyer joke cycle and the humor of disaster. *Midwestern Folklore* 14: 81–89.

Bronner, S. J. (2005). Contesting tradition: The deep play and protest of pigeon shoots. *Journal of American Folklore* 118: 409–452.

Brown, J. D. (1991). The professional ex-. *Sociological Quarterly* 32: 219–230.

Brown, P. (1992). Popular epidemiology and toxic waste contamination: Lay and professional ways of knowing. *Journal of Health and Social Behavior* 33: 267–281.

Brunsma, D. L. (2004). *The school uniform movement and what it tells us about American education.* Lanham, MD: ScarecrowEducation.

Burgess, A. (2004). *Cellular phones, public fears, and a culture of precaution.* Cambridge, UK: Cambridge University Press.

Burns, S. L., & Peyrot, M. (2003). Tough love: Nurturing and coercing responsibility and recovery in California drug courts. *Social Problems* 50: 416–438.

Burstein, P. (1991). Policy domains: Organization, culture, and policy outcomes. *Annual Review of Sociology* 17: 327–350.

Burstein, P. (1998). Bringing the public back in: Should sociologists consider the impact of public opinion on public policy? *Social Forces* 77: 27–62.

Burstein, P., & Bricher, M. (1997). Problem definition and public policy: Congressional committees confront work, family, and gender, 1945–1990. *Social Forces* 75: 135–169.

Burstein, P., Bricher, M., & Einwohner, R. L. (1995). Policy alternative and political change: Work, family, and gender on the congressional agenda, 1945–1990. *American Sociological Review* 60: 67–83.

Burstein, P., & Linton, A. (2002). The impact of political parties, interest groups, and social movement organizations on public policy: Some recent evidence and theoretical concerns. *Social Forces* 81: 380–408.

Butterfield, F. (1998, August 3). As crime falls, pressure rises to alter data. *The New York Times,* p. A1.

Campion-Vincent, V. (2005). *Organ theft legends.* Jackson: University Press of Mississippi.

Campo-Flores, A. (2005, August 8). "I felt my face just melting." *Newsweek* 146: 44–45.

Chambliss, D. F. (1996). *Beyond caring: Hospitals, nurses, and the social organization of ethics.* Chicago: University of Chicago Press.

Chesters, G., & Welsh, I. (2005). Complexity and social movement(s): Process and emergence in planetary action systems. *Theory, Culture and Society* 22: 187–211.

Clarke, A. E., Shim, J. K., Mamo, L., Fosket, J. R., & Fishman, J. R. (2003). Biomedicalization: Technoscientific transformations of health, illness, and U.S. biomedicine. *American Sociological Review* 68: 161–194.

Cline, W. R. (2004). Climate change. In B. Lomborg (Ed.), *Global crises, global solutions* (pp. 13–43). Cambridge, UK: Cambridge University Press.

Conrad, P. (1992). Medicalization and social control. *Annual Review of Sociology* 18: 209–232.

Conrad, P., & Potter, D. (2000). From hyperactive children to ADHA adults: Observations on the expansion of medical categories. *Social Problems* 47: 559–582.

Csaszi, L. (2003). World Trade Center jokes and their Hungarian reception. *Journal of Folklore Research* 40: 175–210.

Davis, J. E. (2005). *Accounts of innocence: Sexual abuse, trauma, and the self.* Chicago: University of Chicago Press.

Davis, P. W. (1994). The changing meanings of spanking. In J. Best (Ed.), *Troubling children* (pp. 133–153). Hawthorne, NY: Aldine de Gruyter.

De Vaus, D. A. (1986). *Surveys in social research.* London: Allen & Unwin.

DeNavas-Walt, C., Proctor, B. D., & Lee, C. H. (2005). *Income, poverty, and health insurance coverage in the United States: 2004* (U.S. Census Bureau, Current Population Reports, P60-229). Washington, DC: U.S. Government Printing Office.

Dicker, J. (2005). *The United States of Wal-Mart.* New York: Penguin.

Dickson, D. T. (1968). Bureaucracy and morality: An organizational perspective on a moral crusade. *Social Problems* 16: 143–156.

Donovan, P. (2004). *No way of knowing: Crime, urban legends, and the Internet.* New York: Routledge.

Downs, A. (1972). Up and down with ecology—The "issue-attention cycle." *Public Interest* 28: 38–50.

Dundes, A. (1987). *Cracking jokes.* Berkeley, CA: Ten Speed Press.

Dundes, A., & Pagter, C. R. (2000). *Why don't sheep shrink when it rains? A further collection of photocopier folklore.* Syracuse, NY: Syracuse University Press.

Eckholm, E. (2006, May 17). For the neediest of the needy, welfare reforms still fall short, study says. *The New York Times*, p. 18.

Ellis, B. (1991). The last thing said: The *Challenger* disaster jokes and closure. *International Folklore Review* 8: 110–124.

Ellis, B. (2001). *Aliens, ghosts, and cults: Legends we live*. Jackson: University Press of Mississippi.

Ellis, B. (2003). Making a Big Apple crumble: The role of humor in constructing a global response to disaster. In P. Narváez (Ed.), *Of corpse: Death and humor in folklore and popular culture* (pp. 35–79). Logan: Utah State University Press.

Erchak, G. M., & Rosenfeld, R. (1989). Learning disabilities, dyslexia, and the medicalization of the classroom. In J. Best (Ed.), *Images of issues: Typifying contemporary social problems* (pp. 79–97). Hawthorne, NY: Aldine de Gruyter.

Erikson, K. T. (1976). *Everything in its path: Destruction of community in the Buffalo Creek flood*. New York: Simon and Schuster.

Featherstone, L. (2006, January/February). Watching Wal-Mart: Four documentaries, four perspectives. *Columbia Journalism Review* 44: 58–62.

Fetner, T. (2001). Working Anita Bryant: The impact of Christian anti-gay activism on lesbian and gay movement claims. *Social Problems* 48: 411–428.

Fields, G. (2000, March 15). Victims of identity theft often unaware they've been stung. *USA Today*, p. 6A.

Filler, D. M. (2000). Random violence and the transformation of the juvenile justice debate. *Virginia Law Review* 86: 1095–1125.

Fine, G. A. (1992). *Manufacturing tales: Sex and money in contemporary legends*. Knoxville: University of Tennessee Press.

Fine, G. A. (2006). The chaining of social problems: Solutions and unintended consequences in the age of betrayal. *Social Problems* 53: 3–17.

Fine, G. A., Campion-Vincent, V., & Heath, C. (Eds.). (2005). *Rumor mills: The social impact of rumor and legend*. New Brunswick, NJ: AldineTransaction.

Fine, G. A., & Christoforides, L. (1991). Dirty birds, filthy immigrants, and the English sparrow war: Metaphorical linkage in constructing social problems. *Symbolic Interaction* 14: 375–393.

Fine, G. A., & Khawaja, I. (2005). Celebrating Arabs and grateful terrorists: Rumor and the politics of plausibility. In G. A. Fine, V. Campion-Vincent, & C. Heath (Eds.), *Rumor mills: The social impact of rumor and legend* (pp. 189–205). New Brunswick, NJ: AldineTransaction.

Fine, G. A., & Turner, P. A. (2001). *Whispers on the color line: Rumor and race in America*. Berkeley: University of California Press.

Fischer, D. H. (1989). *Albion's seed: Four British folkways in America*. New York: Oxford University Press.

Fisher, D. R., Stanley, K., Berman, D., & Neff, G. (2005). How do organizations matter? Mobilization and support for participants at five globalization protests. *Social Problems* 52: 102–121.

Freedman, D. H. (1998, February). When is a planet not a planet? *Atlantic Monthly* 281: 22, 24, 32–33.

Freidson, E. (1986). *Professional powers: A study of the institutionalization of formal knowledge.* Chicago: University of Chicago Press.

Frohmann, L. (1998). Constituting power in sexual assault cases: Prosecutorial strategies for victim management. *Social Problems* 45: 393–407.

Fujiwara, L. H. (2005). Immigrant rights are human rights: The reframing of immigrant entitlement and welfare. *Social Problems* 52: 79–101.

Fumento, M. (1990). *The myth of heterosexual AIDS.* New York: Basic Books.

Fumento, M. (2005, November 21). Fuss and feathers: Pandemic panic over the avian flu. *Weekly Standard.* Retrieved from www.fumento.com/disease/flu2005. html.

Furedi, F. (2001). Bullying: The British contribution to the construction of a social problem. In J. Best (Ed.), *How claims spread: Cross-national diffusion of social problems* (pp. 89–106). Hawthorne, NY: Aldine de Gruyter.

Gallagher, J. (2000, June 25). Identity theft puts victim in her own never-ending story. *St. Louis Post-Dispatch*, p. E1.

Gamson, W. A. (1992). *Talking politics.* New York: Cambridge University Press.

Gamson, W. A., & Modigliani, A. (1989). Media discourse and public opinion on nuclear power: A constructionist approach. *American Journal of Sociology* 95: 1–37.

Gans, H. J. (1979). *Deciding what's news.* New York: Pantheon.

Garvey, M., & Lin, R.-G., II. (2005, May 3). Road shooting probe intensifies. *Los Angeles Times*, p. A1.

Gitlin, T. (1983). *Inside prime time.* New York: Pantheon.

Goedeke, T. L. (2005). Devils, angels, or animals: The social construction of otters in conflict over management. In A. Herda-Rapp & T. L. Godeke (Eds.), *Mad over wildlife: Looking at social conflict over wildlife* (pp. 25–50). Boston: Brill.

Goldstein, D. E. (2004). *Once upon a virus: AIDS legends and vernacular risk perception.* Logan: Utah State University Press.

Gunter, V. (2005). News media and technological risks: The case of pesticides after *Silent Spring. Sociological Quarterly* 46: 671–698.

Gusfield, J. R. (1967). Moral passage: The symbolic process in public designations of deviance. *Social Problems* 15: 175–188.

Gusfield, J. R. (1981). *The culture of public problems: Drinking-driving and the symbolic order.* Chicago: University of Chicago Press.

Haines, H. H. (1984). Black radicalism and the funding of civil rights. *Social Problems* 32: 31–43.

Hamilton, J. T. (2004). *All the news that's fit to sell: How the market transforms information into news.* Princeton, NJ: Princeton University Press.

Harris, S. R. (2006). *The meanings of marital equality.* Albany: State University of New York Press.

Hawkins, G., & Zimring, F. E. (1988). *Pornography in a free society.* New York: Cambridge University Press.

Head, S. (2004, December 16). Inside the Leviathan. *New York Review of Books* 51: 80–89.

Heath, C., Bell, C., & Sternberg, E. (2001). Emotional selection in memes: The case of urban legends. *Journal of Personality and Social Psychology* 81: 1028–1041.

Herda-Rapp, A., & Marotz, K. G. (2005). Contested meanings: The social construction of the mourning dove in Wisconsin. In A. Herda-Rapp & T. L. Godeke (Eds.), *Mad over wildlife: Looking at social conflict over wildlife* (pp. 73–96). Boston: Brill.

Hilgartner, S., & Bosk, C. L. (1988). The rise and fall of social problems. *American Journal of Sociology* 94: 53–78.

Holstein, J. A., & Miller, G. (Eds.). (1993). *Reconsidering social constructionism.* Hawthorne, NY: Aldine de Gruyter.

Holstein, J. A., & Miller, G. (Eds.). (2003a). *Challenges and choices: Constructionist perspectives on social problems.* Hawthorne, NY: Aldine de Gruyter.

Holstein, J. A., & Miller, G. (2003b). Social constructionism and social problems work. In J. A. Holstein & G. Miller (Eds.), *Challenges and choices: Constructionist perspectives on social problems* (pp. 70–91). Hawthorne, NY: Aldine de Gruyter.

Huddy, L., Khatib, N., & Capelos, T. (2002). The polls-trends: Reactions to the terrorist attacks of September 11, 2001. *Public Opinion Quarterly* 66: 418–450.

Hymowitz, K. S. (2006, April 30). How welfare reform worked. *Chicago Sun-Times*, p. B1.

Intergovernmental Panel on Climate Change. 2007. "Climate change 2007: The physical science basis." Retrieved from www.ipcc.ch/SPM2Feb07.pdf.

Irvine, J. M. (2002). *Talk about sex: The battles over sex education in the United States.* Berkeley: University of California Press.

Irvine, L. (2003). The problem of unwanted pets: A case study in how institutions "think" about clients' needs. *Social Problems* 50: 550–566.

Jenkins, P. (1998). *Moral panic: Changing concepts of the child molester in modern America.* New Haven, CT: Yale University Press.

Jenkins, P. (1999). *Synthetic panics: The symbolic politics of designer drugs.* New York: New York University Press.

Jenkins, P. (2000). *Mystics and messiahs: Cults and new religions in American history*. New York: Oxford University Press.

Jenkins, P. (2001). *Hidden gospels: How the search for Jesus lost its way*. New York: Oxford University Press.

Jenkins, P. (2006). *Decade of nightmares: The end of the sixties and the making of eighties America*. New York: Oxford University Press.

Jenness, V. (1993). *Making it work: The prostitutes' rights movement in perspective*. Hawthorne, NY: Aldine de Gruyter.

Jenness, V. (1995). Social movement growth, domain expansion, and framing processes: The gay/lesbian movement and violence against gays and lesbians as a social problem. *Social Problems* 42: 145–170.

Jenness, V., & Grattet, R. (2001). *Making hate a crime: From social movement to law enforcement*. New York: Russell Sage Foundation.

Jenness, V., & Grattet, R. (2005). The law-in-between: The effects of organizational perviousness on the policing of hate crime. *Social Problems* 52: 227–259.

Johnson, J. M. (1995). Horror stories and the construction of child abuse. In J. Best (Ed.), *Images of issues: Typifying contemporary social problems* (2nd ed., pp. 17–31). Hawthorne, NY: Aldine de Gruyter.

Judge, T. A., & Cable, D. M. (2004). The effect of physical height on workplace success and income. *Journal of Applied Psychology* 89: 428–441.

Karen, D. (2005). No child left behind? Sociology ignored! *Sociology of Education* 78: 165–169.

Kiel, D. C., & Nownes, A. J. (1994). Political language, causal stories, and pesticide regulation. *American Review of Politics* 15: 491–506.

Kingdon, J. W. (1984). *Agendas, alternatives, and public policies*. New York: HarperCollins.

Kirk, S. A., & Kutchins, H. (1992). *The selling of DSM: The rhetoric of science in psychiatry*. Hawthorne, NY: Aldine de Gruyter.

Kolata, G. (2004, June 8). The fat epidemic: He says it's an illusion. *The New York Times*, p. F5.

Kolata, G. (2005, April 20). Some extra heft may be helpful, new study says. *The New York Times*, p. A1.

Kollmeyer, C. J. (2004). Corporate interests: How the news media portray the economy. *Social Problems* 51: 432–452.

Kurti, L. (1988). The politics of joking: Popular response to Chernobyl. *Journal of American Folklore* 101: 324–334.

Lafer, G. (2002). *The job training charade*. Ithaca, NY: Cornell University Press.

LaFranchi, H. (1987, April 16). Motorcycle safety: Debate over mandatory helmet laws revs up in two dozen states. *Christian Science Monitor*, p. 7.

Langlois, J. (1983). The Belle Isle Bridge incident: Legend, dialectic and semiotic system in the 1943 Detroit race riots. *Journal of American Folklore* 96: 183–196.

Langlois, J. (2005). "Celebrating Arabs": Tracing legend and rumor labyrinths in post-9/11 Detroit. *Journal of American Folklore* 118: 219–236.

Langman, L. (2005). From virtual public spheres to global justice: A critical theory of Internetworked social movements. *Sociological Theory* 23: 42–74.

Lee, E. (2003). *Abortion, motherhood, and mental health: Medicalizing reproduction in the United States and Great Britain.* Hawthorne, NY: Aldine de Gruyter.

Lichtenstein, N. (Ed.). (2006). *Wal-Mart: The face of twenty-first-century capitalism.* New York: New Press.

Link, M. W., & Oldendick, R. W. (1999). Call screening: Is it really a problem for survey research? *Public Opinion Quarterly* 63: 577–589.

Lipsky, M. (1980). *Street-level bureaucracy: Dilemmas of the individual in public services.* New York: Russell Sage Foundation.

Lipsky, M., & Smith, S. R. (1989). When social problems are treated as emergencies. *Social Service Review* 63: 5–25.

Lofland, J. (1993). *Polite protesters: The American peace movement of the 1980s.* Syracuse, NY: Syracuse University Press.

Lofland, J. (2003). *Demolishing a historic hotel: A sociology of preservation failure in Davis, California.* Davis, CA: Davis Research.

Lonsway, K. A., & Fitzgerald, L. F. (1994). Rape myths. *Psychology of Women Quarterly* 18: 133–164.

Loseke, D. R. (2003). *Thinking about social problems* (2nd ed.). Hawthorne, NY: Aldine de Gruyter.

Lowney, K. S. (1999). *Baring our souls: TV talk shows and the religion of recovery.* Hawthorne, NY: Aldine de Gruyter.

Lowney, K. S., & Best, J. (1995). Stalking strangers and lovers: Changing media typifications of a new crime problem. In J. Best (Ed.), *Images of issues: Typifying contemporary social problems* (2nd ed., pp. 33–57). Hawthorne, NY: Aldine de Gruyter.

Lowney, K. S., & Best, J. (1996). What Waco stood for: Jokes as popular constructions of social problems. *Perspectives on Social Problems* 8: 77–98.

Lutzenhiser, L. (2001). The contours of U.S. climate non-policy. *Society and Natural Resources* 14: 511–523.

MacCoun, R. J., & Reuter, P. (2001). *Drug war heresies: Learning from other vices, times, and places.* New York: Cambridge University Press.

Macionis, J. J. (2005). *Social problems* (2nd ed.). Upper Saddle River, NJ: Pearson Prentice Hall.

Matthews, N. (1994). *Confronting rape: The feminist anti-rape movement and the state.* New York: Routledge.

Maurer, D. (2002). *Vegetarianism: Movement or moment?* Philadelphia: Temple University Press.

McAdam, D. (1983). Tactical innovation and the pace of insurgency. *American Sociological Review* 48: 735–754.

McAdam, D. (1994). Culture and social movements. In E. Laraña, H. Johnston, & J. R. Gusfield (Eds.), *New social movements: From identity to ideology* (pp. 36–57). Philadelphia: Temple University Press.

McAdam, D., & Rucht, D. (1993). The cross-national diffusion of movement ideas. *Annals of the American Academy of Political and Social Science* 528: 56–74.

McCarthy, J. D., & Zald, M. N. (1977). Resource mobilization and social movements. *American Journal of Sociology* 82: 1212–1241.

McCombs, M. (2004). *Setting the agenda: The mass media and public opinion.* Cambridge, UK: Polity.

McCright, A. M., & Dunlap, R. E. (2003). Defeating Kyoto: The conservative movement's impact of U.S. climate change policy. *Social Problems* 50: 348–373.

McMullen, C., & Eyles, J. (1999). Risky business: An analysis of claimsmaking in the development of the Ontario drinking water objective for tritium. *Social Problems* 46: 294–311.

Midanik, L. T. (2006). *Biomedicalization of alcohol studies: Ideological shifts and institutional challenges.* New Brunswick, NJ: AldineTransaction.

Miller, G., & Holstein, J. A. (Eds.). (1997). *Social problems in everyday life: Studies of social problems work.* Greenwich, CT: JAI Press.

Mills, C. W. (1959). *The sociological imagination.* New York: Oxford University Press.

Misra, J., Moller, S., & Karides, M. (2003). Envisioning dependency: Changing media depictions of welfare in the 20th century. *Social Problems* 50: 482–504.

Moeller, S. D. (1999). *Compassion fatigue: How the media sell disease, famine, war and death.* New York: Routledge.

Morrill, A. C., & Chinn, C. D. (2004). The obesity epidemic in the United States. *Journal of Public Health Policy* 25: 353–366.

Murray, C. A. (1994). *Losing ground: American social policy, 1950–1980.* New York: Basic Books.

National Highway Traffic Safety Administration. (2005). *Traffic safety facts 2004: A compilation of motor vehicle crash data from the fatality analysis reporting system and the general estimates system.* Washington, DC: NHTSA.

Nelson, B. J. (1984). *Making an issue of child abuse: Political agenda setting for social problems.* Chicago: University of Chicago Press.

Newton, L. (2005). "It is not a question of being anti-immigration": Categories of deservedness in immigration policy making. In A. L. Schneider & H. M. Ingram (Eds.), *Deserving and entitled: Social constructions and public policy* (pp. 139–167). Albany: State University of New York Press.

Nichols, L. T. (1997). Social problems as landmark narratives: Bank of Boston, mass media and "money laundering." *Social Problems* 44: 324–341.

Nichols, L. T. (2003). Voices of social problems: A dialogical constructionist model. *Studies in Symbolic Interaction* 26: 93–123.

Nichols, S. L., & Berliner, D. C. (2005). *The inevitable corruption of indicators and educators through high-stakes testing.* Education Policy Studies Laboratory (EPSL-0503-101-EPRU), Arizona State University. Retrieved from www.asu.edu/educ/epsl/EPRU/documents/EPSL-0503-101-EPRU.pdf.

Oring, E. (1987). Jokes and the discourse on disaster. *Journal of American Folklore* 100: 278–286.

Overbye, D. (2006, August 25). Vote makes it official: Pluto isn't what it used to be. *The New York Times*, p. A1.

Pawluch, D. (1996). *The new pediatrics: A profession in transition.* Hawthorne, NY: Aldine de Gruyter.

Pearson, G. (1983). *Hooligan: A history of respectable fears.* London: Macmillan.

Pfohl, S. J. (1977). The "discovery" of child abuse. *Social Problems* 24: 310–323.

Preves, S. E. (2003). *Intersex and identity: The contested self.* New Brunswick, NJ: Rutgers University Press.

Rauch, J. (2006, June 4). Families forged by illness. *The New York Times*, p. 15.

Ravitch, D. (2003). *The language police: How pressure groups restrict what students learn.* New York: Vintage.

Reinarman, C. (1994). The social construction of drug scares. In P. A. Adler & P. Adler (Eds.), *Constructions of deviance* (pp. 92–104). Belmont, CA: Wadsworth.

Reinarman, C., & Levine, H. G. (1995). The crack attack: America's latest drug scare, 1986–1992. In J. Best (Ed.), *Images of issues: Typifying contemporary social problems* (2nd ed., pp. 147–186). Hawthorne, NY: Aldine de Gruyter.

Rich, A. (2004). *Think tanks, public policy, and the politics of expertise.* Cambridge, UK: Cambridge University Press.

Rosenfeld, R., Fornango, R., & Baumer, E. (2005). Did *Ceasefire, Compstat,* and *Exile* reduce homicide? *Criminology and Public Policy* 4: 419–450.

Rossi, P. H., Lipsey, M. W., & Freeman, H. E. (2004). *Evaluation: A systematic approach* (7th ed.). Thousand Oaks, CA: Sage.

Rudy, D. R. (1986). *Becoming alcoholic: Alcoholics Anonymous and the reality of alcoholism.* Carbondale: Southern Illinois University Press.

Saguy, A. C. (2003). *What is sexual harassment? From Capitol Hill to the Sorbonne.* Berkeley: University of California Press.

Saletan, W. (2003). *Bearing right: How the conservatives won the abortion war.* Berkeley: University of California Press.

Sasson, T. (1995a). African American conspiracy theories and the social construction of crime. *Sociological Inquiry* 65: 265–285.

Sasson, T. (1995b). *Crime talk: How citizens construct a social problem.* Hawthorne, NY: Aldine de Gruyter.

Schneider, A. L., & Ingram, H. M. (1993). Social constructions of target populations: Implications for politics and policy. *American Political Science Review* 87: 334–347.

Schneider, A. L., & Ingram, H. M. (Eds.). (2005). *Deserving and entitled: Social constructions and public policy.* Albany: State University of New York Press.

Schudson, M. (2003). *The sociology of news.* New York: Norton.

Schurman, R. (2004). Fighting "Frankenfoods": Industry opportunity structures and the efficacy of the anti-biotech movements in western Europe. *Social Problems* 51: 243–268.

Scotch, R. K. (2001). *From good will to civil rights: Transforming federal disability policy* (2nd ed.). Philadelphia: Temple University Press.

Scott, L. (2005, April 7). Wal-Mart's impact on society [Advertisement]. *New York Review of Books* 52: 6–7.

Shibutani, T. (1966). *Improvised news: A sociological study of rumor.* Indianapolis, IN: Bobbs-Merrill.

Silver, I. (2006). *Unequal partnerships: Beyond the rhetoric of philanthropic collaboration.* New York: Routledge.

Smith, M. (2005). The politics of same-sex marriage in Canada and the United States. *PS* 38: 225–228.

Snow, D., & Benford, R. (1988). Ideology, frame resonance, and participant mobilization. *International Social Movement Research* 1: 197–217.

Snow, D., & Benford, R. (1992). Master frames and cycles of protest. In A. D. Morris & C. M. Mueller (Eds.), *Frontiers in social movement theory* (pp. 133–155). New Haven, CT: Yale University Press.

Snow, D. A., Rochford, E. B., Jr., Worden, S. K., & Benford, R. D. (1986). Frame alignment processes, micromobilization, and movement participation. *American Sociological Review* 51: 464–481.

Spector, M., & Kitsuse, J. I. (1977). *Constructing social problems.* Menlo Park, CA: Cummings.

Squires, S. (1998, June 4). Optimal weight threshold lowered: Millions more to be termed overweight. *The Washington Post*, p. A1.

Staller, K. M. (2006). *Runaways: How the sixties counterculture shaped today's policies and practices.* New York: Columbia University Press.

Starr, P. (1982). *The social transformation of American medicine.* New York: Basic Books.

Steffens, L. (1931). *The autobiography of Lincoln Steffens.* New York: Harcourt, Brace.

Stein, R. (2004, March 10). Obesity passing smoking as top avoidable cause of death. *The Washington Post*, p. A1.

Stone, D. A. (1989). Causal stories and the formation of policy agendas. *Political Science Quarterly* 104: 281–300.

Strang, D., & Meyer, J. W. (1993). Institutional conditions for diffusion. *Theory and Society* 22: 487–511.

Taylor, V. (1989). Social movement continuity: The women's movement in abeyance. *American Sociological Review* 54: 761–775.

Tierney, K. J. (1982). The battered women movement and the creation of the wife beating problem. *Social Problems* 29: 207–220.

Toulmin, S. E. (1958). *The uses of argument*. Cambridge, UK: Cambridge University Press.

Troyer, R. J. (1989). The surprising resurgence of the smoking problem. In J. Best (Ed.), *Images of issues: Typifying contemporary social problems* (pp. 159–176). Hawthorne, NY: Aldine de Gruyter.

Tuchman, G. (1978). *Making news: A study in the construction of reality*. New York: Free Press.

Turow, J. (1997). *Breaking up America: Advertisers and the new media world*. Chicago: University of Chicago Press.

U.S. Census Bureau. (1975). *Historical statistics of the United States: Colonial times to 1970*. Washington, DC: Government Printing Office.

Useem, B., & Zald, M. N. (1982). From pressure groups of social movement: Organizational dilemmas of the effort to promote nuclear power. *Social Problems* 30: 144–156.

Viguerie, R. A., & Franke, D. (2004). *America's right turn: How conservatives used new and alternative media to take power*. Chicago: Bonus Books.

Weinberg, D. (2000). "Out there": The ecology of addiction drug abuse treatment discourse. *Social Problems* 47: 606–621.

Weisner, C., & Room, R. (1984). Financing and ideology in alcohol treatment. *Social Problems* 32: 167–184.

Welch, M. (2000). *Flag burning: Moral panic and the criminalization of protest*. Hawthorne, NY: Aldine de Gruyter.

Werum, R., & Winders, B. (2001). Who's "in" and who's "out": State fragmentation and the struggle over gay rights, 1974–1999. *Social Problems* 48: 386–410.

White, L. (2000). *Speaking of vampires: Rumor and history in colonial Africa*. Berkeley: University of California Press.

Williams, F. O. (2001, April 24). Is ID theft overhyped? *The Buffalo News*, p. D1.

Zegart, A. B. (2004). Blue ribbons, black boxes: Toward a better understanding of presidential commissions. *Presidential Studies Quarterly* 34: 366–393.

Index

Note: Page numbers in italics refer to charts, illustrations, and examples.